Cases and Problems

in

INVESTMENTS

Cases and Problems

in

INVESTMENTS

by

FRANCIS J. CALKINS

Professor of Finance
Marquette University

PRENTICE-HALL, INC.

Englewood Cliffs, N. J.

PRINTED IN THE UNITED STATES OF AMERICA

11854

Preface

Without practical examples and cases, theory and description often lead only to a confusion of concepts and principles and cannot be of value to the potential investor of the future. To make these concepts and principles meaningful, concentration on specific firms and securities is essential. Unfortunately, it is difficult to select specific, appropriate examples from the vast array of materials and sources that exist, and anyone interested in increasing his grasp of the subject will have difficulty finding suitable cases and problems that will enable him to apply his theoretical knowledge to practical situations.

To attack these difficulties, this volume offers a sizable number of problems, readings, and cases of a practical nature. The basic problems relate the working out of management and analysis principles through use of issues of ten industrial companies, for which relatively complete data are here given. This procedure will lend to the subject of investments a unified approach that will be of value to the reader. The readings are chosen chiefly from *The Analysts Journal, Journal of Commerce,* and *Moody's Stock Survey* and *Bond Survey,* not only for their own merit, but as representative of what the intelligent investor should look for among other sources that might have been used: *Wall Street Journal, Commercial and Financial Chronicle, Financial World, Barron's, Journal of Finance, The Outlook,* and the vast library of books on investments, securities, and the securities markets.

Through the use of these problems, readings, and cases, the veil of mystery surrounding the subject may be drawn back, so that not only may the future American economy be insured of development, but each individual may find his own personal security through securities.

I suggest a liberal diet of these cases and problems. They are not geared to follow any single text, but are adaptable to almost every volume popular in the current market. More emphasis has been placed on questions of investment policy and decision and on security analysis than on the more definitive phrases of the field, in accord with my desire to keep to the practical, rather than the theoretical. The variety should permit the volume's use either in the traditional approach to investments or in the more modern approach through risk-bearing and portfolio management.

Each problem is introduced by a short statement of its purpose and concludes with a number of provocative questions, some of an elementary nature, others quite advanced. The variety of items also varies from the relatively simple to the complex. Thus, the reader of this volume should feel free to use the problems and cases in any order desirable and, in any given case, to omit any of the questions that do not suit his particular purpose. Calculation work has been held to a minimum consistent with practicality; however, some rather long, laboratory-type cases have been included.

Certain topics have not been covered in this volume. I believe, for example, that investment banking properly belongs in the field of corporation finance; analysis of United States government securities is more theory than practice, since their prices can be treated in other ways; and the impact of taxation on investment management and policy can be introduced at any time, despite changing rates and taxes.

The stock price indexes of the Securities and Exchange Commission are used in this volume as more representative than other available measures. Through the cooperation of the Division of Trading and Exchanges, I have worked out monthly averages for many of the series. Monthly average prices of the ten individual stocks were compiled from data in *Commercial and Financial Chronicle*. Comparative financial statement materials derived from *Moody's Industrials* are also included.

I wish to express my sincere gratitude to many persons and firms for use of other materials: to Merrill Lynch, Pierce, Fenner & Beane; to Carl M. Loeb, Rhoades & Co.; to General Mills, Inc.; to Standard and Poor's Corporation, from whom I received my first interest in the field of investment analysis; to J. M. Galanis; and to the *Chicago Journal of Commerce*. My deepest appreciation goes to H. E.

Luedicke of the *Journal of Commerce* and to Pierre R. Bretey of *The Analysts Journal* for their kindness in permitting extensive use of materials from their publications. Only I can tell how much my colleagues and students have helped with their advice, criticism, and work, and how great has been the encouragement and assistance unselfishly given by my wife.

I shall welcome comments and views on this endeavor in a new approach to investments, and I hope that these cases and problems will help others better to understand the lore of investment.

FRANCIS J. CALKINS

Contents

Part I

Part II

Part III

Part IV

CONTENTS

Part V

Cases and Problems

in

INVESTMENTS

Part I

---

1. Investment and Speculation

A short case involving a distinction between investment and speculation affords a preliminary discussion of the objectives of saving and of the purchase of various classes of assets.

Henry Northman graduated from the high school of a medium-sized town in 1930. Starting to work in his father's garage, he took over operation of the business upon his father's death in 1936 and added an automobile dealership for a medium-priced line of cars. This venture proved to be quite successful, but to round out his business interests in 1938 Northman became a partner in a used car sales lot located on the outskirts of the town. He has taken little active interest in the lot, but it does afford a place at which he can put his trade-in cars on sale.

During the war, Northman served on various local governmental boards and was exempt from service because of an injury he had received in the garage some years earlier. Because of the pattern of war financing he was able to subscribe to a number of new government bond issues at par and to sell them within two weeks or a month at 103 or better. He did this some six or seven times.

Following the war Northman sold some real estate his father had bought in the 1920's. The sale to a home builder gave Northman a 300 per cent profit on the cost of the land to his father. He then built a $30,000 home on which he now has a mortgage of $20,000.

Known as a highly successful businessman in the community, Northman now lists his investments as including $15,000 cash value of endowment life insurance ($60,000 face value), $25,000 face value U.S. Treasury Savings Bonds, 100 shares Chrysler Corporation common, 200 shares American Motors Corporation common, one share Local Telephone Company common, and ten shares each in Fraternal Building Corporation common and Local Country Club common.

1. Would you class Northman's business interests and home as investments? Why?
2. Was the real estate transaction an investment or speculation? How about the government bond transactions?
3. Which of his securities holdings would you class as speculative?
4. If Northman were to have an additional $10,000 in cash to invest, should it be in stocks or bonds? Or should other questions be answered before such a decision can be reached?

2.   Terminology in Investments

A short problem typical of the answers that many investment men get from customers and also that teachers receive from students.

John Doreme is 23 years old, a veteran of the Korean conflict, and is working for a large manufacturing concern. He comes to a brokerage office and seeks advice about his financial plans. When the customer's representative asks about his present position, he replies:

I have a checking account of about $500 and some war bonds I bought while in service in 1951 and 1952. They're worth $1,750. I've got my service insurance but don't know whether it's any good now, so I bought $2,000 term life insurance and paid $200 for three years' premium. Then I've got some securities. I have ten shares of General Motors I got at $50 a share, and ten shares of Brooklyn Union Gas 4 per cent debentures for 105. Then I bought ten shares of Westinghouse Air Brake for $12 and ten shares of New York Central 4 per cent mortgages for $65. And I've got a house I paid $10,000 for, but it's got a G.I. mortgage on it.

1. Can you find all the mistakes that John evidently has made in stating his financial condition?

3.   Legal Description of a Mortgage Bond

The importance of knowing terminology in investments cannot be overlooked. This problem deals with many terms often found in mortgage bonds.

Southwestern Public Service Company *registered* for *negotiated* public offering on February 4, 1953, $12,000,000 *first mortgage bonds*, due February 1, 1978. The *proceeds* of the issue, together with those from the sale of 20,000 shares of $100 par *preferred stock* and 293,462 shares of *common stock* were to be used to *retire* most or all of the outstanding *short-term debt* of the corporation. The borrowing had been incurred for construction purposes. Plant additions for the *fiscal* year to end August 31, 1953, were estimated at $23,400,000 of which about $13,00,000 was for new electric generating facilities. Further financing was expected in succeeding years.

Security. The new bonds are *secured equally* with the seven *series* of first mortgage bonds outstanding under a *direct lien* on substantially all properties and franchises. The total mortgage debt thus outstanding would be about 57.5 per cent of net plant and *pro forma* working capital, with total debt about 63.9 per cent of the same amount.

Interest. The new bonds would bear an interest rate of 3½ per cent. Interest requirements, before income taxes, would have been met in previous years as follows:

Fiscal years	*1952	1952	1951	1950	1949	1948
Times earned on mortgage	4.39	4.17	3.30	2.78	2.57	2.30
Times earned on all debt	3.89	3.70	2.92	2.46	2.28	2.04

 * Twelve months ended November 30, 1952.

Improvement Fund. Payments, beginning in 1954, to be made at the rate of 1 per cent a year on the greatest amount of 1978 series bonds outstanding. Such payments may be made in cash (applied to purchase or redemption of bonds) or in bonds, or by certifying net additions, taken at 60 per cent.

Maintenance Fund. The *indenture* provides for deposit on or before October 1 of each year of cash equal to the excess of 15 per cent of revenues, as defined, over maintenance charges.

Pro Forma Capitalization (as of November 30, 1952).

	Actual	Pro Forma
Mortgage bonds	$69,545,000 (56.5%)	$81,545,000 (56.8%)
Debentures	10,000,000 (8.1%)	10,000,000 (7.0%)
Preferred stock	10,487,000 (8.5%)	12,487,000 (8.7%)
Common and surplus	33,060,000 (26.9%)	39,510,000 (27.5%)

1. Define the italicized terms in the summary given above.
2. Is it usual to include a mortgage on franchises? Of what value is such a mortgage to investors?
3. What is the intent of the improvement fund? What is meant by the provision permitting certification of net additions to property, taken at 60 per cent?
4. What is the purpose of the maintenance provision?

4. Bond Terminology

Another problem in terminology, this time couched in more legal form.

The following information is taken from the *prospectus* for an issue of $162,098,500 Phillips Petroleum Company 3.70 per cent Sinking Fund Debentures due 1983, convertible into Common Stock until June 1, 1963, unless previously redeemed, *at conversion prices of Common Stock* as follows: $65 to June 1, 1958, and $72 thereafter to June 1, 1963. Subject to a Sinking Fund commencing June 1, 1955, sufficient to retire 100 per cent of the Debentures by maturity. (Prospectus dated May 26, 1953.)

Conversion. The 3.70 per cent Sinking Fund Debentures due 1983 ("Debentures") will be convertible into Common Stock until June 1, 1963, unless previously redeemed, at conversion prices of Common Stock (with Debentures taken at their principal amount) as follows: $65 to June 1, 1958, and $72 thereafter to June 1, 1963, such conversion prices being subject to adjustment as described herein.

Sinking Fund. The Sinking Fund, commencing June 1, 1955, provides for annual retirement of $5,590,000 principal amount of Debentures by redemption (at 100 per cent, plus accrued interest) or by purchase or otherwise. Debentures converted prior to April 15, 1955, and in each subsequent 12 month period to April 15, 1963, may be applied to reduction of Sinking Fund installments on a *non-cumulative* basis.

Redemption. Redeemable, at the option of the Company, *in whole or in part*, on 30 days' notice, at redemption prices as follows, plus accrued interest, in annual periods to and including June 1 of the years shown: (table showing 103⅝ per cent for 1954, decreasing ⅛ per cent annually to 1983.)

Denominations. Debentures will be issued *in bearer form* in denominations of $100, $500 and $1,000 only and *in fully registered form* in denominations of $1,000, $5,000 and multiples of $5,000.

Description of Debentures

The Debentures are to be issued under an *Indenture*, dated as of June 1, 1953, between the Company and Manufacturers Trust Company, *Trustee.* The Indenture does not authorize the issuance of any debentures thereunder in addition to the Debentures offered hereby, but does not limit the amount of other securities, secured or unsecured, which may hereafter be issued by the Company.

Conversion Provisions. The holder of any Debenture or Debentures will have the right at his option, exercisable at any time to but not including June 1, 1963, to convert the principal thereof into such number of *full-paid and non-assessable shares* of Common Stock as the principal amount of the Debenture or Debentures surrendered for conversion is a multiple of the conversion price, i.e., the then applicable conversion price as set for earlier, as adjusted if such adjustments shall have been required pursuant to the provisions of the Indenture providing for such adjustments in certain events, such as the issuance of additional shares of Common Stock for less than the conversion price, or a *combination* or *split up* of the Common Stock. There will be no adjustment of interest or dividends upon the conversion of any Debenture. No fractional shares of stock will be issued upon any conversion of Debentures, but in lieu thereof there will be issued non-dividend bearing and non-voting *scrip*, exchangeable during such period (not less than two years from the issue thereof) as the Board of Directors may determine, for full shares when combined with other such scrip.

Certain Restrictions on the Company. The Indenture provides that, if the Company shall at any time mortgage or subject to a lien or pledge any property then owned by it (including stock and other securities of subsidiaries), it will make effective provision to secure the Debentures, and any other indebtedness of the Company then entitled thereto, equally and ratably with all other indebtedness secured by such mortgage, pledge, or lien, so long as any such other indebtedness shall be so secured. This covenant is not applicable to certain types of liens, including *purchase money mortgages*, liens existing on property at the time of acquisition, the pledge of current assets to secure current liabilities, liens on property to secure obligations payable out of the production from such property or the proceeds of such production, liens on the production from property or the proceeds thereof, and mortgages or other liens on property owned by a subsidiary of the Company, whether or not transferred to it by the Company.

Concerning the Trustee. The Indenture provides that the Trustee, prior to the occurrence of a default and after the *curing* of all defaults that may have occurred, undertakes to perform such duties and only such duties as are specifically set forth in the Indenture. In case a default has occurred (which has not been cured) the Trustee shall exercise such of the rights and powers vested in it by the Indenture, and use the same degree of care and skill in their exercise, as a *prudent man* would exercise or use under the circumstances in the conduct of his own affairs. The holders of a majority in aggregate principal amount of the Debentures at the time outstanding shall have the right to direct the time, method, and place of conducting any proceeding for any remedy available to the Trustee or exercising any trust or power conferred upon the Trustee; provided, however, that the Trustee shall have the right to decline to follow any such direction if advised by counsel that such action may not lawfully be taken, or if the Trustee in good faith shall by a responsible officer or officers of the Trustee determine that the proceedings so directed would be unjustly prejudicial to the holders of Debentures not joining in such direction.

Modification of the Indenture. The Indenture contains provisions permitting the Company and the Trustee, with the consent of the holders of not less than 66⅔ per cent in aggregate principal amount of the Debentures at the time outstanding, evidenced as in the Indenture provided, to execute supplemental indentures modifying in any manner the provisions of the Indenture or of any supplemental indenture or the rights of the holders of the Debentures and coupons; provided, however, that no such modification may be made that will permit any change in the principal amount, maturity date, or interest rate of the Debentures or in the provisions governing the payment of principal or interest on the Debentures or any change in such percentage of holders.

Defaults and Notice Thereof. The Indenture provides that the following events are "defaults": (a) failure to pay any instalment of interest on any Debenture for a period of 30 days after the same shall become payable; (b) failure to pay principal of any Debenture whether at maturity, by call for redemption, by declaration as authorized in the Indenture, or otherwise; (c) failure to pay any sinking fund instalment for a period of 60 days after the same shall become payable; (d) failure to observe or perform any of the covenants, conditions, or agreements of the Company and such failure shall continue for a period of 90 days after written notice to the Company from the Trustee or to the Company and the Trustee from not less than 25 per cent of the Debentureholders; (e) occurrence of a default under any mortgage, indenture, or instrument under which there may be issued or by which there may be secured any indebtedness of the Company if such indebtedness shall then become due and payable prior to the date on which it would otherwise become due and payable or the failure by the Company within 30 days of maturity of any indebtedness to pay, extend, or refund the same; (f) adjudication of the Company as a bankrupt, or the appointment of a receiver of the Company for substantially all of its property if such adjudication or appointment shall continue unstayed on appeal or otherwise for a period of 60 days; (g) admission in writing by the Company of inability to pay its debts as they become due, or the filing of a voluntary petition in bankruptcy or the making of an assignment for the benefit of creditors or the consenting to the appointment of a receiver of a substantial part of its property; (h) filing by the Company of a petition under the provisions of Chapter X of the Federal Bankruptcy Act or of an answer seeking the relief therein provided; or (i) entry of an order by a court of competent jurisdiction approving a petition filed against the Company under the provisions of Chapter X of the Federal Bankruptcy Act if such order shall not be stayed within 60 days. The Indenture provides that the Trustee shall, within 90 days after the occurrence of a default (as above defined, but not including any period of grace therein mentioned), give to the Debenture holders notice of all defaults known to the Trustee. In the case, however, of a default of the character described in subdivisions (d), (f), and (i) above, no such notice shall be given until at least 60 days after the occurrence of the default.

Description of Common Stock

The Common Stock, *without nominal or par value*, is entitled to receive such dividends as the Board of Directors may from time to time declare. Each *holder of record* of shares of Common Stock is entitled to *one vote for each share* so held and is entitled to a proportionate part of the net assets of the Company upon liquidation in accordance with the number of shares so held. The *preemptive right* of each holder of shares of Common Stock has not been restricted and there are no subscription or conversion rights, or redemption provisions, applicable to, and there is no liability for further calls with respect to, the Common Stock.

1. Define each of the italicized words or phrases.
2. What is the purpose of the adjustment clause in the conversion privileges? What is this clause often called?
3. Why are these bonds not registered as to principal?
4. What is the term usually used to describe the clause giving certain restrictions on the company? What is its purpose?
5. Why should any provision for modifying the indenture be provided?
6. Are the default provisions of the Indenture of great value to the

investor? What is the reason for including so many possible events?

7. Why is the description of the common stock included?

5. Terminology of Preferred Stocks and Common Stocks

This problem involves use of investment manuals, and is designed to show the type of information given on provisions of security issues.

Commonwealth Edison Company has been noted for its comparatively simple capitalization. However, the provisions of the outstanding issues are of some interest. By reference to Moody's *Public Utilities* or Standard & Poor's *Corporation Records*, investigate the provisions of the preferred stock of Commonwealth Edison for the answers to the following points:

1. What is meant by "Preferred Stock in Series?"
2. What is the intent of the provision prohibiting sinking fund payments if any dividend accumulations are present?
3. Why is the provision of adjustment of the conversion price made?
4. Why does the right to convert continue after the notice of redemption is given? Of what value is this to the holder of preferred?
5. Why is there a limitation on the redemption and purchase of preferred stock? Why are tenders required for purchase of shares?
6. What is meant by cumulative voting? Could the holders of preferred stock ever control the company? What is the minimum and maximum control power holders of the issue, acting in concert, could exercise?
7. If the preferred stock has voting rights, why does it not have a preemptive right? Is this of material importance?
8. What is the common term given to the powers stated under "Restrictions on Certain Corporate Action?"

Now examine the provisions of the various classes and series of preferred stocks of El Paso Natural Gas Company, noting that this company has acquired a much greater amount of its funds through sale of senior securities.

9. What differences exist between the two classes of preferred stock? between the various series of preferred stocks? How did this come about?

10. What is the effect of the provision approved in 1953 permitting reissue of converted preferred stock? Is this harmful to the holders of outstanding shares of preferred? to holders of common?

11. Looking at the provisions of the common stock, what is the intent of the restrictions on payment of dividends? Does the restriction made in the Indenture of the First Mortgage Pipe Line bonds and Debentures detract from the potential dividend increases on the common stock?

12. Examine the voting rights of the two classes of preferred stock in case of defaults on dividends. Does this effectively pass control to either class in case of default? Does the preferred stock also possess "veto powers?" On what items? Why?

13. What is the difference in preemptive rights of El Paso preferred and those of Commonwealth Edison? Can you find out why this provision was made?

Examine the provisions of the Reading Railroad $2.00 2nd Preferred and Wabash Railroad $4.50 Preferred stocks, found in *Moody's Transportation* or *Standard Corporation Records*.

14. What unusual features do you find in these issues? Do they have any effect on the common stocks of the roads?

6. Income Characteristics of Bonds

This problem involves a comparison of the income characteristics of coupon and discount bonds.

Until 1952, U. S. Treasury War Savings Bonds and Defense Bonds, Series E, were sold on the basis of $3 invested bringing $4 at the end of ten years. Competitively, Treasury bonds paid 2½ per cent in semi-annual coupons, while Series G Defense Bonds paid 2½ per cent in semi-annual installments, but were subject to a small discount if presented for redemption prior to maturity.

Mr. Michael has no need for liquidity but desires to use one of these three types of bonds as a method of providing a regular income to him during his later years in life. He could (1) buy Series E bonds, starting at age 55, monthly and cash them at redemption date ten years later, whereupon he could reinvest the principal and use the difference for current living expenses. If he estimates that he needs $300 a month to cover living expenses after he reaches age 65, how much must he invest each month from age 55 on? How much each year? How much over the whole ten-year period?

Alternatively, he might (2) buy Treasury bonds to get the same amount of income. What would be the difference in the flow of income to him? How much need he invest in this type of bond assuming that he needs $300 a month income?

Assume that Mr. Michael follows either plan. What would he have left in his estate at age 75? Would any risks of income change be present? What risks, other than of income change, would be present?

7.   Changes in Bond Yields and Prices

Since it is important that the relative changes in bond yields and prices for different quality classes of bonds be recognized, this problem of a rather simple nature is presented to open the question of the market characteristics of various classes of securities.

There are relatively few bonds that afford possibilities of tracing price movements over a considerable period of time, particularly in the industrial and utility fields. However, a very small sample may be used for illustrative purposes. Complete the following table for the bonds listed, using bond guide books, current periodicals such as *Commercial and Financial Chronicle*, or current newspapers. The issues are:

1. Bethlehem Steel purchase money 6s, 1998, rated Aa by Moody,
2. New England Telephone & Telegraph 1st 4½s B, 1961, rated Aa,
3. Atchison, Topeka & Santa Fe adjustment 4s, 1995, rated A,
4. Atlantic Coast Line unified 4½s, 1964, rated Baa,
5. Baltimore & Ohio refunding & general 2.4-6s, J, 1995, rated B,
   which replaced a former issue of 6s, C, 1995.

	1929	1933	1937	1940	1946	1948	1950	Current
Bond 1:								
Avg. Price	116-1/2	105-1/2	136-1/2	147	165	161-1/2	167-3/8	
Yield	4.95	5.61	3.96	3.53	2.88	2.95	2.75	
Bond 2:								
Avg. Price	98-1/4	102	115-3/4	126-3/8	125-3/8	117	116-3/8	
Yield	4.64	4.34	3.32	2.57	2.24	2.73	2.59	
Bond 3:								
Avg. Price	83-3/4	82-5/8	111	83	122-5/8	110-3/4	120-1/4	
Yield	4.81	5.19	3.43	5.19	2.89	3.41	2.95	
Bond 4:								
Avg. Price	96-1/4	66-3/4	86-7/8	52-1/4	110-1/4	102-3/8	104-3/4	
Yield	4.79	8.35	5.75	12.42	3.57	4.25	3.97	
Bond 5:								
Avg. Price	107-3/4	60-1/4	73-1/4	30-1/8	86-7/8	72-3/4	77-5/8	
Yield	5.46	11.02	8.82	24.13	7.21	9.04	8.26	

1. Compare the relative changes in average prices from 1929 to 1933, from 1933 to 1937, from 1937 to 1946, from 1946 to 1950, and from 1950 to date for the first and second bonds. If the two are of equal quality, why are there differences? Is quality of a bond relative to one industrial group or to the whole bond category?

2. Compare in similar fashion bonds 3, 4, and 5. What conclusions can you draw concerning the relative changes in prices and yields for various quality bonds within the same industry?

3. Refer to the tabulations given in Problem 8. Are the bonds listed in this problem representative samples of their quality groupings?

8. The Patterns of Security Yields

This introductory problem in the field of security yields will reward the student with a comprehension of the cyclical swings in the yields of various types of issues.

Table I-1 presents the record of yields on bonds of the U. S. Treasury, municipals, and different industrial groups of corporations from 1919 through 1952. Some explanation of the different yields may be necessary. From 1919 through 1941 Treasury issues were generally either not subject to Federal income taxes, or were subject only to surtax rates. From 1942 most Federal issues have been wholly taxable and are, therefore, used in the tabulation. The tax rates at the time of the change were 16 per cent for individuals and 38 per cent for corporation incomes. Two series of municipal bonds are included for comparisons: The Bond Buyer series includes both state and city issues, while the series from Standard & Poor's is only for cities. The industrial yields, prepared by Moody's, cover 40 bonds in each group of industrials, rails and utilities, evenly divided in quality ratings among the top four ratings, except for industrials and rails in the last few years when there was a lack of sufficient highest grade bonds to include in the yield computations.

Table I-2 presents a tabulation of a composite yield of the four top quality ratings of corporate bonds, with industrial, rails, and utilities given equal weight, except as noted above.

Table I-3 presents data on preferred and common stocks, the latter for the period, 1929 to 1952, the former for the full period running back to 1919. The yields on preferred stocks, compiled by Standard & Poor's are for high grade industrials only, while those for common stocks, prepared by Moody's, are for a composite and for various types of industrial groupings.

Data to bring these tables up to date can be found in the *Federal Reserve Bulletin*, the *Survey of Current Business*, and other sources.

TABLE I-1
COMPARISON OF BOND YIELDS, 1919-1953*

| | U. S. Treasury | | Municipals | | Corporate | | | |
	Non-taxable	Taxable	Bond Buyer	S. & P.	Composite	Industrial	Utility	Rail
1919	4.72	---	4.50	4.46	6.27	6.18	6.21	6.42
1920	5.32	---	5.04	4.98	7.08	6.94	7.19	7.12
1921	5.09	---	5.42	5.09	7.04	7.04	7.17	6.91
1922	4.30	---	4.21	4.23	5.95	6.04	5.93	5.89
1923	4.36	---	4.27	4.25	6.04	6.04	5.84	6.24
1924	4.06	---	4.21	4.20	5.80	5.90	5.61	5.90
1925	3.86	---	4.13	4.09	5.47	5.61	5.29	5.51
1926	3.68	---	4.14	4.08	5.21	5.37	5.11	5.13
1927	3.34	---	3.99	3.98	4.97	5.10	4.96	4.83
1928	3.33	---	4.05	4.05	4.94	5.10	4.87	4.85
1929	3.60	---	4.31	4.27	5.21	5.31	5.14	5.18
1930	3.29	---	4.12	4.07	5.09	5.25	5.05	4.96
1931	3.34	---	4.07	4.01	5.81	6.08	5.27	6.09
1932	3.68	---	4.77	4.65	6.87	6.71	6.30	7.60
1933	3.31	---	5.14	4.71	5.89	5.34	6.25	6.09
1934	3.12	---	4.22	4.03	4.96	4.52	5.40	4.96
1935	2.79	---	3.38	3.41	4.46	4.02	4.43	4.95
1936	2.65	---	2.93	3.07	3.87	3.50	3.88	4.24
1937	2.68	---	3.03	3.10	3.94	3.55	3.93	4.35
1938	2.56	---	2.99	2.91	4.19	3.50	3.87	5.21
1939	2.36	---	2.82	2.76	3.77	3.30	3.48	4.53
1940	2.21	---	2.52	2.50	3.55	3.10	3.25	4.30
1941	1.95	---	2.15	2.10	3.34	2.95	3.11	3.95
1942	---	2.46	2.25	2.36	3.34	2.96	3.11	3.96
1943	---	2.47	1.90	2.06	3.16	2.85	2.99	3.64
1944	---	2.48	1.64	1.86	3.05	2.80	2.97	3.39
1945	---	2.37	1.49	1.67	2.87	2.68	2.89	3.06
1946	---	2.19	1.51	1.64	2.74	2.60	2.71	2.91
1947	---	2.25	1.93	2.01	2.86	2.67	2.78	3.11
1948	---	2.44	2.35	2.40	3.08	2.87	3.03	3.34
1949	---	2.31	2.15	2.21	2.96	2.74	2.90	3.24
1950	---	2.32	1.90	1.98	2.86	2.67	2.82	3.10
1951	---	2.57	1.97	2.00	3.08	2.89	3.09	3.26
1952	---	2.68	2.20	2.19	3.19	3.00	3.20	3.36
1953	---	2.93	2.40	2.72	3.43	3.30	3.45	3.55

*Sources: U. S. Treasury bonds: Federal Reserve System
Municipal bonds: Bond Buyer and Standard & Poor's
Corporate bonds: Moody's

TABLE I-2
CORPORATE BOND YIELDS,
BY QUALITY RATINGS, 1919-1953*

	Composite	Aaa	Aa	A	Baa	U. S. Treasury	
						Non-Taxable	Taxable
1919	6.27	5.49	5.86	6.48	7.25	4.73	
1920	7.08	6.12	6.59	7.41	8.20	5.32	
1921	7.04	5.97	6.55	7.28	8.35	5.09	
1922	5.95	5.10	5.95	6.03	7.08	4.30	
1923	6.04	5.12	5.26	6.17	7.24	4.36	
1924	5.80	5.00	5.44	5.93	6.83	4.06	
1925	5.47	4.88	5.20	5.55	6.27	3.86	
1926	5.21	4.73	4.97	5.24	5.87	3.68	
1927	4.97	4.57	4.77	5.04	5.48	3.34	
1928	4.94	4.55	4.71	5.01	5.48	3.33	
1929	5.21	4.73	4.93	5.28	5.90	3.60	
1930	5.09	4.55	4.77	5.13	5.90	3.29	
1931	5.81	4.58	5.05	6.01	7.62	3.34	
1932	6.87	5.01	5.98	7.20	9.30	3.68	
1933	5.89	4.49	5.23	6.09	7.76	3.31	
1934	4.96	4.00	4.44	5.08	6.32	3.12	
1935	4.46	3.60	3.95	4.55	5.75	2.79	
1936	3.87	3.24	3.46	4.02	4.77	2.65	
1937	3.94	3.26	3.46	4.01	5.03	2.68	
1938	4.19	3.19	3.56	4.22	5.80	2.56	
1939	3.77	3.01	3.22	3.89	4.96	2.36	
1940	3.55	2.84	3.02	3.57	4.75	2.21	
1941	3.34	2.77	2.94	3.30	4.33	1.95	
1942	3.34	2.83	2.98	3.28	4.28	---	2.46
1943	3.16	2.73	2.86	3.13	3.91	---	2.47
1944	3.05	2.72	2.81	3.06	3.61	---	2.48
1945	2.87	2.62	2.71	2.87	3.29	---	2.37
1946	2.74	2.53	2.62	2.75	3.25	---	2.19
1947	2.86	2.61	2.70	2.87	3.24	---	2.25
1948	3.08	2.82	2.90	3.12	3.47	---	2.44
1949	2.96	2.66	2.75	3.00	3.42	---	2.31
1950	2.86	2.62	2.69	2.89	3.24	---	2.32
1951	3.08	2.86	2.91	3.13	3.41	---	2.57
1952	3.19	2.96	3.04	3.23	3.52	---	2.68
1953	3.43	3.20	3.31	3.47	3.74	---	2.93

*Sources:　Corporates:　Moody's
　　　　　　Treasury:　　Federal Reserve System

TABLE I-3
PREFERRED AND COMMON STOCK YIELDS, 1919-1953*

	Preferred	Common Stocks					
	Industrial	Composite	Industrial	Rails	Utility	Banks	Insurance
1919	6.31						
1920	6.79						
1921	6.80						
1922	6.14						
1923	6.12						
1924	6.08						
1925	5.90						
1926	5.78						
1927	5.51						
1928	5.12						
1929	5.12	3.41	3.84	4.36	2.10	1.65	2.96
1930	4.95	4.54	4.93	5.55	3.45	2.81	4.36
1931	5.04	6.17	6.37	7.83	5.20	5.01	6.70
1932	6.13	7.36	7.28	6.15	7.53	6.96	9.35
1933	5.75	4.42	3.71	2.68	5.81	6.09	5.38
1934	5.29	4.11	3.43	3.01	5.86	5.59	3.92
1935	4.63	4.06	3.52	3.97	5.11	4.77	3.70
1936	4.33	3.50	3.36	2.24	3.66	3.53	3.26
1937	4.45	4.77	4.79	4.29	5.40	3.59	3.85
1938	4.34	4.38	3.86	5.29	6.27	4.98	4.34
1939	4.17	4.15	3.85	3.75	5.31	4.43	4.13
1940	4.14	5.31	5.30	5.41	5.99	4.45	4.41
1941	4.10	6.25	6.33	6.47	8.02	4.74	4.17
1942	4.31	6.67	6.44	7.73	9.75	5.42	4.67
1943	4.06	4.89	4.54	6.93	6.84	4.07	3.68
1944	3.99	4.81	4.56	6.75	6.28	3.57	3.75
1945	3.70	4.19	4.00	5.51	4.99	3.35	3.34
1946	3.53	3.97	3.75	5.38	4.22	3.75	3.31
1947	3.79	5.13	5.06	6.16	5.32	4.47	3.59
1948	4.15	5.78	5.87	6.04	5.85	4.62	3.37
1949	3.97	6.63	6.82	8.47	5.86	4.63	3.27
1950	3.85	6.27	6.51	6.50	5.66	4.49	3.39
1951	4.11	6.12	6.29	6.31	5.77	4.68	3.42
1952	4.13	5.50	5.55	5.88	5.39	4.40	3.24
1953	4.27	5.49	5.51	6.48	5.33	4.46	3.34

*Sources: Preferred Stocks; Standard & Poor's
                Common Stocks: Moody's

1. Assuming that government bonds represent relatively riskless investments, compute the arithmeticical differences between governments and other types of bonds for selected years, such as 1920, 1927, 1932, 1936, 1940, 1946, 1950, and 1952. Since bonds in some classes are priced only in terms of yields, the variations are known "in the trade" in terms of points or hundreths of one percent. What is the "spread" between governments and other types of bonds in points during years of low yields? What is the "spread" in years of high yields? Does this pattern afford any ideas of the comparative swings in bonds of different industries? From Table I-2 can you derive, in similar manner, ideas of the comparative swings in bonds of different qualities? If yields vary inversely to prices, when would you want to hold high quality issues? Low quality issues?

2. The variation between Aaa and Baa bonds is often used as a measure of confidence in the securities markets. Divide the yields on Baa bonds in Table I-2 by those for Aaa bonds for the 1919-1952 period. Do you find any tendency toward a "normal" spread? Does the fact that the spread is low indicate a potential change in the direction of yields?

3. Compute the spread between Baa bonds and the composite of common stocks. Is there a greater relation of these medium grade bonds to common stocks than there is between medium grade bonds and high grade bonds?

4. Compare the spread found in question 3 with that between Baa bonds and preferred stocks. Would you agree with a contention that bonds are always of better quality than preferred stocks?

5. Compare the yield patterns for the various groups of common stocks given in Table I-3. Which has the least cyclical change? Which the most? Do you find any similar pattern of variations in the changes in bond yields of the same industrial groupings as shown in Table I-1?

6. Many writers of investment books and articles refer to the changes in security prices that result from changes in basic bond yields as those arising from money rate or interest rate risks. Do common stock yields show that money rate risks are

important in the prices of common stocks, or do other factors also appear to bear some influence? What about medium grade (Baa) bonds? High grade bonds?

9. The Patterns of Bond Yields and Prices

The relative variations in bond prices and yields afford an interesting advanced problem. Comparisons of various types of bonds, maturities, and quality can reward the student with a workable knowledge of the characteristics of the bond markets.

The tables on pages 18–23 present lists of bonds in the public utility, railroad, and industrial fields, arranged by maturities into ten year groups (allowing some idea of short-term, intermediate, and long term bonds) and by quality ratings. For each bond listed the overall coverage of charges is given for 1952 and for the five-year period, 1948-52, together with the price ranges in 1950, 1951, and 1952. The student can, by reference to bond yield tables, work out the approximate yields, if desired.

1. What relation do you find between the average coverage and quality ratings? This is often called the vital factor in bond analysis.

2. What relation do you find in the price ranges of bonds in the 1955-65 list compared to the ranges of bonds in the 1965-75, and the 1975 and later groups? In theory, short-term bonds should show less variation in price than longer-term bonds, and also have a lower yield. Is this theory borne out by the data?

3. Are there many observable differences in price levels (or yields) between the various groups of industries?

4. Is there any observable difference between yields or prices of mortgages over debentures? Do convertibles offer a special problem?

5. Could you set up yield curves for each of the various categories of bonds? Consider whether separate curves should be derived for each quality classification and each industrial group.

TABLE I-4

Rating	Issue	Amount (millions)	Overall Coverage 1948-52 average	1952	Price Range 1950	1951	1952
			A. Public Utilities				
			1. Maturities 1955 to 1965				
Aaa	Bell Tel. Co. of Pa.				122.4	116.4	112.6
	1st & ref. 5s C, 60	50.0	4.41	4.54	116	110	109.4
	Wash. Gas Lt. Co.				123.6	119	115.6
	gen 5s, 60	5.2	3.00	3.28	120	114.4	112
Aa	Conn. River Pwr.				105.4	104.6	104.4
	1st 3-3/4s A, 61	14.0	2.12	1.98	102.4	102.2	101.6
	New Eng. T. & T. Co.				119.2	113.7	111.2
	1st 4-1/2s B, 61	40.0	3.10	3.98	113.4	108.6	108
A	Atlanta Gas Light Co.				102	101	98.4
	1st 3s, 63	6.3	5.34	3.71	101	98	97.4
	Penn. Wtr. & Pwr. Co.				106.4	104.4	103.6
	ref. & coll. 3-1/4s, 64	9.5	3.46	4.20	104.2	101.4	100.4
	Pub. Serv. Elec. & Gas Co.				105.2	103.7	101.4
	deb. 3s, 63	47.0	3.37	3.53	102.5	97.6	99.3
Baa	Calif. Elec. Pwr. Co.				---	97	97.4
	deb. 3s. 60	2.0	3.97	4.37	---	93	93
	Laclede Gas Lt. Co.				104.6	104.4	102.5
	1st 3-1/2s, 65	19.0	3.14	3.45	103	99.4	100
	Shawinigan W. & P. Co.				100.6	97	93.4
	1st & coll. 3s L, 61	12.4	2.27	2.32	99	92	91.4
	Rochester Tel. Corp.				104.7	102.2	100.4
	s. f. deb. 4s, 63	7.7	2.81	3.31	104.4	98	97
Ba	Western Union Teleg. Co.				103	104.7	104.3
	5s 60	35.0	2.02	1.65	85	99.7	100.4
	United Transit Co.				98	97.4	95
	deb. 4s, 60	3.6	2.84	3.25	92	92	93
	Gatineau Pwr. Co.				102	96	96
	deb. 2-3/4s 61	9.0	2.38	2.56	94	90	70
	General Tel. Corp.				105.4	104	101.4
	deb. 4s, 64	9.6	1.94	2.15	102	100	100
	Green Mtn. Pwr. Corp.				104.4	104.4	102.1
	1st & ref. 3-3/4s, 63	7.6	2.30	2.19	102.5	97.1	99
			2. Maturities 1965 to 1975				
Aaa	Cleve. Elec. Ill. Co.				107.6	106.6	103.2
	1st 3s, 70	50.0	6.59	5.20	104.6	98.6	100.2
	Phila. Elec. Co.				104.5	102.2	99.2
	1st & ref. 2-3/4s, 67	65.0	5.09	5.38	100.4	94.6	96.2
	Cincinnati G. & E.				104.2	102.3	98.2
	1st 2-3/4s, 75	45.5	7.73	6.68	100.6	93.4	94.4
	Conn. L. & P.				107.5	105.6	100.6
	1st & ref. 3s I, 74	10.0	6.36	6.31	106.2	98	98
Aa	Amer. Tel. & Tel.				100.5	99	94
	deb. 2-3/4s, 70	140.0	6.07	7.26	99	96	92
	Detroit Ed. Co.				108.2	105.4	101.6
	gen. & ref. 3s H, 70	50.0	3.47	3.22	104.4	98	99
	Ohio Pwr.				107.6	106.6	104.4
	1st 3-1/4s, 68	55.0	3.95	4.35	104.4	101	102.5
	Pac. G. & E.				107	105.3	100.4
	1st & ref. 3s L, 74	109.5	3.70	3.90	103.2	95.6	97.4
	Consumers Pwr.				106	104.1	99
	1st 2-7/8s, 75	113.8	4.97	4.82	102.1	93.7	96

18

TABLE I-4 (Continued)

Rating	Issue	Amount (millions)	Overall Coverage 1948-52 average	1952	Price Range 1950	1951	1952
A	Appalachian E. P. Co.				109.2	107.2	103.5
	1st 3-1/4s, 70	70.0	3.98	3.98	106.3	99.2	101.2
	Columbus & So. Ohio Elec.				108.7	107.2	102.1
	Co. 1st 3-1/4s, 70	26.8	4.20	3.55	106.1	98.1	99.6
	Alabama Pwr. Co.				107	105.4	105
	1st 3-1/2s, 72	79.0	3.58	3.71	104.5	99.4	102.4
	Columbia Gas Sys.				102.7	102.6	99.2
	deb. 3s A, 75	110.0	4.28	2.93	101.6	95	94
	Wis. Pub. Serv. Corp.				107.4	105.7	102.4
	1st 3-1/4s, 71	24.3	3.49	3.38	105.2	97	98.6
Baa	Gatineau Pwr. Co.				102.5	100.2	93
	1st 3s C, 70	45.0	2.38	2.56	101	86.4	86.4
	Mich. Cons. Gas Co.				106.4	105.2	103
	deb. 3-7/8s, 67	24.0	2.89	2.46	105.2	102	100.2
	Milw. Gas Lt. Co.				103	103.2	96
	1st 3-1/8s, 75	27.0	2.49	2.53	101.6	94	93
	Portland Gen. Elec. Co.				104.4	103.2	96
	1st 3-1/8s, 75	34.0	3.14	3.47	102.4	90	89
	Tenn. Gas Trans. Co.				---	102.4	107
	deb. 4-7/8s, 71	25.0	4.31	2.97	---	102.1	103.4
Ba	Northeastern Wtr. Co.				105.4	104.5	102.6
	coll. 5s, 68	9.3	2.38	2.15	101.2	100.2	100.2
	Calgary Pwr., Ltd.				99	97.4	90
	1st 3-1/4s, 72	11.0	3.67	3.56	97.4	90	84
	Winnipeg Elec. Co.				102.6	101.6	92.4
	1st 3-3/4s, 71	13.0	2.89	4.91	101.2	91	90
	3. Maturities 1975 and later						
Aaa	Commonwealth Ed.				---	96.4	94.2
	deb. 2-7/8s, 2001	48.0	3.47	3.63	---	90.2	91.5
	Mich. Bell Tel.				107.5	106.2	101.4
	deb. 3-1/8s, 88	75.0	6.48	7.71	106.2	100	100
	Consol. G. E. L. & P. Balt.				106.4	104.2	100
	1st & ref. 2-7/8s U, 81	41.8	4.28	4.23	103.2	95.7	95.4
	Phila. Elec.				103.5	102.3	97
	1st & ref. 2-3/4s, 81	30.0	5.09	5.38	100.4	92.3	94.4
	Duke Pwr. Co.				105.2	104.4	98.2
	1st & ref. 2-7/8s, 79	40.0	6.29	4.86	103.4	97.4	95
Aa	Cons. Ed. N. Y.				102.5	101.4	95.4
	1st & ref. 2-3/4s A, 82	100.0	3.89	3.65	99.7	91.4	92
	Detroit Ed. Co.				103.4	101.3	96.4
	gen. & ref. 2-3/4s I, 82	60.0	3.47	3.22	100.2	92.3	93
	New York P. & L.				103	101.4	97
	1st 2-3/4s, 75	48.8	4.43	4.63	100.4	92	93.4
	Gulf States Util. Co.				100.4	98.7	94
	1st 2-5/8s, 76	27.0	5.54	4.20	99	91.6	91.4
	Wis. Elec. Pwr. Co.				100.6	99.3	94.2
	1st 2-5/8s, 76	50.0	4.68	5.02	98.4	91.2	91
A	Ill. Pwr. Co.				---	---	105
	1st 3-1/2s, 82	20.0	4.31	4.21	---	---	103.4
	Pub. Serv. E. & G. Co.				165	165	150
	deb. 6s, 98	18.2	3.37	3.53	160.6	140	142

TABLE I-4 (Continued)

Rating	Issue	Amount (millions)	Overall Coverage 1948-52 average	1952	Price Range 1950	1951	1952
A	Scranton-Sp. Bg. Wtr. Serv.				102.4	99.6	95
	1st 2-7/8s, 76	23.9	2.96	2.79	99	91	91.4
	Indpls. P. & L. Co.				104	102.2	96
	1st 2-7/8s, 79	40.0	4.06	4.66	99.4	93	93
Baa	Pac. Pwr. & Lt.				---	---	102.4
	1st 3-5/8s, 82	12.5	3.91	6.04	---	---	100.4
	Interstate Pwr. Co.				105.3	105	103
	1st 3-3/4s, 78	20.0	2.48	3.27	103.6	100	102
	New Eng. Elec. Sys.				101.4	101.4	97
	deb. 3-1/4s, 77	50.0	2.48	2.29	101	92	92
	S. Car. E. & G. Co.				103.2	103	94.4
	1st & ref. 3s, 80	22.2	2.50	2.61	101	93	92
Ba	Am. & Fgn. Pwr.				99.4	99.3	93
	Inc. deb. 5s, 2030	50.0	2.89	2.68	88	90.4	74.6
	Seattle Gas Co.				108.4	102	101
	1st 3-5/8s, 76	5.1	2.70	2.69	95.4⁻	95	95
	Sierra Pac. Pwr. Co.				101.2	101.2	101
	deb. 3-3/8s, 75	2.5	3.92	3.55	101.2	100.2	101
			B. Railroads 1. Maturities 1955 to 1965				
Aaa	Winston-Salem Sthbd. Ry.				115.3	113.1	105
	1st 4s, 60	5.0	guaranteed		113	106.2	102
Aa	Can. Natl. Ry. Co.				114	109.6	107.5
	guar. 4-1/2s, 56	67.4	guaranteed		109	105.3	105.2
A	L. & N., Atla., Kn. &				109	107.4	104
	Cin. Div. 4s, 55	24.6	3.57	3.88	107	102.2	102.2
	C. B. & Q.				112.6	111.5	107.2
	gen. 4s, 58	24.6	5.38	5.85	110	104	104
	Gt. Northern Ry. Co.				97.4	96	95
	gen. 2-1/4s R, 61	25.0	4.21	4.48	94	90	91
	Chgo. Un. Stat. Co.				106.6	105.6	101.2
	1st 2-7/8s G, 63	37.8	guaranteed		103	100	97.4
	Atla. & Charl. Air Line Ry.				105.4	104	101.6
	1st 3-3/4s, 63	14.0	guaranteed		102.4	101	100.6
Baa	Chgo. Ind. & So. RR				100	101	100
	1st 4s, 56	14.2	guaranteed		89	96	98
	Penn. RR.				115	114.4	110
	cons. 4-1/2s, 60	48.8	1.64	1.91	112	105.4	106.2
	So. Pac. RR				96.6	96.4	96
	1st 2-1/4s G, 61	21.4	guaranteed		93	91	92.2
	Atl. Coast Line				108	109	108.1
	gen. un. 4-1/2s A, 64	32.6	3.34	3.75	101.4	102	104.7
Ba	So. Ry.				98.4	101	103
	dev. & gen. 4s A, 56	39.9	2.56	3.15	90	97.5	98.2
	Boston & Me. RR				84	90.6	76.2
	1st 4s RR, 60	51.4	2.09	1.77	69.4	66	66.5
	Me-Kan-Tex.				100.5	102.4	103.6
	pr. ln. 5s A, 62	12.5	3.55	3.80	84.7	93.6	94.1
	Penn. RR				107	109.4	105.4
	gen. mtg. 4-1/2s A, 65	124.1	1.91	1.72	99.3	94	97.4

TABLE I-4 (Continued)

Rating	Issue	Amount (millions)	Overall Coverage 1948-52 average	Overall Coverage 1952	Price Range 1950	Price Range 1951	Price Range 1952
Ba	Jamestown, Frank. & Cl.				85.6	94.6	90.4
	1st 4s, 59	10.8	guaranteed		70	79	79.1
	2. Maturities 1965 to 1975						
Aaa	Cinc. Un. Term. Co.				110.5	110	105.4
	1st 3-3/4s E, 69	11.0	guaranteed		110	101.4	102.4
	Kas. Cy. Term. Ry.				103.3	98.2	96.4
	1st 2-3/4s, 74	27.5	guaranteed		101	95.4	94.4
Aa	Monongahela Ry.				104	103	100.1
	1st 3-1/4s B, 66	10.0	1.64	1.17	102.5	102.4	98
	St. Paul Un. Depot Co.				104.4	104	100.1
	1st & ref. 3-1/8s B, 71	13.1	guaranteed		100.6	100	100
	Virginian Ry. Co.				104.4	104.4	103
	1st & ref. 3-1/4s C, 73	9.0	4.02	4.31	102.7	98.4	98.6
	Alabama Gt. So.				104.4	101.4	102
	1st 3-1/4s A, 67	8.6	9.11	9.51	103	100.4	100.3
	Wheel. & L. E. Ry. Co.				99	98	95
	gen. & ref. 2-3/4s B, 74	6.7	assumed		97	92	93
A	Central Pac. Ry. Co.				104.4	105.2	103.2
	1st 3-3/4s B, 68	36.7	guaranteed		101.4	101.3	100.6
	C. B. & O.				101.2	101	97.6
	1st & ref. 2-7/8s, 70	47.9	5.38	5.85	99	93	93.4
	Ches. & O. Ry.				107	107.1	105.1
	ref. & imp. 3-7/8s H, 73	39.0	3.74	4.49	103.5	101	102.1
	Kas. Cy. So. Ry.				106	105.4	105.4
	1st 4s A, 75	39.2	3.83	3.57	103.4	100.4	101.6
Baa	Tex. & N. O.				102	103	98
	1st & ref. 3-1/4s B, 70	14.7	4.38	5.52	97.4	96.4	94
	Ill. Term. RR.				99.4	99.2	93
	25-yr. 1st 4s A, 70	11.9	2.35	1.94	96	94	82
	Wabash RR Co.				101.6	103.2	99
	1st 3-1/4s B, 71	45.4	4.10	4.11	97.4	93	94
Ba	Am. Airlines,				99.6	98.4	94.2
	Inc. deb. 3s, 66	30.0	6.62	13.9	90.2	89	91
	So. Pac. Co.				102.4	103.2	104.6
	4-1/2s, 69	63.2	3.22	4.01	92	93.4	96.4
	Ill. Cent. RR. Co.				100	99	104.4
	4-3/4s, 66	34.7	3.14	3.30	95	99	99
	Balt. & O. RR. Co.				98.6	100.2	97.2
	1st 4s A, 75	73.7	2.29	2.83	82	79.7	84
	Pitt., Cinn., Chgo. & St. L.				111.6	115	108.4
	gen. 5s B, 75	26.0	guaranteed		100	99	100
	3. Maturities 1975 and later						
Aaa	Un. Pac. RR.				97.2	96.6	91.2
	ref. 2-1/2s C, 91	78.1	11.65	12.45	93.2	84	86
	A. T. & S. F. Ry.				131.3	129.7	121.1
	gen. 4s, 95	150.9	9.16	9.79	125.4	116.2	116.5
	Norfolk & W. Ry. Co.				133.4	132	122.4
	1st cons. 4s, 96	32.4	17.87	20.25	126	117.3	118
	Term. RR. Assn. of S. L.				105	104	98
	ref. & imp. 2-7/8s D, 85	37.7	guaranteed		103	93.4	94

TABLE I-4 (Continued)

Rating	Issue	Amount (millions)	Overall Coverage 1948–52 average	1952	Price Range 1950	1951	1952
Aa	Un. Pac. RR.				105	104.6	100.2
	deb. 2-7/8s, 76	44.5	11.65	12.45	101	95	95.3
	St. L. Southwstrn. Ry. Co.				106	106	112
	1st 4% cert., 89	20.0	7.93	12.44	99.4	100	110.4
	Virginian Ry.				101	100.4	96.4
	1st & ref. 3s B, 95	56.7	4.02	4.31	94.2	92.4	92
A	Chgo. R. I. & P.				100.6	100	96.4
	1st 2-7/8s A, 80	52.7	9.66	8.18	98.4	95	93.2
	Gt. Northern Ry.				102.2	101.2	93
	gen. 3-1/8s O, 2000	37.5	4.21	4.48	95.4	87.4	86
	N. Y., Ch. & St. L.				104	104	99
	ref. 3-1/4s E, 80	54.0	4.90	4.73	100	95	95
	A. T. & S. F. Ry.				121	121.5	114.1
	adj. 4s, 95	48.8	9.16	9.79	119	106.4	108
	L. & N.				100.2	103.2	95.4
	1st & ref. 3-3/8s F, 2003	51.9	3.57	3.88	89.4	86	86.2
Baa	So. Pac. Co., Oregon Lines				105	105.2	105
	1st 4-1/2s A, 77	61.3	3.22	4.01	97.1	97	98.3
	Tex. & Pac. Ry.				106	106	104.4
	gen. & ref. 3-7/8s E, 85	34.6	3.75	4.95	100	98	99
	So. Pac. RR. Co.				97.2	97	89
	1st 2-7/8s E, 86	50.0	guaranteed		87.6	82	82.5
	No. Pac. Ry. Co.				113	114.2	110.6
	prior lien 4s, 97	100.9	2.43	2.73	100.6	100	101.4
	So. Ry.				123.4	125.3	120.4
	1st cons. 5s, 94	92.0	2.56	3.15	111	107	109.1
Ba	B. & O. RR., Pitt., L.E. &				92.4	98.3	96
	W. Va. ref. 4s A, 80	35.0	2.29	2.83	81	78	81.4
	Penn. RR.				103	107.5	98.4
	gen. 4-1/4s D, 81	50.0	1.64	1.91	90.6	87.4	89.4
	N. Y. Cent.				73.3	75	67.4
	cons. 4s A, 98	69.0	1.37	1.51	55	58.4	60.1
	West Shore RR.				70.6	71.6	67
	1st 4s, 2361	46.3	assumed		56	57	58.2
	No. Pac. Ry.				73	76	76
	gen. lien 3s, 2047	53.9	2.43	2.73	60.4	63	69.1

C. Industrial
1. Maturities 1955 to 1965

Rating	Issue	Amount (millions)	Overall Coverage 1948–52 average	1952	Price Range 1950	1951	1952
Aaa	Texas Corp.				106.4	105	102.6
	deb. 3s, 65	60.0	31.49	28.65	104	101.6	100.2
Aa	Dow Chem.				101	100.2	97.4
	deb. 2.35s, 61	27.0	17.05	12.32	99.2	94.5	94.7
	Skelly Oil				103.2	101.7	99.4
	deb. 2-3/4s, 65	10.0	87.29	87.10	101	97.2	97
	Quaker Oats				102.6	101.3	99.4
	deb. 2-3/4s, 64	10.0	21.57	11.93	100.4	97.1	96.5
A	Allis-Chalmers				101	99.7	99
	deb. 2s, 56	15.0	22.24	10.92	98.6	97	96.2
	York Corp.				104	102.2	101
	1st s.f. 3-1/4s, 60	1.9	9.73	8.90	102	99	100.2

TABLE I-4 (Concluded)

Rating	Issue	Amount (millions)	Overall Coverage		Price Range		
			1948–52 average	1952	1950	1951	1952
A	Amer. Tob.				104.4	103	101.5
	s.f. deb. 3s, 62	66.1	5.49	4.44	101.7	98.4	99.1
	Lorillard (P.) Co.				105.1	103	101.6
	deb. 3s, 63	16.0	6.05	3.81	102.1	99	99.4
Baa	Celotex Corp.				102	102.2	100
	3-1/4 deb. (45), 60	3.4	13.74	8.54	100.4	98.1	99
	Celanese				104.4	103.6	101.1
	deb. 3s, 65	31.0	11.85	3.70	102.6	97.4	98
Ba	Bush Term. Bldgs.				106.4	105	105.1
	1st 5s, 60	3.2	3.85	2.77	104	103	104.2
		2. Maturities 1965 to 1975					
Aaa	Atlantic Refining				102.6	101.2	100.6
	deb. 2-5/8s, 66	25.0	35.44	30.76	100.4	96.4	93.3
	Shell Union Oil				99.5	98.2	95.3
	deb. 2-1/2s, 71	117.3	29.10	23.27	97.4	90.6	92.4
	St. Oil (N.J.)				98.3	96.6	94.4
	deb. 2-3/8s, 71	85.0	39.05	38.40	96	89.6	90
Aa	Beth. Steel				102.1	101.7	98
	cons. 2-3/4s I, 70	72.4	19.01	12.46	100.3	93.4	94.4
	Minn. Min. & Mfg.				103.5	101.5	100
	deb. 2-3/4s, 67	9.3	60.8	65.0	101.4	101.4	98.7
	May Dept. Stores				101.3	100.2	96.7
	deb. 2-5/8s, 72	14.4	30.72	18.48	99.4	96.6	93
A	Amer. Tob.				105.7	104.4	101
	s.f. deb. 3s, 69	75.4	5.49	4.44	103	97.4	98
	Union Oil Co.				103.4	102.5	98.7
	deb. 2-3/4s, 70	23.6	13.39	10.53	101.1	95	96.1
Baa	Union Oil Co.				---	---	109.6
	conv. deb. 3-1/8s, 72	35.0	13.39	10.53	---	---	103.4
Ba	Peabody Coal				---	100	102
	s.f. deb. 4-7/8s, 66	6.0	4.74	2.84	---	98.4	100
	Warren Petrol.				---	105.4	114.2
	conv. deb. 3-1/2s, 66	15.0	9.98	6.38	---	103.6	103.6
		3. Maturities 1975 and later					
Aaa	Socony Vacuum				99.4	98	94.5
	deb. 2-1/2s, 76	93.1	34.45	32.98	97.4	89.2	91.2
Aa	Beth. Steel				105.4	104.4	100.4
	s.f. deb. 3s K, 79	46.0	19.01	12.46	103.4	97.6	98.2
A	Amer. Tob.				---	---	102.2
	s.f. deb. 3-1/4s, 77	50.0	5.49	4.44	---	---	100
Baa	Celanese				---	---	103.6
	s.f. deb. 3-1/2s, 76	50.0	11.85	3.70	---	---	100.6
Ba	Cities Serv.				101.4	100.6	97.7
	s.f. deb. 3s, 77	78.1	5.39	5.18	99.7	90.5	91.6
	Walworth				95.2	96.4	85
	conv. deb. 3-1/4s, 76	5.0	9.88	8.47	87.4	80	76

10. Common Stock Price Fluctuations

It is important to realize that varied types of common stocks, even when classed into broad industry groups, do not all follow the same patterns of price change. This elementary problem is intended to emphasize the risks involved in thinking of common stock investment in terms of averages.

The Securities and Exchange Commission has prepared and issues weekly stock price indexes for a selected sample of issues traded on the New York Stock Exchange. Those industries, classified according to the Bureau of the Budget's standard industrial classification, which accounted for more than one percent of the volume or value of common stock trading in 1949, were selected for representation in the index. For each industry, the most active stocks, volume or valuewise, were chosen to give a coverage of 65 per cent of volume and value of trading in the industry in 1949. At least five issues were included in each industry to give a representative index. 204 of these stocks were listed on the New York Stock Exchange on January 1, 1939, while the other 61 were listed at various later times. The composition of the index has remained the same since 1949 except for changes due to mergers, reorganizations, and so forth. The method of computing the index is to multiply the closing price for each week by the number of shares outstanding for each stock, add these market values and divide by the number of shares. The resulting weighted averages for industries, groups, and the composite are then related to a base average for 1939 to give the index number for the week. An unweighted average of weekly indexes gives the monthly and annual averages. Due to some slight adjustments made at a later date, the indexes for some industries in 1939 vary slightly from 100, but the deviations are not considerable and do not alter the significance of changes. The S.E.C. index is similar to that prepared by Standard & Poor's Corporation. The latter includes some unlisted common stocks and uses different industry group classifications.

Annual averages for these stock price indexes are presented in Table I-5 for the composite, industrial groups and selected industries. Examination of the tabulations shows that from the 1942

TABLE I-5
STOCK PRICE INDEXES, 1939-1953 (1939 equals 100)*

Year	Compos-ite	Manufac-turing	Durable Goods	Iron & Steel	Motor Veh.	Non-Durables	Foods	Chemi-cals	Tex-tiles
1939	100.0	100.0	100.0	100.0	100.0	100.0	100.0	100.0	100.0
1940	94.2	93.4	92.5	99.4	101.2	94.2	93.3	101.0	103.5
1941	85.7	84.8	81.6	92.2	80.5	88.0	83.9	90.0	91.4
1942	74.9	75.5	73.7	78.2	76.4	77.1	75.0	77.3	85.7
1943	99.1	99.0	94.7	87.1	105.0	103.5	104.0	94.1	124.9
1944	108.0	106.8	104.5	91.4	124.5	109.1	120.6	93.9	144.0
1945	131.2	129.0	129.0	117.6	148.1	129.2	152.3	107.4	201.8
1946	149.4	146.6	138.6	146.0	143.1	154.4	192.4	125.8	280.8
1947	130.9	132.4	119.9	130.5	126.8	144.6	163.0	119.1	234.0
1948	132.8	136.9	124.5	142.8	129.7	148.7	149.9	118.9	259.4
1949	127.7	132.1	116.1	125.7	129.7	147.1	146.7	127.1	222.1
1950	154.1	165.7	150.2	180.3	181.5	180.2	169.9	172.3	277.0
1951	184.8	206.8	178.5	222.2	206.5	233.1	171.6	222.8	356.4
1952	195.0	220.2	188.8	204.9	232.8	249.2	165.1	225.6	303.9
1953	193.3	220.0	192.6	203.6	244.2	245.2	175.0	234.8	236.7

Year	Trans-portation	Rails	Air-lines	Utili-ties	Telecom-munications	Electric and Gas	Trade, Fi-nance, Service	Mining
1939	100.0	100.0	100.0	100.0	100.2	100.0	100.0	99.7
1940	99.2	96.5	154.4	99.9	101.4	96.0	90.4	95.6
1941	96.5	95.1	122.9	89.1	94.4	75.1	82.0	71.1
1942	90.8	89.0	123.3	69.8	74.5	57.4	71.3	59.7
1943	125.7	120.2	215.9	90.4	94.7	79.1	100.9	83.4
1944	140.5	135.5	231.2	98.9	103.1	87.6	117.1	93.2
1945	190.0	179.9	356.3	112.9	114.4	108.8	149.3	114.3
1946	202.4	190.7	378.9	119.6	119.7	124.2	204.3	125.5
1947	149.1	143.9	228.2	105.5	101.5	114.3	162.8	117.2
1948	158.4	156.3	190.1	99.4	96.1	106.1	157.0	133.3
1949	136.2	132.7	184.1	98.1	90.5	110.6	160.5	129.2
1950	160.0	155.7	217.9	108.9	99.6	122.8	183.8	143.5
1951	199.0	191.8	298.0	112.6	103.3	126.8	207.9	205.1
1952	220.6	216.2	278.6	117.9	102.9	142.5	205.8	275.7
1953	218.7	215.2	265.6	121.5	103.8	151.8	206.6	240.5

*Source: Securities and Exchange Commission (calculations by the author.)

lows, the market rose to 1946, declined about 20 per cent to 1949, and then soared upward to the end of 1952. Such was not the pattern, however, of the different group averages nor for all the individual industries. And, not only was the timing of the cyclical swings different, but, more importantly, the relative variations differed greatly. Note, for example, the relatively small variation in the telecommunications industry as compared with that for the airlines or for the mining industries. The evident basic forces underlying such diversity of movement must be different. One of the problems of investment in common stocks is to appraise these forces adequately. For purposes of speculation, such an analysis is paramount.

1. Tabulate the years in which the early war lows, postwar highs, and 1950-1953 highs were reached. Can you find any consistency in the lead or lag of certain groups or industries when compared with the composite?

2. Calculate the percentage of decline or advance recorded by each series between the years tabulated in the above question. What industries have shown better than the composite? Which ones did worse?

Part II

---

11.   Calculation of Stock Yields

Every investor should become familiar with at least the basic mathematics used in securities valuation. This simple problem calls attention to some of the more important points involved in the computation and interpretation of common stocks yields, and yields on preferred stocks.

Mr. S. Ward is a conscientious investor who follows a policy of trying to achieve the highest possible rate of return on his securities consistent with good quality issues. In October 1951 he decided that the textile industry offered some rather high yields. Burlington Mills, paying a dividend of $1.35 a year, was selling at 19, Celanese sold at 47 while paying a $3 dividend on each share, and Industrial Rayon paid a $3 dividend and sold at 60. On the basis of yield, he purchased 100 shares of Burlington Mills common stock. At the end of 1952 the prices and dividend rates were found to be: Burlington Mills, 16¾ and $1; Celanese, 38 and $2.25; Industrial Rayon, 55 and $3. The market in textile shares continued to decline in 1953. On June 18, Mr. Ward consulted his customers' representative at a local brokerage office and found that Burlington Mills was selling at 12½ with an expected dividend of $.60 a share; Celanese was selling at 23 on an anticipated $1 dividend for the year; and Industrial Rayon was expected to continue its $3 dividend rate and was selling at 44. On the basis of the current yields at the time, a switch to Industrial Rayon was indicated.

However, Mr. Ward calculated his yields in a different way. He used the current dividend rate and the purchase price for his Burlington Mills, to get a rate of 3.2 per cent. He knew that many

27

stocks could give him a better return, although the 4.8 per cent yield at the current date was about average for good quality issues.

1. Was Mr. Ward correct in his method of calculating yields, or was his customers' representative correct?

   When deciding between alternative securities, should the current yield on both be used, or should the current yield on one be compared with the yield on cost for the other?

2. How should the yield on a portfolio be calculated? Should it be on the basis of cost prices against income, or current prices against income?

   If your answers to these two questions are not the same, can you explain the use of inconsistent methods?

3. In the case of cumulative preferred stocks, should accumulated and unpaid dividends be included in the computation if they are likely to be paid during the coming year, or should only the regular dividend rate be considered in computing a yield? What should be done in the case of a cumulative preferred stock when no dividend appears likely for some time? What would you do if only part of a cumulative dividend were to be declared during the year?

12.   Bond Yield Calculations

A knowledge of the methods of calculating bond yields, and even of the use of bond yield tables, is an invaluable tool for the investor. This problem involves only simple calculations.

1. On June 6, 1952, Montana-Dakota Utilities 1st 3s of 1965 were quoted in the over-the-counter market at 88 bid, while the 3⅝s of 1976 were quoted at 92 bid. Which bond had the higher current yields? Which had the higher net yield or yield to maturity, if both paid interest on April 1 and October 1, and fell due on April 1?

2. United States Government short-term issues are quoted in the market in terms of yields. If Treasury bills are quoted on the basis of 2.63 for 91 day maturities, what would the price of $10,000 of bills be? Can you calculate this easily, or should reference be made to yield tables?

3. Indianapolis, Indiana, gas revenue bonds mature serially. In mid 1952 they were quoted at 1.65%-1 for 4½ per cent bonds, for 3⅛ bonds, and for 2⅞ per cent bonds, respectively, all maturing in five years, and at 2.25%-1 for bonds maturing in 15 years. Calculate the prices for each of these bonds. Why would anyone be willing to pay such high prices for bonds maturing in such a short time?

13. Calculation of Conversion Privileges

The calculation of conversion rights is often bewildering to the investor. If the basic principles are known, however, the methods are simple.

1. Southern California Edison Co. has outstanding a series of 4.48 per cent cumulative convertible preference stock ($25 par) and another at 4.56 per cent. Each share of the former is convertible into 0.85312 common share, and the latter into 0.921 share. From a current source, secure quotations for the issues, and determine if it is profitable to convert. Under what conditions might the preferreds sell far above the common? Could the common sell far above the preferreds? Why?

2. Phillips Petroleum Company has outstanding 3.70 per cent sinking fund debentures, due 1983, convertible into common stock at $65 to June 1, 1958, and $72 thereafter to June 1, 1963. From a current paper secure the quotations on these issues. Compute whether it is profitable to buy the bonds and convert into common. Why is the conversion rate set in terms of dollars instead of shares? What is done about fractional shares? What is the conversion parity of the bonds? Of the stock? What is likely to occur shortly before June 1, 1958? Before June 1, 1963? Why? Is it usual to have a restricted term for conversion?

3. Look up the provisions of Houston Lighting & Power Co. convertible 3¼ per cent debentures, due 1967. What uncommon type of conversion privilege exists in this issue? Can the value of this privilege be calculated readily? Why?

14. Exercising Rights to Subscribe to New Issues

The valuation and handling of rights is often difficult for the small investor. An opportunity to examine various types of situations involving rights is presented here. Note the difference from warrants, as well as the similarities.

The summer of 1953 was distinguished by protracted periods of heat and dryness in most sections of the United States. Large numbers of city residents turned to air conditioning units for relief and comfort. Available supplies were quickly exhausted; factories operated at above-capacity limits in vain efforts to meet the consumer demand. New companies and old projected plans for expansion and looked to the capital markets for funds.

One of the largest manufacturers of air conditioning equipment, Carrier Corporation, had experienced many difficulties during its history; its management determined that funds should be acquired while the popularity of its products was active in the minds of potential buyers of stock. In early September the company filed with the Securities and Exchange Commission registration statements covering offerings of new preferred stock and of new common stock. It was said that the company would, in view of the unsettled condition of the stock market at the time, defer announcement of just what would be offered until shortly before the registrations became effective, and would then withdraw the unwanted registration.

On September 22 announcement was made that 278,422 shares of common stock would be offered for subscription at $31.75 a share to holders of common stock on September 22, on the basis of one new share for each four old shares held. The rights were to be exercised before 3:30 P.M., Eastern Standard Time, on October 7, 1953. Trading of rights on the New York Stock Exchange began on September 24, with the stock to be traded ex-rights on the following day. The closing prices each day for the stock and for the rights were as follows:

Date	Stock	Rights
September 24	36	$1\frac{3}{16}$
25	$35\frac{1}{8}$	$1\frac{3}{16}$

Date		Stock	Rights
	28	35¾	1
	29	35⅞	1¹⁄₁₆
	30	36⅜	1⅛
October	1	36⅞	1⁵⁄₁₆
	2	37½	1⅜
	5	36½	1⅛
	6	36½	1¼
	7	36⅝	1³⁄₁₆

1. What is a right? Are rights always issued when new stock is being offered?
2. What is the usual period available for exercise of rights? What happens to unexercised rights?
3. Calculate the theoretical value of a right on: September 24, September 25, October 1, October 5, and October 7.
4. Why are the actual and theoretical values of a right often different? Is the difference usually great?

Stockholders of Sinclair Oil Corporation received, as of January 9, 1953, rights to subscribe at par to $101.8 million of new convertible subordinated debenture 3¼ per cent bonds, due 1983, at the rate of $100 principal amount for each 12 shares of common stock held. The new issue was convertible into common at $44 a share through January 18, 1958, with the conversion price increasing thereafter in intervals of five-year periods. The maximum potential dilution of the common from conversion of the new debt was 19 per cent. The common stock at the time was selling at about 41¼, to yield 6.30 per cent on the $2.60 dividend then being paid.

The rights were selling at about ¹⁵⁄₃₂ and were to expire January 26. On January 19, a leading investment service advised sale of the rights and the purchase of shares directly, for they appeared to offer the average common stock investor a better participation in the company's longer term future. Graded Baa by Moody, the bonds were classed as good medium grade, but eligible for legal investment in some states.

At the time, Baa industrial bonds were selling in the market at an average yield of 3.26 per cent. However, one service indicated that they believed the yield on the Sinclair debentures without a conversion privilege would be about 3.35 per cent, equal to a price of about 98⅛. The difference between the bonds and common stock was thus about 3.0 per cent yield basis.

The conversion price for the bonds, $44, was 3¼ points above the going market price for the common. Multiplying this difference by 2.28 ($100 divided by $44) we get 7.41 points for the value of the conversion privilege. This, added to the nonconvertible yield price of 98⅛ results in a price of 105⅝, approximately, as the when-issued value of the bonds.

The actual when-issued market valued the bonds at 105⅞. Thus, the premium asked by the market did not seem excessive at the time.

Sinclair common stock earnings for 1952 were estimated at about $7.00 a share, covering amply the $2.60 dividend rate. There was also a possibility that should the need for cash for expansion purposes decline, the dividend rate might be increased with subsequent higher valuation for the common. In view of these factors, the service advised: "we regard the debentures as having moderate near term attraction to those investors who cannot hold common stocks but can purchase share privilege obligations at prices above their straight investment value."

5. Why is the advice to stockholders negative while that to bond buyers is conditionally positive? What kind of bond buyer would especially be interested in this type of issue? Why? Did the corporation have these buyers in mind when it prepared the indenture provisions on conversion?

Reference is occasionally made in investment circles and books to arbitraging during the period when rights are being traded. As an illustration of one of the most complex of these situations, the following quotation from the *Journal of Commerce*, May 23, 1952, may prove of interest and value.

The new American Telephone offering of convertible debentures to be made to stockholders was well received in financial circles. In arbitrage quarters it was predicted that the new rights, based on last night's closing of 156 for the stock, might have a value of close to $2 each. It was also indicated that the new debentures might be valued at around 113 or more. In determining these values the arbitrage houses have to consider a number of factors. The new bonds are not convertible until Oct. 1 which means that in selling the stock short as a hedge, two dividends of 2¼ points each must be absorbed. Also to be considered is the cost of the rights, brokerage and interest. In buying the bonds, when-issued, there would be interest from Aug. 1 at an annual rate of 3½ per cent which would be partly cancelled by the interest paid on money borrowed. The sum involved is 7¾ points. This amount subtracted from the 156 selling price results in a figure of 148¼. The new issue is convertible at 136 and the exercise of the rights involves an expenditure of $100. The difference between 148¼ and 36 is a possible price of 112¼ for the new issue. Arbitrageurs work on a current return basis instead of a yield to maturity as the issues never mature.

6. The calculations of arbitrageurs is allied to that used by the investment service for the Sinclair bonds, but is more complicated for the amateur investor. But with these professionals in

the market, is it likely that the values of rights to issues which have an active market will offer any spectacular profits except through actual exercise for the rights and holding of the new stock? Would the same apply for inactive issues?

7. For a classic example of pricing of a new issue involving rights, look up in the *Commercial and Financial Chronicle* the case of Phillip Morris & Co., Ltd., Inc. 3.60 per cent preferred stock, rights on which expired January 28, 1946. The new stock was offered on the basis of one new share at $100 for each ¾₀ common share held. Of a maximum of 149,883 shares offered, only 19,543 shares were actually issued, with 142,563 of the remaining shares subscribed withdrawn under a rescinding offer of February 18, 1946. Does the pricing of this issue offer any reason why so few shares were taken up by the common stockholders?

8. What is "stand-by" underwriting? How would the market for rights in each of the above cases be affected by such underwriting? Is it ever possible to find situations in which rights are traded for value when the rights have no theoretical value? Why?

15. Brokerage House Services

The purpose of this problem is to familiarize the reader with the various services offered by a brokerage house, including those of transacting orders. The types of orders that may be entered are also considered.

1. Make a visit to a brokerage house or investment firm in your city. Check off on the following list the services that are offered.

(a) Transaction of orders.
(b) Research facilities:
    (1) In the office.
    (2) By wire or correspondence.
(c) Firm analyses and publications:

    (1) Available only at the office.
    (2) For general distribution.

(d) Advisory service to customers or general public regarding investment programs.

(e) Collection of dividends and bond interest without charge.

(f) Handling of transfers, redemption, and exchange of securities without charge.

(g) Safekeeping of securities without charge.

(h) Custodian service for investment accounts.

(i) News services and publications.

(j) Interest paid on cash balances left with firm.

2. Secure a copy of the confirmation forms used by the firm to notify customers of the completion of a transaction. If any items are unclear, ask for an explanation. In particular, ask about the amount of postage fees and when they are charged. What is the "settlement date?" Must securities or cash be in the broker's hands before the order, or by the settlement date?

3. What forms must be completed to open an account? Will added forms be necessary for a joint account? a partnership account? a corporate account? an estate or trust? What particular differences can be made in joint accounts? Are these of significance in your state? under Federal law?

4. Secure a copy of the margin agreement used by the firm. Examine its terms carefully. What rights does it give to the broker over your account? What margin does the broker ordinarily require be maintained after the initial purchase? Can this agreement be used only on the securities purchased on margin or does it cover the whole account? If it covers the whole account, it might explain why the broker might transfer title to his name for purposes of convenience. Can you prevent this? How? Is this a wise policy?

5. Suppose you were to open an account, then purchase or deposit some common stocks with the broker. After a few days the issuer of one of the stocks announces rights to purchase additional shares will be issued. Will these rights be sent to you or to the broker? Will the broker do anything if you do not instruct him to exercise or to sell the rights? Is this of any value to customers?

6. Is it possible to have an account with a brokerage firm and, while traveling, place an order with an entirely different house for a transaction by your broker? Suppose you have some securities in a safety deposit box and, while vacationing, decide that they should be sold. How can this be done?

7. Is there any minimum size order accepted by the broker? Does this apply to all accounts and types of orders? Can he take orders for issues that are listed on exchanges of which his firm is not a member? Does the broker do an over-the-counter business? Does he sell investment fund shares? On what basis, dealer or broker?

8. What is meant by an "open order"? a "day order"? are there any other types of orders commonly used? Why must a broker know whether an order to sell is "long" or "short"? What is a "market order"? In the event you place an open order to buy a stock, does the broker automatically change the price set after the issue sells "ex-dividend"? What about "ex-rights"? What is a "stop order"?

9. What are "special offerings"? How do they affect the net purchase price of odd lots to individuals? When are they made? In what issues? (Refer to the monthly Statistical Bulletin of the Securities and Exchange Commission, particularly February issues.)

10. What is a secondary distribution? How does it differ from a "special offering"? What is the difference to the individual investor in odd lots? In what type of issues and markets are they likely to occur?

11. What is the "monthly investment plan"? Of what advantage is it to the small investor? How do its total costs compare with those for odd-lot trading?

12. Considering the "load" on purchase of investment company shares as equal to a maximum of 8.1 per cent plus postage charges, and the cost of selling equal to the taxes involved, what advantages are there in the "monthly investment plan" for buying corporate stocks over a regular purchase of investment company shares?

16. Brokerage Calculations

This problem takes up the various charges made by brokers on types of transactions, compares them with over-the-counter pricing, and concludes with a comprehensive question.

1. Mr. Walter McCann had been watching the price movements of International Harvester Company common stock, and decided

one day to purchase 100 shares. The current price was 30. He gave the order to a brokerage firm and received a confirmation of the purchase at 29¾. What amount would he have to pay the brokerage firm, assuming that he decided to leave the certificate in the broker's hands?

2. Some time later Mr. McCann decided to purchase an additional 50 shares of International Harvester stock. The confirmation he received read that the purchase was made at 30⅝, but on reading the papers for the day, Mr. McCann noted that the high price listed was only 30½. Could this occur? Could he have bought 50 shares of Oliver Corporation common stock on a day when no trades were made in the issue on the New York Stock Exchange? How? What amount would Mr. McCann pay to his broker for the 50 shares of Harvester? What amount for a purchase of 50 shares of Oliver at 12⅛?

3. At a still later date Mr. McCann decided to sell his 100 shares of Harvester stock. He received a confirmation of the sale at 32. What would be the proceeds of the sale? What would have been the proceeds had he sold only 50 shares of Harvester stock? Of 50 shares of Oliver Corporation common at a price of 13⅝? Why is there a sizeable difference in the transfer taxes charged?

4. Suppose, alternatively, that Mr. McCann wished to give 60 shares of stock to his alma mater. What procedure would be necessary? Would a transfer tax be paid? How much?

5. In the case of the purchase and sale of 100 shares of Harvester stock at the prices given above, what amounts would Mr. McCann put on his income tax report in reporting his capital gain?

COMMISSION RATES
Stocks
New York Stock and most other exchanges, (effective November 9, 1953).

1. Round lots of single transactions in a unit of trading:

Money Involved	Commission
Under $100	As mutually agreed or 6%
$100 to $1,999	1% plus $5
$2,000 to $4,999	½% plus $15
$5,000 and over	0.1% plus $35

2. Odd lots of less than a unit of trading: same as above, less $2.00.

3. Minimum. When amount involved exceeds $100, no more than $1

per share or $50 per single transaction, but in no case can commission be less than $6.00.

4. "In and Out" Rate. On purchase and sale of a single security within 30 calendar days, commission rates on the liquidating transaction are 50 per cent of the regular rate.

American Stock Exchange

For stocks selling at $10 to $142 a share, $14.50 plus ¼ per cent of the total amount involved in the transaction.

Bonds   *U.S. Government Bonds*

For $1,000 to $25,000 par value, ¹⁄₁₆ point plus shipping cost.

Corporate Bonds

1 or 2 bonds selling at $10 or more per bond	$5.00 each
3 bonds selling at $10 or more per bond	4.00 each
4 bonds selling at $10 or more per bond	3.00 each
5 or more bonds selling at $10 or more per bond	2.50 each

TRANSFER TAXES

Note: In all cases, no par stock is taken as equivalent of $100 par. Odd-lot purchases are usually subject to the same transfer taxes as are normally charged against the seller.

Federal Taxes

Stocks: 5¢ per $100 of total par value, if selling under $20 a share; 6¢ per $100 of total par value, if selling at $20 or over a share.

Bonds: 5¢ per $100 par value, but government and municipal bonds are exempt.

State Taxes

Note: The following taxes are levied on all transactions in stocks taking place within the state. All bond transactions are exempt.

New York: If price is

under $5 a share	1¢ a share
between $5 and $10 a share	2¢ a share
between $10 and $20 a share	3¢ a share
$20 and over a share	4¢ a share

Pennsylvania:

2¢ per $100 of total market value, but not in excess of 2¢ per $100 of total par value of the transaction.

Texas:

3¢ per $100 of total par value of the transaction.

Note: The following are taxes levied on all transfers of stock made within the state.

Florida:

10¢ per $100 of par value of stock being transferred.

South Carolina:

4¢ per $100 of par value of stock being transferred.

6. The National Quotations Bureau issues daily, weekly, and monthly offers to buy and sell over-the-counter securities. From a copy of one of these issues, select a common stock, e.g., Kaiser Steel Corporation common. Compare the quotation given in the N.Q.B. sheets with those published in the *Wall Street Journal* or *Journal of Commerce* for the same day. Do you find any difference? Compute what the total price per share would be on a purchase of 25 shares of the stock if the dealer charged a commission, then compare this with the price listed in the paper. Do over-the-counter dealers work on a commission basis or a mark-up basis (percentagewise) in their direct dealings with customers? Under what circumstances might a dealer be able to get a better mark-up?

7. For each of the following securities, compute the approximate difference in gross cost and net proceeds from buying on September 26 and selling at the same price on October 27. Do these calculations offer grounds for some conclusions as to the minimum feasible amount of any investment commitment? Of a speculative trading commitment? What differences would there be if the trades took place within thirty days?

       100 shares General Foods Corp. common @ 55
        10 shares Borden Co. common @ 55
         1 share American Telephone & Telegraph common @ 155
        10 shares Panhandle Eastern Pipe Line 4% cum. pfd. @ 96
        10 shares Fireman's Fund Insurance Co. common @ 62
       100 shares Chase National Bank common @ 50
    $1,000 Gulf Mobile & Ohio Ry. 4s B, 1975 @ 102
    $2,000 Portland General Electric 1st 3½s, 1977 @ 96

17.   Margin Transactions

A knowledge of the working of margin transactions is often a valuable tool in the kit of every investor. This simple problem serves as an introduction to the subject.

On July 5, 1952, Mr. Brown deposited the sum of $3,600 with his broker, and gave an order to buy 100 shares of United States Steel common stock, then selling at 47. On August 7 he received a call from the broker asking for more margin because the price of Steel had fallen to 35.

1. How much additional margin would the broker require?
2. Is this call mandatory?
3. In case Mr. Brown could not meet the broker's request, how much would he get back from the broker after he was "sold out?"
4. Would the broker sell out all the shares, or merely enough to re-establish the satisfactory margin level?
5. Mr. Brown was paying 5 per cent on borrowed funds. What would he have lost on the transaction, assuming he was "sold out?"

18. Short Sales

The operation of short selling is often misunderstood. This simple problem is intended to afford an introduction to the technique and purpose of short selling.

Late in 1952, Mr. Blake, buyer of piece goods in a department store, came to the decision that the textile field was heading for a down swing. He found from the daily newspaper that Celanese common stock was currently selling at 47. Since this large manufacturer of rayon had shown large swings of earnings in the past, Mr. Blake reasoned that a repetition could well occur. Accordingly, he instructed his broker to sell 100 shares of Celanese common short the next morning. The confirmation slip showed the transaction took place at 47. Subsequent events showed that Mr. Blake's analysis had been correct. By June 1953, Celanese common was selling at 25. Mr. Blake decided to "close out" his short sale.

1. What were the proceeds of the short sale? Could Mr. Blake have withdrawn any of these funds from the broker?
2. How did the broker make delivery of the shares sold short?
3. What was the cost of "covering" the short sale? What net profit resulted from the transaction?

4. Could Mr. Blake have lost on his transaction? Why? How much?
5. What was the maximum possible gain for Mr. Blake? Compare this with the maximum possible loss. How could Mr. Blake have guarded against a quick, unfavorable turn in the market?
6. Was Mr. Blake speculating? Was he gambling? What was the effect on the market at 47 of Mr. Blake's selling? Of his buying at 25? Is this of any significance to the market? To the economy?

19. Over-the-Counter Transactions

Since the unlisted or over-the-counter market is an important segment in the securities market, a firm understanding of its operation and function is essential to all investors.

The stocks of many important companies in various lines of industry are not traded on the national or regional exchanges. Among such companies are: Time, Inc., and Meredith Publications (*Better Homes & Gardens*), Kellogg Co. (cereals), Gerber Products (baby foods), Tennessee Gas & Transmission, and Texas Eastern Transmission (pipelines), West Point Mfg. Co. (textiles), P. R. Mallory (hats), and Anheuser Busch (beer). Since there is a nation-wide interest in many of these securities, it is often believed that the fact that they are not listed means that the public cannot purchase shares in them. Is this true? Why are they not listed? Is this of any importance to the investor?

From daily financial papers or from *Barron's* or the *Commercial and Financial Chronicle*, note that no record of transactions in over-the-counter securities is given. Who are those bidding or offering in the market? Do they actually own shares? In what quantities are the bids and offers given? What is known as "making a market?" Can an investor buy only from the house making a market?

1. Compare the relative variations in price over a few years, getting the data from a security price record or Moody's manuals, for the following pairs of issues:

a. West Point Mfg. Co. and Cannon Mills
b. Kansas Nebraska Natural Gas and Northern Natural Gas
c. Time, Inc. and Curtis Publishing Co.
d. Miles Laboratories and Bristol-Myers
e. Central Illinois Electric & Gas and Central Illinois Light

2. Why are practically all insurance company and bank stocks not listed? Operating subsidiaries of public utility holding companies?
3. Can listed securities ever be traded over the counter? Under what conditions would this type of market be preferable? What alternative exists on the exchanges, particularly the New York Stock Exchange and the American Stock Exchange?
4. Why are equipment trust obligations and municipal bonds traded in the over-the-counter market? Do the factors pointed out in the discussion of stocks above hold for the bond market?

20. Options

The speculative devices of options are not widely known or used. This problem is included for those who want to learn something about these volatile procedures.

On July 9, 1951, 90-day options were offered on 100 share units, at current market prices, for a number of issues. Among these were New York Central common, then at 16, at $137.50 and $200, and U.S. Steel common, at 39¾, at $187.50 and $250. Subsequent high and low prices within the 90 day period were: for New York Central, 20⅞ and 15¾, and for U.S. Steel, 43¼ and 39⅛, but with a dividend payable to holders of record August 8, amounting to $.75 a share. The high price for U.S. Steel was reached after the ex-dividend date.

1. What are puts and calls?
2. Why is there a variation in option prices between puts and calls? When might the price of a put be higher than that of a call? What time intervals are covered by options? Can special options be arranged?

3. What gain or loss would have occurred if a put were purchased on New York Central and not exercised? When would this be done? What gain if it were exercised at 15¾? (Note the commissions and taxes involved differ from those on stock trading.) What would have been the gain or loss if a call had been purchased and not exercised? When would this be done? If it were exercised at 20⅞? (Assume you held 100 shares of the stock when buying the call.)

4. What would be the results for similar transactions in a put in U. S. Steel, exercised Aug. 16 at 39⅛? A call exercised Sept. 5 at 43¼?

5. Who is likely to use options? Would an investor ever use them? Are options a device for large or small investors? speculators? Can you ever lose on option deals? What is a straddle?

Part III

21. Supply and Use of Personal Savings

The broader economic aspects of investment in securities is a subject with which investors as well as economists must be familiar. This problem, the first of a series dealing with the general economic aspects of investment, presents for consideration some rough measures of the flow of savings into the securities markets.

Aggregate measures of economic activity have become familiar statistical materials since the early 1930's. In national income analysis, all personal income received is either spent on personal consumption or is considered saved. Savings may be viewed as a combination of liquid or capital personal assets and a reduction of outstanding personal debts. The following data present estimates of personal savings and their uses since 1933, measured in billions of dollars, as made by the Department of Commerce and the Securities and Exchange Commission.

1. What relation can you discern between personal income and savings from 1933 to 1941? Through the war years? 1946 to 1950? From 1950 to date? What reasons can you give to explain the lower savings rates in the 1950's over those of the war period?

2. To what extent do you find any evidence of an increasing importance of institutional investing?

3. To what extent are aggregate estimates of personal savings and their use deceptive measures of the availability of savings for purchase of securities? (Remember that the values shown are evidently on a cash basis for current value, rather than on a cost value. Thus little can be done to estimate the change in aggregate values of personal portfolios.)

43

TABLE III-1

ESTIMATES OF THE SUPPLY OF PERSONAL SAVINGS AND THEIR
USE IN LIQUID ASSETS, 1933-1953* (In billions of dollars)

Year	Personal Income	Personal Savings	Change in Liquid Assets				
			Total	Banks & Sav. & Loan	Insur-ance	Secur-ities	Debt Payment
1933	47.2	- 0.6	- 0.97	- 1.77	0.68	- 0.71	0.83
1934	53.6	0.1	2.67	1.47	1.49	.23	- .52
1935	60.2	2.0	1.60	2.11	1.79	- 1.76	- .54
1936	68.5	3.6	4.30	3.45	2.22	- .34	- 1.03
1937	73.9	3.7	4.09	.48	3.14	1.02	- .55
1938	68.6	2.0	3.12	.35	2.64	- .38	.51
1939	72.9	2.9	4.37	3.06	3.01	- .41	- 1.28
1940	78.7	4.2	4.29	3.09	3.14	- .01	- 1.94
1941	96.3	11.1	10.22	5.18	4.01	2.94	- 1.91
1942	123.5	27.8	29.84	11.24	5.04	10.38	3.20
1943	151.4	33.0	39.07	16.77	6.77	13.87	1.66
1944	165.7	36.9	41.61	18.36	8.17	15.14	- .07
1945	171.2	28.7	37.66	20.12	8.59	9.97	- 1.02
1946	178.0	12.6	12.32	11.76	6.97	.11	- 6.54
1947	190.5	4.0	6.30	3.24	7.08	3.43	- 7.45
1948	208.7	10.0	4.34	.02	7.31	4.12	- 7.11
1949	206.8	7.6	3.04	.21	6.05	2.90	- 6.13
1950	227.1	12.1	1.59	5.73	5.03	1.11	-10.37
1951	255.3	17.7	12.03	7.81	8.23	2.78	- 6.94
1952	271.2	18.4	14.44	10.24	9.38	4.55	- 9.76
1953	286.1	20.0	13.4	8.4	8.3	6.2	- 9.5

*Sources: Survey of Current Business, 1951 National Income Supplement,
and July Issues, 1952-1954 (table 6). Securities and Exchange
Commission, Statistical Bulletin, July, 1954.

Note: Negative savings mean aggregate consumption exceeds income.
Negative change in liquid assets means a decrease in the aggregate
or individual type of liquid assets. Negative debt payment means
increase in consumer debt under mortgages or other types of credit.

22. The Supply of Savings and the Demand for Securities

This problem is presented chiefly as an alternative to the preceding problem, but it also examines the choices made in the selection of specific types of securities as liquid assets.

Since 1933 the Securities and Exchange Commission has been preparing estimates of savings of individuals, classified into various types of liquid assets holdings and into changes in consumer debt. These data afford a fair measure of the amount of savings that are available to the investment market when we consider both the direct and indirect investment processes available to individuals. Thus, we may examine the changes in holdings of life insurance and assume that these amounts were invested institutionally. Correspondingly, we may assume that changes in bank balances were available either for a loan or investment base. Direct investment in securities are usually considered made on a cash basis, omitting changes in the amount of margin trading.

It appears important to note that the perplexing anomaly of the 1950's, of consumer credit rising at the same time as personal holdings of liquid assets is not unreasonable. The reverse might just as easily occur.

The accompanying table presents the record of changes in holdings of liquid assets yearly since 1933, according to the form of holding or type of debt paid or incurred. Note that negative debt payment means an actual increase in debt.

1. What discernible trends in aggregate amounts of savings used in specific channels do you find? What cyclical pattern, if any, do you find, considering 1937-1938 and 1946-1948 as periods of relative recession?
2. Consider the relative importance of each form of liquid asset holding annually for the span of years since 1934. Does this cause you to change any of your answers to the preceding question? Of what importance is this to the individual investor? To the institutional investor? To the economy in general?
3. Why would the aggregate public decide to increase their debt burden and at the same time increase their liquid asset holdings? Would this be more likely to occur between two segments

TABLE III-2

ESTIMATES OF LIQUID SAVINGS BY INDIVIDUALS, 1933-1953
(billions of dollars)*

Year	Liquid Assets	Currency & Bank Deposits	Savings & Loan Assns.	Life Insur- ance	Securities			Debt Payment	
					U. S.	Munic- ipal	Corpo- rate	Mort- gage	Other
1933	- .97	- 1.17	- .60	.68	.14	- .93	.08	.73	.10
1934	2.67	1.78	- .31	1.49	1.14	- 1.11	.20	- .12	- .40
1935	1.60	2.34	- .23	1.79	- .59	- .13	- 1.04	.29	- .83
1936	4.30	3.61	- .16	2.22	1.00	- .55	- .79	.28	- 1.31
1937	4.09	.39	.09	3.14	1.06	- .01	- .03	.04	- .59
1938	3.12	.31	.04	2.64	- .08	- .14	- .16	- .20	.71
1939	4.37	3.00	.06	3.01	.06	- .23	- .24	- .50	- .78
1940	4.29	2.88	.21	3.14	.51	- .46	- .05	- .78	- 1.16
1941	10.22	4.80	.38	4.01	3.47	- .28	- .25	- .94	- .97
1942	29.84	10.96	.28	5.04	10.37	- .22	.22	- .06	3.26
1943	39.07	16.18	.59	6.77	14.15	- .12	- .16	.36	1.30
1944	41.61	17.54	.82	8.17	15.74	- .08	- .52	.12	- .19
1945	37.66	19.06	1.06	8.59	10.49	- .18	- .34	- .20	- .82
1946	12.32	10.58	1.18	6.97	- .15	- .35	.61	- 3.24	- 3.30
1947	6.30	2.04	1.20	7.08	2.09	.36	.97	- 4.06	- 3.39
1948	4.34	- 1.23	1.25	7.31	1.52	1.03	1.57	- 4.64	- 2.47
1949	3.04	- 1.27	1.48	6.05	1.24	.60	1.06	- 3.83	- 2.30
1950	1.8	3.6	1.5	5.0	0.0	0.7	1.4	- 7.2	- 3.2
1951	11.8	6.0	2.1	8.3	- 1.0	0.4	3.2	- 6.5	- 0.5
1952	13.6	7.1	3.1	9.3	- 0.4	0.9	3.7	- 6.3	- 3.8
1953	13.4	4.7	3.7	8.3	1.3	1.8	3.0	- 6.7	- 2.8

*Source: Securities and Exchange Commission. Statistical Bulletin (monthly).

of the public, one increasing assets while the other goes into debt, or could it occur simultaneously in the general public?

23.   Supply of New Securities

The flow of new securities into the marketplace is of importance to the investor and to the economist. This problem considers some of the underlying causes affecting the sale of security issues.

One of the most important factors in the development of American industry is the supply of new securities offered. Data for issues of securities offered publicly since 1919 are available. The record shows that there have been noticeable cyclical swings in the value of security offerings, but with a rather pronounced upward trend.

The advancing cost of plant facilities, as well as the higher price levels, has forced additional working capital requirements on business firms. The interactions of inflationary influences and the increased mechanization of industry can be cited as causes for the upward trend. The cyclical changes, however, are equally important for they reflect the changing supply of securities that in turn reflects the demand for funds. It is with this factor that we are presently interested.

The data for total security offerings, as shown in Table III-3, conceal relatively important forces that affect investors, personal as well as institutional. In particular it is important to see the relative changes in the supply of issues for new capital and those arising from a mere refunding of existing issues. The supply of new issues is more closely related to the swings in general business activity, while that for refunding issues is influenced more by interest rates than business activity. It would appear that at the start of a business cycle, while interest rates in the capital market are low, refunding of outstanding debt and senior equity obligations occurs, followed by a surge of new capital issues which tapers off as the cycle declines.

Yet, even within the totals for new capital and refunding issues, there are observable differences between the offerings of various types of issuers. In particular, we find that Federal agencies will tend to issue new securities in a contracyclical pattern, and to refund issues and other debts rather regularly in conformance with the maturity pattern desired in the handling of Federal debts. On the other hand, municipalities appear to borrow new money in a cyclical pattern related to business activity, and refund existing issues when new money is not necessary. Foreign issuers have withdrawn substantially from the Americal capital markets, but have sold issues in a relatively close cyclical pattern. The downward trend in foreign issues may be due, at least in part, to the changed policy of direct governmental loans and grants, rather than one of political indifference such as obtained prior to 1930.

The impact of new and refunding issues on the particular segments of the securities markets is more observable since 1934, when the Securities and Exchange Commission began to furnish more detailed information than was available in earlier years. Because of the almost steady upward trends involved, with the exception of 1937-1938, and the effects of war financing by government and in-

TABLE III-3
CORPORATE, MUNICIPAL AND FEDERAL FINANCING,
MONTHLY AVERAGES (in millions of dollars), 1919-1952*

Year	Grand Total	New Financing					Refunding			
		Total	Corporate	Federal Agencies	Municipal	Foreign	Total	Corporate	Federal Agencies	Municipal
1919	357	299	187	26	57	29	58	35	--	1
1920	334	303	214	--	56	33	31	19	--	1
1921	350	298	142	11	100	46	52	47	--	1
1922	437	360	185	29	90	57	77	61	3	2
1923	416	359	220	28	87	24	57	44	5	2
1924	529	466	252	15	115	84	63	41	--	2
1925	594	518	300	14	113	91	75	51	2	4
1926	619	529	313	8	112	96	91	68	3	2
1927	828	649	388	7	123	131	179	154	8	3
1928	833	676	446	5	115	110	156	132	--	3
1929	966	849	667	--	118	64	117	115	--	1
1930	640	585	374	7	120	85	54	40	--	4
1931	335	260	129	6	103	21	76	68	4	2
1932	144	99	27	6	64	2	45	27	8	7
1933	88	59	13	5	40	‡	29	18	2	3
1934	184	116	15	34	67	--	69	26	26	11
1935	396	118	34	13	71	‡	278	155	82	30
1936	521	164	99	2	61	2	357	282	29	32
1937	333	175	102	13	59	1	158	101	23	16
1938	372	196	73	40	81	2	175	106	55	11
1939	488	192	32	77	78	5	296	144	128	16
1940	400	163	61	38	63	‡	238	169	29	40
1941	462	238	89	106	43	‡	224	130	58	36
1942	176	90	52	9	29	--	87	35	37	15
1943	186	54	31	7	15	1	132	57	44	22
1944	358	78	54	1	20	3	280	206	35	34
1945	671	148	105	2	39	1	523	411	76	27
1946	727	387	296	11	79	1	340	246	61	17
1947	813	641	400	17	186	36	172	123	35	4
1948	871	776	495	25	217	40	95	24	64	7
1949	819	687	424	19	234	10	133	37	79	9
1950	925	700	369	33	281	18	225	112	83	9
1951	1006	818	481	39	273	28	203	44	135	24
1952	1245	1023	606	45	330	33	222	59	134	28
1953	1267	1144	633	25	452	28	122	15	97	8

*Source: Survey of Current Business from Commercial and Financial Chronicle
‡Less than one million

dustry, the cyclical changes are not as apparent as in longer series of data, as revealed in Tables III-4 and III-5. Nevertheless, some tentative conclusions may be drawn from the more detailed data.

TABLE III-4
SECURITIES FINANCING, 1934-1953 (in millions of dollars)*

Year	Gross Total	Federal	State & Municipal	Corporate Total	Bonds	Pref. Stock	Com. Stock
1934	4,910	3,567	939	397	371	6	19
1935	6,683	3,044	1,232	2,332	2,225	86	22
1936	9,982	4,142	1,121	4,572	4,029	271	272
1937	5,328	1,938	908	2,310	1,618	406	285
1938	5,926	2,594	1,108	2,155	2,044	86	25
1939	5,687	2,345	1,128	2,164	1,980	98	87
1940	6,564	2,625	1,238	2,677	2,386	183	108
1941	15,157	11,504	956	2,667	2,390	167	110
1942	35,438	33,847	524	1,062	917	112	34
1943	44,518	42,816	435	1,170	990	124	56
1944	56,310	52,425	661	3,202	2,669	369	163
1945	54,712	47,859	795	6,011	4,855	758	397
1946	18,685	10,573	1,157	6,900	4,882	1,127	891
1947	19,941	10,589	2,324	6,477	5,036	762	779
1948	20,250	10,327	2,690	7,078	5,973	492	614
1949	21,110	12,020	2,907	6,052	4,891	425	736
1950	19,893	9,717	3,532	6,361	4,920	631	811
1951	21,265	9,888	3,189	7,741	5,691	838	1,212
1952	27,209	13,036	4,401	9,534	7,601	564	1,369
1953	28,824	14,062	5,558	8,898	7,083	489	1,326

Year	Net Total Corp.	Cost of Financing	Uses of Funds			
			New Money	Refund Bonds	Refund Debt	Refund Pfd. Stk.
1934	384	14	57	231	84	--
1935	2,266	66	208	1,794	170	71
1936	4,431	141	858	3,142	154	226
1937	2,239	71	991	911	111	190
1938	2,110	45	681	1,119	215	87
1939	2,115	49	325	1,637	69	59
1940	2,615	62	569	1,726	174	128
1941	2,623	44	868	1,483	144	100
1942	1,043	20	474	366	138	30
1943	1,147	23	308	667	73	72
1944	3,142	60	657	2,038	49	351
1945	5,902	109	1,080	4,117	134	438
1946	6,757	143	3,279	2,392	379	476
1947	6,466	111	4,591	1,155	356	196
1948	6,959	119	5,929	240	488	67
1949	5,959	92	4,606	360	637	41
1950	6,261	100	4,006	1,149	620	122
1951	7,607	134	6,531	391	363	96
1952	9,380	154	8,180	583	459	21
1953	8,755	143	7,960			

*Source: Securities and Exchange Commission Annual Reports and Statistical
Bulletin

TABLE III-5
PUBLIC FINANCING AND PRIVATE PLACEMENT OF
SECURITIES ISSUES, 1934-1953 (in millions of dollars)*

Year	Total Bonds	Public Financing	Private Sale	Stocks Sold to Limited Group
1934	372	280	92	--
1935	2,225	1,840	385	2
1936	4,029	3,660	369	4
1937	1,618	1,291	327	3
1938	2,044	1,353	691	1
1939	1,979	1,776	703	3
1940	2,386	1,628	758	7
1941	2,389	1,578	811	2
1942	917	506	411	10
1943	990	621	369	3
1944	2,670	1,892	778	9
1945	4,855	3,851	1,004	17
1946	4,881	3,019	1,862	54
1947	5,035	2,888	2,147	88
1948	5,973	2,963	3,010	79
1949	4,890	2,435	2,455	49
1950	4,920	2,360	2,560	166
1951	5,691	2,364	3,326	130
1952	7,601	3,645	3,957	99
1953	7,083	3,806	3,228	

*Source: Securities and Exchange Commission Statistical Bulletin.

The trends of securities issued from the United States Government and its agencies and the various municipal borrowers have reflected the wartime needs for armaments and the postwar requirements of "catching up" with necessary expenditures and expansion due to population shifts. It would appear, however, that municipalities tend to take advantage of comparatively low interest rates in their financial plans.

Turning to corporate offerings, the most easily recognized tendency has been the growth of private offerings to a limited group of investors, usually institutions such as life insurance companies. Particularly noticeable since 1948, but a major factor since 1940, private placements have exercised great influence on the form of securities issued by corporations in the postwar period. The substantial totals of senior securities, bonds and preferred stocks, issued since 1948 are in sharp distinction to the lower totals of common stock issues that bulked so large in the great new securities markets of the 1920's.

One of the reasons often advanced for the sizable amount of private placements has been the cost of flotation of securities issues. The record reveals that costs have declined from 3.4 per cent in 1934, and above 3 per cent in 1937, to less than 2 per cent since 1947. The cost of flotation of corporate issues in 1952 amounted to only one sixth of one per cent of the gross proceeds. Since private placements are included in these totals, however, it is impossible to say whether the costs of public flotation have decreased as a result of the institutional competition, have remained steady, or have increased.

The totals of securities issued for new money purposes has grown to impressive figures, reflecting the increased costs of plant, needs for working capital, and inflationary influences noted earlier. The changes in amounts of issues devoted to retirement of existing issues appear to indicate that shifts in interest rates and capital costs are important factors, rather than the usual cyclical influences.

1. Prepare a brief commentary on the amount and type of new securities available to the individual investor, taking into account the securities primarily directed toward institutional investors. Be sure to deal with both long-range and cyclical factors and consider the question of whether institutional demand affects the type of financing or whether the opposite is true.

24. The Effect of Economic Changes on Investments

This problem is intended to summarize the long-run effects of various types of economic change on the primary forms of investment available to the individual, bonds, real estate or mortgages, and common stocks. Such changes may help to explain in considerable degree the price and yield changes noted in preceding problems.[1]

All types of economic change leave their effects upon the structure

---

[1] This problem is based upon a suggestion from John C. Clendenin.

of business, sometimes permanently, often only temporarily. The impact of news of impending changes often causes relatively violent swings in the securities markets, and until the real effects of the change are considered, the market may, for quite a period of time, be unduly or incorrectly influenced. Witness for example, the market in 1939-1941 when the outbreak of hostilities in Europe caused a sudden rise in stock prices, followed by a slow, gradual decline, and then a drastic drop as the full effects of the "blitzkrieg" were felt. To appraise the effects of differing types of economic change on types of securities and on business, the investor must look either at the short-run results or the long-run, more permanent effects.

A series of events is given for analysis of their effects on business activity, profits, bank credit, bond yields, mortgage interest rates, real estate prices, and industrial common stocks. Each event is to be viewed separately in its long-run (six months or more) implications on each of the economic or investment situations given. It is suggested that the problem be set up in tabular form, with the seven columns, one line for each event (a-l, as listed below). Leave sufficient space in each block thus formed for a short comment, when necessary.

The events are:

(a) Continued increase in institutionalization of savings, but at a stepped-up rate.

(b) Legislation to permit increased depreciation allowances to be taken by business.

(c) Extension of legislation to permit greater investment in stocks and real estate by insurance companies and pension trusts.

(d) A resumption of the continued use of deficit financing by the Federal Government.

(e) Decision by the Federal Reserve authorities to support the long-term Government bond market at par.

(f) A reduction in initial margin requirements on listed securities.

(g) Revolution in the Ukraine and the European satellite nations of Russia.

(h) Institution of a "mortgage bank" that will discount any credits offered by institutions in the field, using such discounted mortgages as collateral for borrowing from the Federal Reserve System.

(i) Legislation to set up a series of investment funds to assist small business development.

(j) Reduction in the rate of taxation of personal incomes.

(k) Shortening of the holding period for short-term capital gains.

(l) Elimination of personal income taxation on dividends received, but with a 5 per cent increase in the rate of corporate income taxes.

Note that the effects may be: Increase, Decrease, No Direct Effect, or Indeterminate. For example: for (f), the answer might well be— no direct effect on real estate prices; for (a), it might show conflicting or indeterminate results on business as competitors would be financed more easily, thus reducing profits and stock prices. At the same time savings institutions might also bid against each other and raise stock prices. In the case of indeterminate results, it would be advisable to give a brief explanation of the alternatives and the probabilities of each.

25. Security Prices and Cyclical or Price Risk

This is the first of a series of problems dealing with the basic factors affecting security prices in general. A firm understanding of the risks of investment and the ways in which different types of securities meet these risks is necessary for intelligent investing.

Risk may be defined as a probability of loss in any venture. The greater the possibility of loss, the greater the risk involved in holding a specific security. The risks apply to both the safety of the value of the security and to the flow of income arising from it.

These risks affect all assets, not only securities, but cash, real estate, insurance, and all others. It is, therefore, impossible to avoid the risks of holding assets. The risks can only be met head on in an attempt to take advantage of them or minimized in their effects by trying to reduce their impact on the assets held at any given moment by varying the relative amounts of assets as one or another of the risks of investment are held to carry weight. This latter form of handling risks is known as the principle of diversification.

Three basic risks of investment in assets have been classed by most writers: cyclical or price risk, associated with the changes in the earnings of business and the activity of the economy; price level or purchasing power risk, associated with the changes in the level of commodity prices and particularly the level of consumer prices; and interest or money rate risks, associated with changes in the level of the costs of money. This problem deals with the way in which the various types of securities are affected by the first of these risks. Other risks will be considered in later problems. It must, nevertheless, be understood that all three risk factors are continually operating to affect security prices and the values of all assets.

1. Examine the data presented in Table III-6. Do you find any close relation between the prices of bonds and the index of industrial production? Next, do you find any close relation between preferred stock prices and the index of industrial production? Finally, do you find any close relation between the common stock price index and that of industrial production? Which relation appears the closest?

2. Which of the three long-term price series, corporate bonds, preferred stocks, or common stocks, exhibits the greatest variation through the various cycles covered in the period? Which of the series varies the least? Would you now say that price risk is particularly concerned with changes in industrial production? On what theoretical assumption does this answer rest?

3. Assume it is desirable to attempt to take advantage of price risks. Which type of security would you use? What kind of investment policy would be required to attain maximum results?

4. Assume it to be desirable to avoid price risks as much as practicable. Would you invest at all? If you would, in what types of securities?

5. On a graph of the indexes of common stock prices and of industrial production, draw free-hand trend lines. Do you find any great similarity of trends? Is there any reason for this? Of what importance are the implications of this relationship? But, on what assumptions does this rest?

TABLE III-6

RISK ELEMENTS IN SECURITIES INVESTMENT, 1919-1953

Year	Bond Prices		Preferred Stock Prices	Common Stock Prices	Industrial Production	Consumer Prices
	Treasury	Corporate				
1919		81.9	110.9	75	39	74
1920		75.2	103.2	68	41	86
1921		76.6	103.0	58	31	76
1922		85.5	114.0	72	39	72
1923		85.0	114.5	73	47	73
1924		86.6	115.2	77	44	73
1925		88.3	118.6	95	49	75
1926		90.1	121.0	106	51	76
1927		91.6	127.1	125	51	74
1928		91.8	136.7	158	53	73
1929		89.1	136.7	201	59	73
1930		90.8	141.5	158	49	71
1931		92.8	139.4	100	40	65
1932		84.4	114.7	51	31	58
1933		91.2	122.1	67	37	55
1934		98.2	132.5	77	40	57
1935		105.5	151.4	83	47	59
1936		109.6	161.9	118	56	59
1937		110.2	157.6	118	61	61
1938		111.7	161.4	88	48	60
1939		114.7	167.5	94	58	59
1940		116.3	169.2	88	67	60
1941		117.7	171.9	80	87	63
1942	100.7	117.4	162.4	69	106	70
1943	100.5	118.3	172.7	92	127	74
1944	100.3	118.7	175.8	100	125	75
1945	102.0	121.6	189.1	122	107	77
1946	104.8	123.4	198.5	140	90	83
1947	103.8	122.1	184.7	123	100	96
1948	100.8	118.2	168.6	124	104	103
1949	102.7	121.0	176.4	121	97	102
1950	102.5	121.9	181.7	146	112	103
1951	98.8	117.7	170.4	177	120	111
1952	97.3	115.8	169.7	188	124	114
1953	93.9	112.1	164.0	189	134	114

Sources:
Bond Prices: Standard & Poor's, estimated price of a 4%, 20-year
bond rated A1+. Long-term Treasury 2-1/2%, maturing
in 15-12 years, as computed by Federal Reserve Board.
Preferred Stocks: Standard & Poor's, price for 7%, cumulative non-
callable stock, average of 14 issues.
Common Stocks: Standard & Poor's Index of 402 issues, 1935-39 equals
100.
Industrial Production: Federal Reserve Board, 1947-49 equals 100.
Consumer Prices: Bureau of Labor Statistics, 1947-49 equals 100.

26. Security Prices and Purchasing Power Risk

The second problem on the risks of investment is intended to provide a background for use in investment management. It here is used to help describe the movements of prices of different types of securities.

A second risk of investment is present in the holding of any asset, that is, purchasing power change. This risk involves not only the risk of loss through change in the purchasing value of the principal invested, but also through changes in the purchasing value of the flow of income derived from asset. Its impact is best measured by the changes in consumer prices.

Writers in investments have held that this risk can best be minimized by holding assets whose value changes with consumer prices. Since this is impossible of practical achievement, another solution might be to hold foreign balances and then, after a price change, to repatriate funds. This assumes, however, that foreign prices do not themselves change and that a perfectly free market in foreign exchange exists. Under present-day conditions, this appears relatively impossible. Hence, it is very necessary for most people to become aware of the methods of handling purchasing power risk within a nation.

It is purchasing power risk of which people talk when they say that although a purchase of $75 of War Bonds in 1941 gave $100 in 1951, the purchasing power of these funds would be only $51. In effect, the investor would have gone without interest on his bond and also lost over 30 per cent of his principal.

1. From an examination of Table III-6 in Problem 25, which of the types of securities shows the closest variation to the changes in consumer prices? Which shows the least protective power against purchasing power changes?
2. Since bond interest and preferred stock dividends are generally constant in amount, whereas common stock dividends tend to

vary with common stock prices, which type of security affords the greatest protection of income against purchasing power risk? Which type is most open to this risk? Would real estate which affords no direct income be of special advantage in combating purchasing power risk?

3. Consider the length of the cycles of industrial production and of consumer prices, and also the extent of variation during the cycles. Do you think it more important to protect savings from changes in industrial production or from changes in consumer prices? This might be of importance to the investor, and deserves consideration.

4. In a very enlightening article in the *Commodity Yearbook, 1953*, on "The Relationship of Commodity and Securities Prices," some interesting relationships are shown. It is said that although business activity and monetary and credit developments exert, in theory, similar influences on the price of common stocks and of consumer prices, this cannot be said to constitute a hard and fast rule because of quite a few divergencies, particularly in the war and post-war periods. "On the basis of the experience of the past 43 years, it is reasonable to assume that the trends of commodity and securities (i.e., common stock) prices should be similar except during war and post-war adjustment periods or when some abnormal event occurs to distort the securities or commodity situations." (p. 13). If we examine prices of common stocks highly sensitive to raw materials prices, further study shows that this statement has been generally true in the cases of copper, lead and zinc, paper, and steel, as well as in certain processers of raw materials, such as leather, textile weavers, and processers of vegetable oils. Examining the short period from 1939 to date, as shown by the tables in Problems 25 and 10, can you find evidence of the ability of certain types of common stocks to vary with consumer prices? Or, could you say that the whole 1939-1953 period is one of abnormalities? Would you conclude that there are some long-term investments which can protect surely against purchasing power risk? Are these commitments also protective against price risk?

27.   Security Prices and Money Rate Risk

This problem examines a third risk of holding assets. Most individual investors overlook the importance of this risk, hence careful examination of it is necessary.

Money rate risk is usually considered to include the hazard of price change in securities caused by changes in interest rates, which in turn reflect the changes in the demand for and supply of credit and investment funds over periods of time. Other factors remaining constant, a rise in interest rates causes an increase in bond yields, which are, for all practical purposes, interest rates, and hence causes a decline in bond prices. A drop in interest rates thus causes a rise in bond prices.

Two important amplifications of money rate risks must be appreciated: one, as maturities decrease the absolute change in bond prices caused by a given change in interest rates decreases; and second, for a given maturity, changes in interest rates will have greater absolute effect at high than at low levels. The proof of these statements can be demonstrated by reexamining Problem 12.

Thus, since interest rates in specific cases and bond yields for specific issues includes both the cost of funds and a premium for risk-bearing, high risk loans and securities will vary more in price than will low risk issues for any given change in money or interest rates.[1] And also, since risks of payment are less for early payments of interest (or dividends) and principal than for those that are more remote, short-term issues will vary less in price than will longer-term issues. Distinctive evidence of the influence of maturity on interest rates is shown in Table III-7.

Nevertheless, the actual market for credit and funds cannot be conceived as including perfectly continuous demand and supply curves; the particular needs of borrowers and institutional influences on lenders prevent such curves. Many of the latter factors affecting securities may be examined in later problems on institutional in-

---

[1] See Problems 8 and 9 where variations in yields for various bond qualities were examined.

TABLE III-7
YIELDS ON TAXABLE GOVERNMENT SECURITIES
OF DIFFERENT MATURITIES, 1942-1953

Year	91-day Bills	3-5 year maturities	6-9 year maturities	15-12 year maturities
1942	0.326%	1.46%	1.86%	2.46%
1943	0.373	1.34	1.90	2.47
1944	0.375	1.33	1.92	2.48
1945	0.375	1.18	1.58	2.37
1946	0.375	1.16	1.39	2.19
1947	0.594	1.32	1.56	2.25
1948	1.040	1.62	2.00	2.44
1949	1.102	1.43	1.63	2.31
1950	1.218	1.50	1.62	2.32
1951	1.552	1.93	2.26	2.57
1952	1.766	2.13	2.48	2.68
1953	1.931	2.57	2.74	2.93

Source: Federal Reserve Bulletin, except 6-9 yr. from Standard Trade and Securities.

vestment policy. It is sufficient here to indicate that the short-term money market affects competitively both short-term, low-risk loans and securities, with less perfect competition existing in longer maturities and higher-risk loans and investments. Data in Table III-8 afford easy comparisons of the effect of risk arising from the legal position of various types of securities.

The contractual interest payments on bonds and regular payment of dividends on high-grade preferred stocks afford adequate measures for determining yields on these types of securities. In the case of common stocks the problem is more difficult, since dividend payments are discretionary in both time and amount. Hence, it is customary to turn to the relation of earnings to price (often expressed as the price-earnings ratio) as a measure of the rate of capitalization of earnings currently expressed in the market. Since the rate of capitalization is merely an expected rate of return, it is of the same category as interest rates, and should, at least theoretically, reflect changes in money rate risk. Both dividend yield and the earnings/price ratio data are included in Table III-8.

1. What factors cause variations in the "spreads" between the bill

TABLE III-8
MONEY RATE RISK FACTORS, 1919-1953

Year	Long-Term Bond Yields			Preferred Stock Yields	Common Stocks	
	Treasury	Municipal	Corporate		Div. Price	Earn. Price
1919	4.72%	4.46%	5.51%	6.31%		
1920	5.32	4.98	6.18	6.79		
1921	5.09	5.09	6.03	6.80		
1922	4.30	4.23	5.17	6.14		
1923	4.36	4.25	5.22	6.12		
1924	4.06	4.20	5.07	6.08		
1925	3.86	4.09	4.93	5.90		
1926	3.68	4.08	4.77	5.78		
1927	3.34	3.98	4.65	5.51		
1928	3.83	4.05	4.63	5.12		
1929	3.60	4.27	4.86	5.12	3.41	6.14
1930	3.29	4.07	4.71	4.95	4.54	4.53
1931	3.34	4.01	4.55	5.04	6.17	2.83
1932	3.68	4.65	5.28	6.13	7.36	----
1933	3.31	4.71	4.69	5.75	4.42	2.78
1934	3.12	4.03	4.14	5.29	4.11	3.78
1935	2.79	3.41	3.61	4.63	4.06	5.45
1936	2.65	3.07	3.34	4.33	3.50	5.87
1937	2.68	3.10	3.30	4.45	4.77	6.80
1938	2.56	2.91	3.20	4.34	4.38	4.39
1939	2.36	2.76	3.02	4.17	4.15	6.36
1940	2.21	2.50	2.92	4.14	5.31	8.16
1941	1.95	2.10	2.84	4.10	6.25	10.28
1942	*2.46	2.36	2.85	4.31	6.67	9.18
1943	2.47	2.06	2.80	4.06	4.89	7.02
1944	2.48	1.86	2.78	3.99	4.81	7.46
1945	2.37	1.67	2.61	3.70	4.19	6.19
1946	2.19	1.64	2.51	3.53	3.97	7.08
1947	2.25	2.01	2.58	3.79	5.13	11.53
1948	2.44	2.40	2.80	4.15	5.78	14.79
1949	2.31	2.21	2.65	3.97	6.63	14.08
1950	2.32	1.98	2.59	3.85	6.27	14.62
1951	2.57	2.00	2.84	4.11	6.12	10.42
1952	2.68	2.19	2.95	4.13	5.50	9.50
1953	2.93	2.72	3.18	4.27	5.49	9.96

*Taxable issues for 1942 and later years.

Source: Federal Reserve Bulletin, Moody's Industrials.

rate and yields on other Government issues shown in Table III-7? Could the bill rate ever be higher than the yield on long-term Government bonds? Why?

2. Money rate risk is described by the changes in yields to maturity of various types of bonds and by current yields on preferred stocks. Is this risk a factor for buyers of bonds who intend to hold them for only a few years? Is it a factor for speculators to consider? Is it present in West Shore R.R. 4s of 2361?

3. In Problem 8 it was found that "spreads" between various grades of bonds, and between bonds and preferred and common stocks, varied from year to year. Examine the "spreads" in Table III-8 to find any cycle of interest rate changes. Comment on your findings.

4. Assume you are manager of an institutional investment agency. How would you plan your security holdings so as to avoid money rate risks? How would you plan to take advantage of money rate risks? What would be the most profitable cyclical plan to follow?

5. Which exhibits the closer relation to Treasury bond yields, the dividend yield or earnings/price ratio? Is the relation of any significance or are other factors more actively at work?

6. What can be the impact of money rates on holders of high-rate bonds and preferred stocks which are callable? Is this of any significance? Is there any recourse in case money rates rise? Does this make the effect of money rate risk on callable issues a "one-way street"?

7. Describe briefly the manner in which Governmental actions can affect the securities markets. Which markets are most easily affected? Does the impact fall on all markets or just on some of them?

28. Investment Characteristics of Securities

To summarize the qualities inherent in specific types of investments is the focal point of this problem. Most amateurs do not realize that no single issue embodies all desirable characteristics, while few have only unfavorable qualities.[1]

---

[1] Adapted from a suggestion by John C. Clendenin.

The purpose of this problem is to analyze the risks and other qualities found in differing types of investment, and can best be achieved by a columnar tabulation. It is suggested that columns be set up with the following headings:

(a) Type of investment.

(b) Price risk, i.e., that change resulting from changes in earnings.

(c) Price-level risk, i.e., that resulting from commodity price shifts.

(d) Money rate risks, i.e., that resulting from changes in interest rates.

(e) Tax position, i.e., with regard to Federal income taxes, estate tax, and so on.

(f) Freedom from care, i.e., ability to be laid away for years without any trouble.

(g) Current yield, i.e., current income divided by current price.

You are asked to analyze the following investment types for each of these qualities, rating them High or Favorable, Good or With Advantages, Fair or with Little Advantage, or Poor or With No Advantages.

1. Savings account at a local bank.
2. Savings and loan account.
3. Life insurance reserves (cash surrender values).
4. Series E Treasury Savings Bonds.
5. Long-term Treasury bonds.
6. Municipal bonds, i.e., those of states, counties or cities.
7. High-grade corporate bonds.
8. Medium-grade corporate bonds.
9. High-grade preferred stocks.
10. Convertible bonds or preferred stocks.
11. Medium grade preferred stocks.
12. High-grade utility stocks.
13. Medium-grade railroad stocks.
14. High-grade industrial stocks.
15. Medium-grade industrial stocks.
16. Bank and insurance company stocks.
17. Home ownership.

The current prices and income can be procured from bond and stock guide books or, with somewhat greater difficulty, from daily newspapers, or from magazines such as *Barron's* or *The Commercial and Financial Chronicle*.

As guides to the price variability of typical issues, the following tabulations are presented.

High and Low Prices, 1946-1954*

5. U. S. Treasury, 2 1/2s, D 72/67. . . .106 1/2 — 90 1/8

6. New York City 3s, 1980 126   — 98

7. Am. Tel. & Tel. 2 3/4s, 75 . . . . . .101 3/4 — 89
   Socony Vacuum Oil 2 1/2s, 76. . . . .100 1/8 — 88

8. Atl. Coast Line un. 4 1/2s, 64. . . . .118 1/2 — 93 1/2
   Sunray Oil Corp. deb. 2 7/8s, 66 . . .103 3/8 — 92

9. Endicott Johnson 4% cum. 111   — 89 1/2
   U. S. Steel 7% cum. 166   — 129 1/2

10. Allis-Chalmers 3 1/4% cum. conv. . .123   — 73
    Worthington Corp. 4 1/2% pr. pfd. . .177   — 62

11. Lehigh Valley Coal $3 n-c. 1st pfd. . . 38 7/8 —   8
    Jones & Laughlin 5% cum. A. 103   — 81 5/8

12. Cleveland Elec. Illum. . . . . 64 3/4 — 34 1/2
    Commonwealth Edison. . . . . 44 3/4 — 25

13. New York Central RR. . . . . 35 3/4 —   9 1/4
    Pennsylvania RR. . . . . 47 1/2 — 13 3/4

14. Intl. Business Machines 306   — 66
    Monsanto Chemical. . . . . .109 1/2 — 38 5/8

15. American Airlines. . . . . 19 7/8 —   6 1/8
    Hunt Foods. . . . . 41 1/4 —   6 5/8
    St. Regis Paper . . . . 32 1/2 —   6 1/4

16. Chase National Bank. . . . . 49 1/2 — 32
    Home Insurance Company . . . . . . 48 1/2 — 22 1/2

*To September 20.

29. Quality and Price as Factors in Common Stock Price Fluctuations

The amateur in investments is often intrigued by low-priced issues. This problem examines the validity of the contention that such issues are good speculative media, and also shows that investors need not avoid low-priced issues entirely.

In December 1951, John C. Clendenin reported on an interesting class experiment in the price fluctuations of common stocks. The question involved a testing of the proposition that low-priced stocks vary relatively more than high-priced issues. A side issue involved the proposition that issues of good quality vary less than those of lower quality.

As measures of quality, the ratings of the *Financial World* and Fitch stock record books were used. The periods studied were 1937-1944, 1946, and 1948. Variations in price were measured in terms of the range for the period as a percentage of the average of midpoint in price, i. e., average of high and low for the period.

We conclude that the often-repeated advice to speculators to select low-priced stocks to obtain wider price movement is mostly nonsense. The proper advice to one who seeks wide price movement is to select a low-quality stock. There are more low-priced than high-priced stocks of low quality, so the tendency for one desiring low quality may be to look among the low-priced stocks; but there is no reason whatever to avoid high-priced ones of comparable quality, if the only object is to trade in stocks whose price movements are characteristically wide.

The same reasoning will indicate that the investment-minded stockholder who prefers a stable market need not avoid low-priced stocks of appropriate quality. There seems to be no greater reason to fear price instability in a $10.00 stock than in a $65.00 one of the same grade.[1]

1. For a recent year or period, using the same source materials, test the validity of Clendenin's conclusions. Could it be that quality ratings have been assigned on the basis of past relative price variability? If so, how can relative price variation be explained by quality ratings?

2. For the same list of stocks used in question 1, prepare a similar comparison of range to average earnings per share for the period 1945 to date. Is there any apparent correlation in results? Would this indicate that variability in earnings is an important criterion of quality, so far as common stocks are concerned?

3. For the same list of stocks, prepare a comparison of range to average dividend payments for the period 1945 to date. Is there any better correlation than that for earnings? Do earn-

---

[1] Clendenin, John C., "Quality versus Price as Factors Influencing Common Stock Price Fluctuations," *Journal of Finance*, VI (December, 1951), pp. 398–405. Quoted from pp. 404–5.

ings, dividends, or price variation appear to be the uppermost factor in appraising the quality of a stock?

30. Growth Stocks

Much has been written about growth stocks, but many investors are uncertain about methods of selecting such issues. This authoritative essay is perhaps one of the best statements extant on this important investment topic.

INVESTING IN GROWTH STOCKS
by Jeremy C. Jenks [1]

The Nature of Corporate Growth

In the normal development of any successful business there are usually one and sometimes several periods of rapid growth preceded by long "make ready" periods, and followed by long "consolidation" periods. The classical growth pattern involves an initial development stage when its sales and profits rise only gradually, a growth phase when its business forges ahead rapidly, and a stage of consolidation or maturity when its growth levels off.

There are several practical and economic reasons for this typical pattern of corporate development, which may be described in terms of human effort. Until comparatively recently the success story typical of many prominent industrialists has involved long hours of work in garage or attic inventing or developing a product, the begging or borrowing of small capital to start the business in such makeshift quarters as available, culminated by the eventual acceptance of the product after years of sales promotion and product development. Then follows expansion of the business through investment of retained earnings and later on, through either sale of equity capital, or consolidation and acquisition of other companies, eventual emergence of the company as an industrial leader. Although this is typical story-book stuff, the actual initiation, development, and success of a great many leading companies have followed such a pattern.

The early stages of a young company are usually characterized by rather slow progress, because: (1) the products and process must be developed; (2) capital must be found to build plants to produce at an economic volume; (3) markets must be laboriously built; and (4) competition must be met.

After those initial steps are accomplished, a period of rapid growth may occur, because: (1) products are established, and markets are expanding rapidly; (2) the company has reached a size and status where capital can be secured more easily, and earnings are large enough to permit expansion from retained earnings; and (3) competition has been met or absorbed. After the period of rapid growth is over, the company

---

[1] *Analysts Journal,* published by N. Y. Society of Security Analysts, vol. 3, 2d quarter 1947, pp. 38–53.

reaches its maturity stage with a resultant slowing down of growth: (1) the market has now reached substantial size and is no longer expanding at the same rate; (2) the company has secured the maximum economic percentage of the over-all market; (3) ownership and management are older and financially secure and no longer have the incentive to take substantial risks; and (4) the business has become so large that the complexities of retaining present markets and fighting off new competition occupies a large portion of the management's time.

Within the framework of a typically classical pattern such as outlined, there is only one period of growth for each successful company. Actually this is a great oversimplification. DuPont, for instance, contraverts such oversimplification, having experienced a series of growth phases in its 100-year history. Growth usually comes in waves similar to the incoming tide on the beach, and progress generally coincides with upturns in the business cycle. The waves may be several years or more apart, or there may be several waves close together, followed much later by another period of rapid growth. . . .

Characteristics of Growth Stocks

In this article the phrase "growth company" means *a company that will eventually be successful and that is now in or entering a phase of rapid development.* A "growth stock" is the common equity of a growth company. The definition of a "growth stock" should perhaps also emphasize that the company's growth must be beneficial to the stockholders through increasing *per share* earnings, dividends, and asset values.

There are a number of generally accepted characteristics of growth stocks: (1) the stock may sell at a high price-earnings ratio as the growth is recognized and investors are willing to pay a price based on future earnings rather than historical or present earnings; (2) the stock may sell on a low yield basis because of the high price-earnings ratio and small dividend payments reflecting retention of earnings for expansion; (3) the stock usually acts better than the market in the advancing phases and to a lesser extent also acts better than the market in the declining market phases, not only because of its favorable trend of earnings, but also because a market following has been built up through the past success of the stock; (4) the stock may have a tendency in bullish phases to outrun itself and outrun the market because of overenthusiastic speculators; (5) subsequent to an important bear phase in the market, the stock may precede major turning points and in the ensuing upward phase outstrip the market, possibly making new highs well in advance of market duplication of previous highs; (6) at successive market peaks the stock may make new highs, and at successive market bottoms the stock may hold above previous lows.

Most of these characteristics are desirable but with growth stocks, as well as with other stocks, substantial losses are incurred through poor timing of purchases and sales. In the early stages of a declining market many growth stocks give ground as fast or faster than cyclical type equities. This stems from the fact that, in the final stages of the preceding bull market, these stocks frequently are bought by relatively uninformed investors impressed with the stock's past "above-average" performance. Also, low dividend payments, because of the capital requirements of the company, frequently contribute to relatively poor market action in the early stages of a decline. Further, the necessity of securing additional capital funds to implement an expansion program occasionally results in poor timing of new stock financing and contributes to unfavorable market patterns.

Market action of growth stocks depends not only on the growth characteristics of an issue but also on the intrinsic quality characteristics and other factors. For example, the common stock of Celanese Corporation, in spite of its excellent growth trend, declined more rapidly than did the general market in two recent bear phases, those of both 1937 and of 1946. During the intervening years, from early 1939 through June of 1946, however, Celanese common outperformed the market threefold. On the other hand, Abbott Laboratories common did better than the market through both the 1937-38 collapse and the 1946 market decline, but did only as well as the market from 1939 through 1945. Consideration of market price patterns of growth stocks and their individual market characteristics in relation to the market as a whole is of value in the timing of purchases and sales. . . .

Recognition of Growth Stocks

There is no simple formula by which growth stocks can be recognized. Perhaps the starting point for any security analyst in selecting growth stocks is to first select industries where growth has been common in the past. . . .

Pre-eminent from the point of view of continuity of growth and the number of companies apparently in a strong growth phase are the chemical and related industries. Had an investor concentrated all his funds in a diversified list of chemical stocks in 1918, his resultant capital improvement would have outstripped a diversified list of securities (as measured by Standard and Poor's market averages) by 300%.

The excellent article by George MacIntosh, "A Method of Valuing Growth Stocks," published in the first issue of the *Analysts Journal* (1945) discusses a number of the factors involved in appraising growth stocks. While trying to avoid covering the same ground as in that article, we may review certain fundamentals. These remarks will be grouped under three general headings: management, products, and earnings.

Management. The intentions and abilities of management are perhaps the primary determinant of a business's success or failure. This applies equally to the growth field and other fields of investment. In any business a move in one direction is often extremely difficult to retrace. A management's decision to introduce a new product or to enter new markets involves expenditure of funds and substantial risk. If these management decisions are wrong or poorly timed, the retrenchment from the attempt is usually expensive and may involve considerable loss and interruption of the growth trend. Not only must basic decisions be sound, but they must also be correctly timed. The decision to build new plants, or temporarily to defer plant construction, for example, will affect many facets of a company's business, such as the competitive sales position, production costs, and finances.

There is no simple method of valuing the effectiveness of a management. All that can be done is to study the record and to know the people involved. . . .

From statistical sources, an examination of reported research expenditures is helpful in evaluating a management's attitude toward the development of the business. In the chemical industry aggressive managements expend 3% of sales or more for research, a substantial dollar sum. Analysis of general, administrative, and selling expenses as a per cent of sales and as a per cent of net before taxes is often a further clue as to the efficiency of management. For example, Pfizer's expenses, amounting to only 5.6% of sales in 1946, while the record of growth in recent years has been exceptional.

Successful management of a corporation entails a proper balance among production, sales, research, and finance, though extra ability in one of these fields may be the means of success in some businesses.

Products. The characteristics of supply, demand, prices, competition, and relative costs for the products are all subject to analysis. They involve a consideration of some broader economic aspects. There are three principal methods used in creating product values: (1) creating a new product possessing both utility and scarcity (for example, the silicones produced by Dow-Corning and General Electric); (2) increasing the utility of something which has scarcity (for example, modern machine tools or air transport planes); and (3) increasing the scarcity of something which has utility (for example, cartel agreements designed to restrict production, as has occurred in coffee, rubber, and other products). The first two methods of creating values are always used by successful companies, and the effectiveness of product and market development is a direct measure of growth possibilities. The third method has not usually been profitable over the longer term and is contrary to the basic philosophy of growth.

For many growth companies the following generalizations about products are frequently true: (1) direct price competition is moderate; (2) the process or production method is low cost in comparison with other methods; (3) the product is susceptible to production in quantity and uniform quality; (4) markets are broad with a large number of potential consumers; (5) the product has characteristics that distinguish it from competing products, or it has special uses; (6) the product is frequently protected by patents or, of equal importance, by superior managerial "know-how."

In many of the pre-eminent growth industries, such as the chemical industry, product analysis is difficult because of the wide number of products and the competition for markets between different products, or similar products made by different processes. It is frequently true in the chemical field, for example, that the characteristics of supply, demand, and price vary materially from period to period, and competitive factors change rapidly. It is usually easier to analyze the outlook for a classification of products, rather than for individual products, and a reasonable diversification of products and markets is generally helpful, although too much diversification frequently limits growth possibilities.

Earnings. When a management is in the process of deciding whether or not to expand plants for further production of new products or for enlarged production of old products, it lays considerable stress on what is usually referred to as the "pay-out." "Pay-out" means the length of time that the expected additional profit from the new operation will take to return the capital investment involved. Expressed in another way, what the management is actually concerned with is how high a return can be made on the new investment. If a return of 25% can be made after all charges, it is the equivalent of a four-year "pay-out."

One characteristic of true growth stocks is the ability to earn a high return on invested capital. There are two principal factors which determine the return on invested capital. The first is the number of dollars of sales that can be generated by a given investment, and the second is the profit margin that can be earned on the sales. The two factors when multiplied give the return on invested capital. It is frequently worth watching fairly closely the development of earning power in relation to invested capital, for companies under analysis for growth characteristics, since changes in rates of return, either upward or downward, may signalize a change in the growth trend.

The combination of a high rate of return on invested capital and the high price-earnings ratios at which recognized growth stocks normally sell creates the opportunity for acceleration of growth through financial management. A common method of increasing per share earnings is to exchange stock for the stock or assets of a smaller company. Monsanto has been an excellent example, having acquired about a dozen properties over the last 15 years. If the exchange can be effected on the basis of relative market prices, and if the growth company stock commands a price-earnings ratio of 20 times earnings while the company to be acquired sells on a 10 times earnings basis, there is an increment in earnings per share to the acquiring company. Similarly, many growth companies can sell additional stock publicly at considerably above the book values per share and employ the new money in such a way that a high rate of return can be earned on new capital. In this way it is in a position to increase per share earnings rapidly and materially. For example, Merck sold common at $50 a share last year when the book value was only $16.18 a share. Thus, with growth companies, success breeds success, and the reputation for growth resulting in a favorable market appraisal of the equity permits growth at a faster rate than could be achieved merely through investment of retained earnings.

Although abnormally high rates of return on invested capital invite competition, there are many companies which, because of protected positions and skillful management, have been in a position to secure unusual rates of return and resulting unusual growth.

Risks in Growth Stocks

However brilliant investment results may be conjured for growth stocks, nevertheless, in all fairness, it should be pointed out that this type of security is particularly subject to special risks. Unless the investor is able to gauge accurately the end of a growth phase, it is conceivable he may, at a given market stage, pay prices for this type of security, which reflect prospects "which no longer exist." In that event, slavish adherence to an otherwise sound investment philosophy may prove costly. Reasons for changes in growth, which may be somewhat obscure to the average investor, may have their genesis in a change in management, competitive factors, markets, or a number of other variables.

For example, the history of Air Reduction will serve to illustrate this. During the '30's this company enjoyed an excellent trend of earnings suggestive of substantial growth. As a consequence, investor enthusiasm was responsible for this stock attaining in 1936 a price of 86½, representing the high of the 1932–37 bull market. Subsequently investors ascertained to their ultimate financial loss that changing business conditions in the 1938–39 depression prevented continuation of its previous growth trend. The possibility that the depression merely served to interrupt the growth trend was negated by heavy wartime taxes, definitely restricting the growth of all chemical companies. To this writing, expectation that such a trend might be resumed has been deferred by changing business conditions, with resultant lower profit margins offsetting the increase in sales volume. Accordingly, Air Reduction common is now selling at a discount of over 50 per cent of its 1936 peak, and at no time since then, despite the substantial market rise in the period 1942–46, has the stock reached, let alone exceeded its previous high.

A further risk in investing in growth stocks results from the nature and processes of growth. Growth does not occur without physical expansions of plant facilities, investment of substantial funds, expansion of personnel, and assumption of larger payrolls and overhead expenses. At times individual growth companies or industries become overexpanded. For example, the air-line industry over the last year incurred substantial losses, primarily as the result of too rapid expansion and miscalculation of demand. With growth companies as with all businesses, there are problems of taxation and labor relations. Growth cannot occur if either the Government or labor takes too high a portion of the available income. Changes in patent laws, antitrust action by the Government, regulation of prices or rates of return, all add to the risk of investing in growth stocks but are not specifically risks confined to growth companies as they affect industry generally. However, owing to the high market appraisal of most growth stocks, such securities are particularly vulnerable to such adverse factors.

There are also psychological hazards in investing in growth stocks. In the parlance of Wall Street, "a tree does not grow to the sky." There is nothing quite so dangerous to the investor as projecting a present trend considerably into the future. Trends have the habit of changing at about the time they become widely recognized and accepted as permanent.

Use of Growth Stocks for Investment and Speculation.

For accounts primarily interested in long term appreciation, there appear to be two principal approaches that will result in better than average market performance: (1) buying selected growth situations; (2) buying selected special situations. To quote Benjamin Graham in the article, "Special Situations" in the fourth quarter issue, 1946, of the *Analysts Journal*, ". . . a special situation is one in which a particular development is counted upon to yield a satisfactory profit in the security even though the general market does not advance." At times the distinction between growth stocks and special situations becomes small, as frequently there exist growth stocks where some particular development may be counted on to yield a profit.

For an investment account, the equities of mature companies which have completed their rapid growth phase also are good investments, particularly where yield is important as well as appreciation on capital. Senior securities such as bonds and preferred stocks are not under consideration in this discussion which is concerned only with the portion of funds devoted to equity investments.

In selecting growth stocks for investment, the choice is wide, and much depends on individual circumstances. High grade investment accounts are usually liberally sprinkled with the recognized growth leaders. If proper selection and reasonably good timing are assumed, the risk in this type of growth equity are not large, as patience is usually all that is required to obtain a profit. However, the security buyer pays a relatively high price-earnings ratio for this type of security and the relative maturity of the company frequently means that the rate of growth is slowing down or will slow down. However, that type of orthodox investment has been profitable for a number of years and should continue successful.

For the account able to take somewhat higher risks, the policy of looking for growth characteristics in smaller younger companies is frequently rewarding. The equities of the smaller companies, where growth is not proved, frequently sell at considerably lower price-earnings ratios than the proved growth equities. The appreciation on an equity of a company in the early stages of a substantial growth phase may be considerably larger than the appreciation in a similar length of time on an established growth equity. In the earlier stages, not only may earnings increase more rapidly, but also price-earnings ratios may lengthen out as the growth trend is more generally recognized. The risks are concomitantly larger, however, and the analysis should be thorough and the market timing sound. Frequently, the equities of companies of this type are not listed, and in some cases, where they are listed, markets are thin, increasing the market hazard. A proper selection and diversification among smaller growth equities will, however, diminish the over-all risk. It is also possible to avoid investing in part in fields that possess a less attractive medium or longer term growth outlook. For example, the investor in duPont buys a widely diversified business as well as about 9/10th of a share of General Motors for each share of duPont. DuPont departments include ammonia, electro-chemicals, explosives, fabrics and finishes, heavy chemicals, organic chemicals, photographic products, pigments, plastics, rayon, and nylon. There is also a substantial investment in partially owned companies such as Remington Arms. If the individual investor believes, for example, that electrochemicals, organic chemicals, and plastics are the most interesting divisions for growth, he might invest an equal amount of funds in selected smaller companies having strong positions in those particular specialty lines. It is frequently true that a specialty company concentrating all its efforts in one line of endeavor is able to compete successfully with the department of a larger company which also operates in that field.

More as a curiosity than as a suggested procedure, the accompanying table shows earnings and dividends per $100 of market value for a combination of smaller specialty chemical companies. In effect, by buying relative amounts of stock in a number of smaller companies, an investment has been built up in companies having total sales of about $100 million, and, in relation to market values, the combination earns a considerably higher return and gives a considerably better yield than an average of leading diversified chemical company stocks.

	1946, Based on Recent Prices	
	Earnings per $100 of Market Value	Dividends per $100 of Market Value
Eight Specialty Chemical Companies		
Durez Plastics & Chemical	$ 6.71	$3.01
Hooker Electrochemical.	7.37	2.67
Lindsay Light & Chemical.	10.87	2.79
National Cylinder Gas	12.20	7.08
Newport Industries.	13.03	6.10
Nopco Chemical	9.92	3.24
Parker Rust-Proof	8.00	6.84
Victor Chemical Works	6.16	2.56
Average	9.28	4.29
Four Large Diversified Chemical Companies		
E. I. duPont	$ 5.39	$4.00
Hercules Powder	5.46	2.70
Monsanto Chemical	4.31	1.97
Union Carbide	6.46	3.18
Average	5.41	2.96

There are, perhaps, four basic methods of investing in or speculating with growth stocks. The method used depends considerably on the individual objectives and abilities of the security purchaser and on the permissable risk and income requirements involved. These four methods are widely applicable to other stocks than growth stocks.

1. Buying for semi-permanent ownership.
2. "Swapping" between stocks on the basis of relative prices of the equity and progress of the company.
3. Trading in stocks primarily on an appraisal of over-all business and stock market prospects.
4. Buying stocks in anticipation of a particularly favorable development that will affect the price.

These methods may be combined in various ways, but they are essentially different, and it is generally desirable for an investor to decide in advance which of the methods he is following. Different types of growth securities are suitable for the different methods involved.

The first method, buying for semi-permanent ownership, is particularly suitable for a business man who is investing in his own company or in a company which he is in a position to follow closely. This type of investing is also suitable for large investment funds where there is the necessity of keeping money at work, or where tax considerations make long term holdings desirable, and is generally suitable for almost any type of account for at least a portion of its funds. The characteristics to look for in an equity which is being bought for semi-permanent ownership are an unusually able and aggressive management and large and rapidly expanding markets for the products. Depending on the risks that may be assumed by the individual, it is also desirable to buy in the early stages of growth, before the growth characteristics are widely recognized. A company with a small capitalization in any interesting field is a candidate for examination although perhaps 19 out of 20 may be rejected. Excellent examples of the profits that could have been made through semi-permanent ownership of growth stocks are Dow Chemical, now selling at over 15 times the price 20 years ago, and Abbott Laboratories, now selling at over 10 times the high in 1929.

The second method, swapping between growth stocks based on current appraisals of value, is particularly suitable for a fairly large account being actively managed by a professional analyst having access to detailed up-to-date information on a relatively wide number of companies. That method of trying to secure superior market performance has considerable appeal to professional investors. For this type of investing, usually medium sized or larger growth companies with fairly good markets for the equities, but not necessarily market leaders, are desirable. In all cases, companies with good growth characteristics are desirable, but it is not necessary to concentrate on maximum growth. Examples are Dow and duPont, which have sold from 10 to 30 points apart in the last 12 months and Pfizer and

Merck where several profitable swap opportunities have occurred in the last year.

The third method, trading in growth stocks on an appraisal of over-all business and market prospects is not especially suitable to growth stocks as against cyclical type equities. However, growth stocks may be used, as generally in a bullish phase of business or markets growth stocks are market leaders. Also growth stocks frequently turn up toward the end of a declining market before other groups and are suitable at that time. The type of equity desirable for this kind of speculation is a fairly large company having active markets for the security and a large and steady market following. The smaller specialty companies are not generally suitable, either because of poor market characteristics for the stock, or unusual economic characteristics which give earnings a pattern not closely similar to the over-all pattern of business.

The fourth method, buying a stock in anticipation of a particular favorable development for a quick small profit, also is not especially suitable to growth stocks, except that growth stocks frequently respond to good news vigorously. There is perhaps no specific type of growth stock that is more suitable than another for this purpose, except that the equity should have a sufficient market following to assure some interest in the news.

The first two methods appear well suited to the characteristics of growth stocks. The second method may be combined with the third or fourth method in an effort to secure superior investment performance.

Generally speaking, the results that can be obtained through skillful management of investment funds, or through skillful speculation, by emphasis on growth stocks, compare favorably with results obtainable with other types of securities. However, not all individuals are so constituted, mentally and emotionally, that investing for growth is the most satisfactory method. Certainly, substantial profits have been made in cyclical type securities or in special situations, as in reorganization rails and holding company utilities. For the professonal or amateur student of security values, however, growth stocks are a rewarding field.

1. What is a growth stock? How are growth stocks characterized?

2. Do growth stocks cluster in industry groups or are they apt to be found in all industries? What industries appear now to be in the growth stage? What companies in non-growing industries appear to be in a growth stage?

3. How can growth be measured? If all companies with high earnings rates and low "pay-out" are classified as growth situations, can they be quickly differentiated from non-growth situations?

4. What are the risks of holding growth stocks? Can an easy appraisal be made when a firm drops its growth characteristics?

5. Are growth stocks proper media for reducing any of the risks of

investment? Which ones? Are they infallible for these purposes?

31. Diversification in Investment

*Since the principles of diversification are often well known but
are relatively difficult to display, this problem is included to show
one form of analysis of a portfolio as a measure of diversification.*

Investment counselors have generally devised forms through
which appraisals of clients' security holdings may be made readily
at periodic intervals. Various classifications are used to differentiate
the types of degrees of risk involved in the fund and its parts. The
accompanying form illustrates one type of a "Supervisory Analysis
Sheet."

In using this analysis sheet some definitions will be necessary.
The *Reserve* is composed of cash and various obligations maturing
within six months. The *Money Rate Risks* are bonds and preferred
stocks falling in the four highest categories of at least one or more
of the securities rating services. The *Earnings Risks* include all
lower grade bonds and preferred stocks as well as all common stocks.
They are divided according to the cyclical variability of earnings
into low, medium, and high volatility. The Earnings Risk issues are
also reclassed according to their qualities as growth issues, stable
issues, or matured or declining industry issues. In another section
they are again classified by industries and grouped into Producers'
Goods, Consumer Durables, Consumer Nondurables, Extractives,
and Services.

Both dollar amounts and percentages of the total fund are requisite materials for proper analysis, as is the current income and yield
on the total portfolio, if not on the larger sections of it.

1. Does this Supervisory Analysis Form omit any important information which might aid in appraising risks? Should this
   data be on the form? Where?
2. Why are only high grade bonds and preferred stocks included
   in Money Rate Risks?
3. Why are lower grade senior securities called Earnings Risk
   issues?
4. Can growth issues have high volatility? Illustrate.
5. Fill in the form from one of the portfolios given in this volume,

SUPERVISORY ANALYSIS FORM

Account_____ Date_____

Part I Risk Classification			Part IV Industry Classification		
	Amount	%		Amount	%
A. Reserve	___	___	Producers' Goods:		
B. Money Rate Risks			_____		
M 1	___	___			
M 2	___	___			
M 3	___	___			
M 4	___	___			
Total	___	___	Total		
			Consumer Durables:		
C. Earnings Risks					
Low	___	___	_____	___	___
Medium	___	___			
High	___	___			
Total	___	___			
Total Fund	___	___	Total	___	___
			Consumer Nondurables:		

Part II Maturity Schedule					
	Under 5	5 to 10	Over 10		
M 1	___	___	___		
%	___	___	___		
M 2	___	___	___		
%	___	___	___		
M 3	___	___	___		
%	___	___	___		
M 4	___	___	___	Total	___ ___
%	___	___	___	Extractives:	
Total	___	___	___	Petroleum	___ ___
%	___	___	___	Natural Gas	___ ___
				Nonferrous Metals	___ ___
Part III Growth Classification				Gold and Silver	___ ___
				Total	___ ___
Growth	___	___		Services:	
Stable	___	___		Banks	___ ___
Matured	___	___		Finance Companies	___ ___
Total Earnings Risks				Insurance Companies	___ ___
	___	___		Electric Utilities	___ ___
				Gas Utilities	___ ___
				Telephone & Tel.	___ ___
				Water Utilities	___ ___
				Pipelines	___ ___
				Railroads	___ ___
Total Fund:	___			Airlines	___ ___
Income:	___			Other	___ ___
Yield:	___%			Total	___ ___
				Grand Total	___ ___

in a later section, and comment on the balance shown in the
fund.

Part IV

32. Investing for a Commercial Bank

*This problem, based on an article by a prominent bank invest-
ment authority, brings into focus not only the background of bank
investment policy but some very pertinent remarks on methods of
implementing the policy.*

Robert W. Storer has succinctly given phrase to the problems of
investing for a commercial bank during a period of low interest
rates.[1] The following abstract, though rather long, should be of
considerable interest.

As a basis for discussion it is suggested that most commercial
banks have the same basic objectives: (1) to meet the reasonable
and legitimate needs for the community for credit and to estimate
the magnitude of those needs; (2) to be able to pay out deposits as
they are demanded and to estimate the probable extent of such
withdrawals; and (3) while taking care of the foregoing primary
responsibilities, to earn as much for their stockholders as possible,
not with perfect safety but with a reasonable minimum of risk.
This third objective should be subordinated to the first two, but
should not be wholly submerged by them.

It thus appears that we must treat any given bank and its investment portfolio as consisting not of one, but of three banks—a bank
of demand deposits, a savings bank, and a bank (almost an investment trust) of capital funds. This treatment appears justified by the
varying characteristics and turnover of each of the three classes of

---

[1] Robert W. Storer, "Bank Portfolio Management — Some Applied History
and Philosophy," *The Analysts Journal*, published by the New York Society of
Security Analysts, Vol. 6, No. 1 (First Quarter, 1950) pp. 23-26.

liabilities, the offsetting assets against which are being lent or invested.

A commercial bank owns short, low-yielding investments not because they return a good income, but in order to be able to sell them quickly and without much loss should loan demands or deposit withdrawals rise. It should be noted that these two contingencies seldom occur at the same time and to the extent that a bank cannot need this over-estimated liquidity, it can hold longer and higher-yielding investments which benefit its stockholders.

Examination of the key ratio of loans to total deposits for the National Banking System since 1863 shows that since 1874 there has been a long downtrend. Whenever the figure has stabilized at a given level for a few years it has never thereafter risen much, nor for long. This has occurred by reason of the rapid rise in investments over the period. Since deposits increase whenever either loans are made or investments purchased, deposit shrinkage has occurred only when loans are paid or investments are sold or paid. The decline to unprecedented lows in 1943-45 arose out of the creation of deposits through bank buying of war-deficit Treasury paper. It would appear quite out of the question for the loans/deposits ratio to reverse its long-term downtrend and revert to the levels characteristic of the years before World War II deficit financing.

Each commercial bank should examine its own loan/deposit ratio which, though it may vary widely from the record of the National Banking System, can give some idea of the potential loan demand. It may well be concluded that the banking system will be most unlikely to lend more than about 35 per cent of its total deposits over the foreseeable future. Many a banker might well be surprised at the amount of "shorts" he is keeping for potential loan demand that need not be held for that purpose.

Taking up the other occasion for liquidity, that is for cash and "shorts," we would look at the record of deposits and investments. The only drastic decline in deposits was in 1930-33 when a 28 per cent decline was rung up. Investments at the same time increased about half a billion dollars. Most of the deposit decline, therefore, appears to have arisen from a liquidation of loans. Individual banks, of course, had experiences departing widely from the average, and any specific banker would find it necessary to consider his own particular record and situation in relationship to the average. The question for the individual banker is whether he can competitively hold his present share of a stable total of deposits. It might well be suspected that many banks have "shorts" in excess of the amounts required to meet probable loan demand and for deposit withdrawal.

Most of the "shorts" and also short loans must be allocated in the bank portfolio against demand deposits. But what about time and savings deposits? Here again the local conditions determine the situation. If time deposits are stable they should be invested accordingly. But how long is that?

Examination of the record since 1892 of commercial deposits, commercial bank time (and savings) deposits, and mutual savings bank deposits reveals that in the 50-year period ended 1948 there were eight years when commercial bank time deposits declined from one year end to the next. Five of those years were 1929-33 when the decline aggregated 45 per cent. Mutual savings bank deposits, on the other hand, not only did not drop but rose slightly in that depression era.

If, therefore, a bank's time deposits are largely true thrift accounts, they might well be invested along the lines of a mutual savings bank.

As for investing capital funds, I suggest that the average life of the investments should be longer than that for savings deposit investments and the rate higher. Capital funds are of course the most stable in the bank.

What kind of investments should be made? Largely Treasuries. For bank investments the liquidity of Treasury paper (especially under conditions when a bank may need to utilize its liquidity) to be so outstandingly superior to that of non-Government obligations, as to counsel the use predominantly of Treasury securities in a commercial bank portfolio. By liquidity is meant saleability at a minimum of loss. "I would rather have to sell any given amount of 2½s of 1967-72 than almost any corporate security, even of shorter term, when others are also selling."

1. Why must the bank consider its loan policy and program in connection with its investment policy and program?
2. Assume that you are working for a bank that is exactly equal in all respects to the average of all National Banks as shown in

the *Federal Reserve Bulletin*. Work out the proportions of "shorts" that you would carry under present-day circumstances, assuming that you have total deposits of $10,000,000.

3. Since mutual savings banks can invest in corporate and municipal securities, is the proposition that savings deposits, after providing for liquidity, be invested according to the mutual savings bank plan inconsistent with the proposition that only Treasury issues should be proper investments for a bank?

33. Life Insurance Company Liabilities as an Investment Determinant

This problem introduces the field of life insurance company investment by examining the character of life insurance company liabilities.

One authority on life insurance has stated that "life insurance companies are practically exempt from the dangers connected with demand obligations," and that "the greater part of their investments need not be so readily salable for cash as those held by most other financial institutions." These statements were made to confirm the ability of life insurance companies to hold only small portions of their assets compared to the amount of effective insurance outstanding. In 1900 the amount of life insurance owned was $8 billions, against which assets held were only $1.7 billions. In 1950 these figures had grown to $234 billions and $64 billions respectively. The statements appear to be somewhat aside the main point that life insurance companies hold only their reserves against policies outstanding, except for term insurance. The flow of premiums on the average should at least equal the outlays required, assuming no growth in the amount of insurance underwritten. Nevertheless, some problems are posed for investment policy making.

1. Under what conditions might a substantial portion, say as much as 40 per cent, of an insurance company's liabilities become demand obligations? How do life insurance companies guard against such a contingency? How could such demands be met? What would be the effect on sizable insurance company liquida-

tions on the securities markets? Would other institutional interests be present to buy such issues, or would they also be in a process of liquidation?

2. On what basic assumptions does the safety of insurance rest? In what respects does a life insurance policy differ from a time deposit? from a savings and loan account? Does this difference permit a substantial variance in the investment policies of life insurance companies from those of banks and savings and loan associations? What would be your answer if the public were to consider life insurance policies as liquid investments rather than more permanent investments?

3. On what assumption would a life insurance company rest its decision to purchase equity securities? Is there any difference between this assumption and that underlying the purchase of debt obligations?

34. Investing for a Fire and Casualty Insurance Company

Because of the relatively unsatisfactory treatment given to the investment policies of these important institutional investors, the following authoritative article by one of the outstanding investment men in the field is presented.[1] The difference of approach is importantly emphasized.

THE POINT OF VIEW OF A FIRE INSURANCE COMPANY BUYER
by Samuel B. Jones

Several months ago I undertook to explore the fire and casualty company common stock buying potential before a group of our Philadelphia analysts. An estimate had attributed to various types of institutions an annual $900 million potential for common stocks, and had assigned $250 million of that amount to the fire and casualty companies. My conclusion at the time, however, was that no immediate likelihood existed that the fire and casualty share of the appetite would be satisfied during the remainder of 1951. I may have been wrong, of course, for the market continued going up for the remainder of the year and then some!

[1] Samuel B. Jones, "Viewpoint of a Fire Insurance Company Investment Buyer," *The Analysts Journal* published by the N. Y. Society of Security Analysts, Vol. 8 (May, 1952), pp. 9-12.

Nevertheless, from kindly comments made, I judge that my remarks, if not convincing, at least were instructive, insofar as they indicated the various criteria by which a fire and casualty company investment buyer plots the limits within which he can prudently operate. Therefore, a review of my reasons for concluding a lack of common stock buying power may be acceptable as a "refresher" to those who appraise the investment merits of insurance company stocks and are interested in the standards of measurement by which the companies themselves judge their investment needs. I would then like to use my own experience last year here at the Fire Association of Philadelphia to illustrate my points, and finally, I would like to venture some criteria of these mechanical guides and suggest some modifications of the time-honored investment approach, in order to preserve investment assets more adequately in the future.

One statistical service lists 372 stock fire and casualty companies, not to mention some 250 mutuals. Obviously, no set of rules has been accepted as an investment guide by all of these, and it is hardly likely that such a decentralized industry could be made to conform to an established investment pattern. As a matter of fact, investment philosophies themselves differ widely. There are, for instance, those companies that in the past have placed primary stress on bonds rather than stocks. In this category we think of the Aetna, Hartford, St. Paul Fire and Marine, the Fireman's Fund, and the great majority of the casualty companies. This group takes the point of view, no doubt, that it operates in the insurance business and must assume considerable risk and liability as it is, without extending risks into another field. There is much to be said for this point of view, particularly for those companies that are without adequate investment facilities or those that carry on unduly high or concentrated insurance risk.

The majority of the fire companies, however, are aggressive common stock investors. They need the better income return to bolster their dividend-paying ability, and they seek through common stocks to ward off, as best they may, the squeeze on surplus from an inflationary rise in liabilities. The larger and more prominent of the stockminded fire and casualty companies include the Continental, Fidelity-Phenix, the Home, and the Insurance Company of North America. To illustrate the contrast between the two groups, the bond companies, such as the Aetna, Hartford, the Fireman's Fund, and St. Paul, judging from last year's reports, hold approximately 15% of their assets in common stocks. Among assets I include cash, receivables, real estate, and all other assets as well as securities. The common-stock-minded companies, on the other hand, hold as much as 40 to 45% of their total assets in common stocks. So that you may judge the color of glasses through which this analysis is made, the Fire Association of Philadelphia, the portfolio of which I manage, is approximately 30% invested in common stocks and, accordingly, by classification joins the stock-minded companies.

However, that one favors common stocks has not necessarily been the controlling factor in choosing between bonds and stocks. The fire and casualty company investment buyer has other concerns than a mere appraisal of the general economic and investment outlook. The big point of distinction between the investment department of a fire and casualty company and the activities of a general investment fund is that the investment department of the fire and casualty company is part and parcel of an institution actively engaged in writing insurance. The investment policies must necessarily be patterned after the requirements of the insurance company's chief purpose in life.

Whereas companies within the industry lack uniformity and whereas some are more aggressive than others in acquiring common stock investments, nevertheless, because of this interrelationship between the insurance activities and investment needs, there are in a general way, certain basic criteria by which the portfolio manager determines his investment requirements.

Specifically and without regard to the investment outlook, I think it is fair to say that the following points crystallize the various considerations to which portfolio managers pay respect:

1. Business liabilities (all liabilities except capital items) should be offset by cash, receivables, and money-rate bonds, be they short or long term.
2. Policy holders' surplus (capital, surplus, and voluntary reserves) should be exposed to no more than a judicious degree of common stock risk, dependent primarily on its relative abundance in relation to premium reserves.
3. A poor underwriting experience or an unfavorable outlook should be compensated by additional investment caution.
4. Net investment income must, in any event, leave no doubt that dividends are covered by a safe margin.

In way of explanation, so far as point one is concerned, it is certainly obvious that a relationship exists between business liabilities and liquid resources. The loss reserve, the tax reserve, the expense reserve, the commission reserve, and a goodly share of premium reserve are surely current liabilities. Some will argue that premium reserves can always be ceded and, therefore, should not be included among current liabilities. Others will draw a similarity to deferred receivables, and again eliminate them from business liabilities. In essence, however, although the premium reserve is established on the principle of future earnings to be drawn down only with the elapse of time, it is in fact the single measure of insurance risk on the balance sheet.

If the business were to be liquidated, it no doubt would be reasonable to consider premium reserves as salable; but the job of the investment department is to keep the company alive and active. If the industry was immune to catastrophe, we could accept the deferred earnings interpretation. The fact of the matter is, however, that catastrophes do occur, and a reserve against the hazards assumed is essential. Moreover, the covering assets must be maintained in readily available form and at well-assured values. Nevertheless, we do know from practice that, if the average loss experience is realized in the period immediately ahead, some future earnings are tied up in the premium reserve. Investment analysts say it is approximately 40% for fire companies and 35% for casualty companies. In deference to this logic, some of us are willing to compromise the first criterion to the extent of substituting money rate preferreds for bonds for that portion of the premium reserve representing anticipated earnings of the future.

The second criterion is a matter for careful thought. How much of a portfolio can be invested in equity risk issues? There is more than the market outlook at stake in the answer to this question. Just as the banker is reluctant to extend loans beyond a certain ratio to his capital funds, so also an underwriter is reluctant to extend sales of insurance policies beyond a certain ratio to his company's policy holders' surplus. The ratio used to be a dollar of policy holder surplus for a dollar of premium reserve. Pressure of circumstances has liberalized this relationship in the minds of most of us to 1 to 1½, or even to 1 of policy holders' surplus to 2 of premium reserves. Whatever the accepted ratio, the capacity of an insurance company to write its business is dependent on its capital funds. Therefore the relative abundance of surplus is all-important in the decision as to what the maximum exposure in equity risks should be. Those companies with an abundance of capital funds are not so much concerned about this matter. Those with less capital abundance, on the other hand, must tread warily.

To illustrate, The Insurance Company of North America, the Fidelity-Phenix, the Continental, and the Hartford Fire, have 50 per cent to 60 per cent of the liability side of their balance sheets in the form of capital funds. These companies enjoy abundance. On the other hand, there are those with a relative scarcity of capital funds such as the Glens Falls, the Aetna, and the Security of New Haven. The former group can afford to practice greater leniency toward common stocks. The North American reports common stocks equal to 94% of policy holders' surplus. The Fidelity-Phenix and the Continental hold common stocks to the equivalent of approximately 80% to 90% of policy holders' surplus. The Hartford Fire shows evidence of adhering less rigidly to its defense of bonds.

On the other hand, those with a less plentiful supply of capital funds in relation to their volume of insurance business, are more likely to guard their position zealously and protect what they have. The Glens Falls, with less than 30 per cent of total liabilities represented by policy holders' surplus, has limited its common stocks to a little over 40 per cent of capital and surplus. The Aetna, in a similar position, holds just about 50 per cent, and the Security approximately 45 per cent of its policy holders' surplus in common stocks.

There is no hard and fast rule of just what the ratio of common stocks to policy holders' surplus should be. To judge by the examples given, if capital funds make up approximately half of total liabilities, commons under favorable circumstances may reach upward toward 90 per cent or 100 per cent. When this is the case, however, every time the stock market averages fluctuate, these companies must expect an equivalent fluctuation in their own policy holders' surplus unless they are more adept than most of us. If capital funds are in the neighborhood of a quarter of the liability side of the balance sheet, then discretion in the use of common stocks is generally accepted as the better part of valor. You will see some exceptions to this generalization in the accompanying table, but for the most part I think it a fair conclusion.

CRITERIA ILLUSTRATIONS
FROM EARLY 1951 ANNUAL REPORTS
OF FIRE AND CASUALTY INSURANCE COMPANIES

Company	(1)	(2)	(3)	(4)	(5)	(6)
Fidelity-Phenix.	53.5	93.5	95.0	73.0	6.6	155.0
Continental	53.4	106.0	82.1	73.5	7.4	150.0
Phoenix, Hartford	49.7	120.0	61.6	51.0	5.1	128.0
Ins. Co. of NA	45.8	79.4	92.0	72.2	6.8	155.0
Great American	41.8	79.0	100.0	51.0	4.3	134.0
Boston	40.4	92.0	72.0	69.0	3.2	114.0
Camden.	37.7	94.8	69.7	57.2	3.7	117.0
Fire Assn.	36.2	80.8	83.5	45.3	2.6	143.0
Agricultural	34.9	97.6	57.3	16.0	2.3	112.0
Hartford Fire	33.4	104.0	43.8	47.0	7.8	114.0
Hanover.	32.2	81.9	79.7	58.5	2.7	124.0
Glens Falls.	29.6	109.0	43.5	58.7	6.6	128.0
Aetna	26.7	108.0	54.7	54.0	3.1	115.0
Security, New Haven . . .	26.6	96.5	45.8	62.0	2.1	103.0
Firemen's, Newark . . .	22.8	66.9	110.0	40.7	3.0	162.0
	*	*	*	*	*	*
U. S. Guarantee.	53.9	147.0	44.7	73.0	19.4	130.0
Continental Casualty . . .	27.7	106.6	53.3	53.0	6.3	161.0
Maryland Casualty	26.1	102.0	53.0	62.2	6.9	246.0

(1) - Percent Policyholders' Surplus of all Liabilities, incl. Capital, etc.

(2) - Percent Cash, Receivables, & High-Grade Bonds to Business Liabilities.

(3) - Percent Common Stocks to Policyholders' Surplus.

(4) - Percent Dividends Paid to Net Investment Income.

(5) - Percent 10-yr. Underwriting Profit Margin, Geyer's 1950 Analyzer.

(6) - Percent 1950 vs. 1945 Liquidating Value, Geyer's 1950 Analyzer.

Then come the last two criteria. They can be disposed of quickly. In a sense, an insurance company is two businesses, even though they be closely interrelated. If risks mount in one, it is only good judgment to curtail the risks of the other. A poor underwriting record is evidence of a disproportionate underwriting risk. The customary proof of this is the best formula: the ratio of losses and loss adjustment expense to earned premiums plus the ratio of expense to written premiums. The difference between the sum of these and 100 per cent is about as near as one can come to approximating a true current year profit margin. Profit margins have suffered of late for various and sundry reasons, such as disasters of Texas City nature, hurricane, inadequate rates, and pioneering activities into multiple line writings. Until profit margins are re-established on firm ground, an investment policy should compensate with conservatism for unusual underwriting risks assumed.

Finally, we must contend with the ever-present doctrine that dividends are paid from net investment income. Far be it from me to explain why one segment of a company's operation alone should be called on to provide the wherewithal for dividend payments, but nevertheless this is the case. It imposes a high degree of inflexibility on portfolio management. Cash is frowned on as a medium of investment. Withdrawing from the market becomes the more difficult. Yet, net investment income must be religiously maintained whatever the investment outlook. . . .

. . . I would like to suggest some modifications to the generally accepted guides as I have outlined them.

1. Political expediency has cast fiscal economy to the winds. As a result, progressive dollar debasement is a major investment factor of the future.

2. The era of planned economy seems to have established money rates on a permanently low yield and unattractive basis.

3. High corporate taxes levied in full against interest and income as compared with an 85 per cent corporate tax exemption applicable to dividend income just about removes all income attraction from taxable bonds as compared with stocks.

4. An accelerated pace of new invention augurs convincingly for a dynamic industrial expansion in years to come. If the insurance industry — regulated as it is — is to fulfill its obligation to the larger economy of the future, it, too, must participate in the growth. The last column of my table shows remarkable achievement in this direction. The industry must continue and improve on this record.

To me the sum total is that the risk in cold cash and money-rate securities is certainly no less in the long run than it is in well-timed purchases of selected equity issues. New kinds of "exposure" have reared up. I question whether the ratio of common stocks to policy holders' surplus any longer measures the chief "exposure" by which a company's capital and surplus is endangered. To be sure, capital and surplus is a dollar figure, and the debasement of offsetting fixed dollar assets will be no different from the debasement of capital values. On the other hand, an inflationary expansion of liabilities would result most certainly in a corresponding decline in the relative value of capital and surplus if anchored rigidly to the best the bond market has to offer. The future may well pose a capital and surplus problem. Not because capital and surplus declines in dollar amount but because capital and surplus fails to keep pace with the economy as a whole. To forestall this is my purpose.

Accordingly, though the principles behind the criteria remain intact, I would suggest modifying the means of providing for the execution of those principles. I would modify the criterion that requires that cash, receivables, and bonds must cover all business liabilities. I would establish from the past record what the maximum claim on assets in the light of present-day conditions might be in the event of a calamitous disaster and then provide an impregnable cash and short-term note, bill, and certificate position to cover any such contingency. I would then look to my capital, as distinct from the combination of capital and surplus which makes up policy holders' surplus, and make sure that a decline of one half to two thirds in stock market values would not jeopardize this figure, even though a poor market converges with a poor underwriting period. Then I would use the greater freedom from mechanical restrictions to build up equities, varying the proportions between the very best of preferreds and common stocks, depending on the last two criteria – the need for caution, the need for income and the investment outlook. I would then spend less time worrying about what my year-end policy holders' surplus would look like. Theoretically, for the Fire Association this would increase our potential use of equities by at least a quarter and permit greater reliance on investment judgment without inhibitions created by rigid mechanical relationships.

1. Compare Jones' suggestions with the customary investment policy for commercial banks and with that suggested in Problem 32.

35.   Investment of Pension Trusts

The pension trust as an investment institution is of recent, but significant importance. This problem highlights some of the larger investment problems attached to the functioning of a trust. Note particularly how it differs from a life insurance company and from an investment company.

The nature of pension funds permits or requires a unique investment pattern. The two significant factors about a pension fund, from an investment point of view, are: (1) the flow of cash into the fund may be used in large measure or wholly to meet any disbursement requirements of the plan, and (2) the absence of a need for sudden or substantial liquidation of the fund at any one time lessens the importance of market values of the securities held relative to their cost. In the first aspect the pension fund is similar to a life insurance company or an open-end investment company; in the latter aspect, neither fully parallels the pension fund since each may, in some respects, be called upon to meet a catastrophic situation.

In theory at least, both the principal and income of a pension fund are available for the payment of benefits. In practice, however, the fund is built up with company contributions over a period of years until the investment income plus the firm's annual contributions about equal the pension fund disbursements. At that time the fund is said to become "fully funded."

Some pension trusts invest only in bonds, others include mortgages as eligible media, some are fully invested in stocks, others hold only a portion in stocks. Of the first group are many municipal pension funds and the retirement fund of the American Telephone & Telegraph company. Of the funds holding stocks there is a noticeable proportion that limit such holdings to 35 per cent of the fund, that figure being equal to the limit set by New York for legal trust portfolios.

The General Electric pension trust, formed in 1912, has assets in excess of $400 millions. In 1946 a substantial revision and extension was made, but the original investment plan of concentrating holdings in U.S. government securities was kept, although the original legal limit was established as inclusive of all securities eligible for investment by insurance companies in New York. The pension trust thus avoided commitments in any corporate or municipal issues and concentrated on U.S. Treasury obligations. In 1950 the policy was revised to adopt a plan for stock purchases under a dollar-averaging program of ⅓ of the annual contributions until a minimum of 20 per cent of the portfolio or a maximum of 30 per cent is reached. In mid-1952 there were some 70 stocks on the list of approved securities which the trustees were authorized to purchase. Actual purchases were made selectively from this list of those issues which appeared lowest priced each week. The portfolio in mid-1952 contained common stocks in the following pattern: oils, 18 per cent; chemicals, 16 per cent; utilities, 13 per cent; autos and accessories, 8 per cent; retail trade, 8 per cent; foods, 7 per cent; building materials, 5 per cent; banks and insurance, 5 per cent; tobaccos, 4 per cent; agricultural implements, 3 per cent; containers, 3 per cent; nonferrous metals, 3 per cent; steels, 3 per cent; drugs, 2 per cent; and office equipment, 2 per cent. The yield on this part of the complete portfolio was 5.84 per cent, as of 1952.

Bonds in the portfolio had an average life of 17½ years to call date and a minimum of A rating, or equivalent. The yield was 2.91 per cent on the bond portfolio, which was distributed as follows: utilities, 59 per cent; industrials, 21 per cent; finance companies, 11 per cent; and equipment trusts, 9 per cent. Government securities amounting to 19 per cent of the total fund had an average life to earliest call date of 12 years, and a yield of 2.24 per cent.

The pension funds of the City of New York at the end of 1951 consisted of:

City employees' retirement system	$ 516.7 millions
Teachers' retirement system	456.3 millions
Board of Education retirement system	24.0 millions
Police Pension Fund	25.5 millions
Fire Pension Fund	9.4 millions
Total	$1,031.9 millions

The funds were invested as a unit in the following manner:

Cash	$ 7.5 millions
Securities of the City of New York	758.3 millions
Securities of N. Y. City Housing Authority	7.6 millions
Securities of U. S. Government	258.5 millions
Total	$1,031.9 millions

Under the pension plan agreement an interest rate of 4 per cent is guaranteed to all employees who were members of the funds prior to June 1947, and a return of 3 per cent to all city employees who entered the funds thereafter. The actual returns on the funds in 1951, with comparisons for 1938, are listed below.

	1951	1938
City Employees' Fund	3.08%	3.85%
Teachers' Fund	2.91%	3.83%
Board of Education Fund	3.12%	3.90%
Police Fund (new)	2.54%	
Fire Fund (new)	2.55%	
Average return	2.98%	

The pension funds for police and fire employees were almost wholly invested in New York City obligations, accounting for the low rate of return. Since 1945, the pension funds, along with city sinking funds, have bought all security issues of the City of New York at a standard yield of 2.5 per cent to each maturity of the serial issues.

The Employee Beneficial Funds of the Springfield, Massachusetts, Republic-Union and the Springfield Daily News each own about 32 per cent of the common stock of Atlas Tack Corporation. This stock has been held for a long period of time with continued additions made periodically. The late Sherman H. Bowles, president of Atlas Tack, was also the owner of the two newspapers and evidently influenced the purchase of the stock. On December 31, 1952, the Republic-Union fund held 31,657 shares, compared with 30,207 shares a year earlier, and with 26,097 shares on March 31, 1948. The Daily News fund held 31,626 shares, 30,171 shares, and 26,196 shares on the same dates. The market price of the stock varied widely from a low of $4 a share in 1940 to a high of $40 in 1946. In 1952 the stock traded as high as $31 and on February 1, 1953, sold at 23½.

From 1946 to 1950, dividends of $2 a share were paid, although earnings of Atlas Tack ranged from a high of $2.06 a share in 1950 to a low of 2 cents a share in 1949. In 1951 earnings were $1.67 a share, but the dividend was raised to $3 share and held at that figure throughout 1952 in spite of a deficit incurred for the first nine months of the year. The natural result was a deterioration of the working capital position of the firm.

The common knowledge within the company that control rested with the funds created the situation whereby directors declared dividends in excess of earnings in the belief that they had an obligation to maintain the trusts' income on their $1.5 millions investment. However, late in January 1953 the directors of Atlas Tack decided to defer the quarterly dividend.

1. Of the three plans outlined which appears to be built on the soundest investment principles? Why?
2. What are the pitfalls of a controlled policy for investment of a fund? Is there any difference between the possible results of the New York City funds and the Springfield newspaper funds under such a controlled plan?

3. Could the experience of the newspaper funds be a criticism of possible results from the Sears Roebuck employees' retirement fund, which owns over 25 per cent of the outstanding Sears stock? Why? Would similar conclusions be drawn for concentrated investment of any pension fund? For example, what would happen if the pension fund of United Mine Workers was wholly invested in stocks of coal mining companies?

4. Should the earnings on an all-bond portfolio over a period of years be able to meet a net yield requirement of 2½ per cent? If common stocks are included, can a company "underfund" a pension plan, on the assumption that the number of covered employees may decline in periods of recession? This naturally would cut down company payment requirements.

5. Appraise the following investment procedures for pension funds: staggered maturities, holdings of preferred stocks, mortgages, sale and lease-back arrangements, private placements, convertible issues.

Sources: J. D. Lockton, "Investing for the Pension Trust," *Analysts Journal*, Aug. 1952, pp. 64-67; N. Belfer and M. Stoller, "The Administration of Municipal Pension Funds: A Case Study," *Current Economic Comment* (University of Illinois Bureau of Business Research), Feb. 1953, pp. 41-46; B. Weberman, "How 1-Stock Investments Pose Income Pitfalls for Trust Funds," *Journal of Commerce*, Feb. 2, 1953, pp. 1, 5.

36. Investing a University Endowment Fund

This problem continues the series of management problems for institutional investors. The scene for endowment and similar funds is somewhat different, however.

Educational institutions that depend to a large degree on endowment income have tended over the past two decades to invest larger proportions of their funds in common stocks. The proportion of endowment funds invested in stocks at 12 large universities in 1947 reveals that close to half of most funds were placed in preferred and common equities. State supported schools have tended to follow the lead of the private schools listed in Table IV-1. For example, California's policy is not to hold over 30 per cent in equities, while Michigan's calls for up to 15 per cent in preferred stocks and 35 per cent in commons.

TABLE IV-1
DISTRIBUTION OF INVESTMENTS
OF SELECTED SCHOOLS, 1947

University	Size of Fund (millions)	Percent invested in		
		Bonds	Preferred	Common
Harvard. . . .	179	48	10	42
Yale.	115	58	12	30
Northwestern.	57	64	5	31
Rochester . .	56	52	18	30
M. I. T. . . .	47	64	2	34
Princeton. . .	45	48	16	36
Cornell	42	57	10	33
Stanford . . .	39	69	7	24
Johns Hopkins	35	53	15	32
Pennsylvania .	33	57	16	27
Vanderbilt . .	32	65	10	25
Dartmouth . .	21	54	5	41

A review of the Harvard Endowment Fund, handled under the "prudent man principle" that is legal in Massachusetts, reveals the gradual shift into equities since 1929. A comparative distribution of selected years since 1929 appears in Table IV-2.

TABLE IV-2

ANALYSIS OF INVESTMENT OF HARVARD UNIVERSITY FUND, 1929-1953

	Percentage of Market Values as of June 30								
	1929	1932	1937	1941	1946	1950	1951	1952	1953
Cash & U. S. Securities. . .	9.0%	6.2%	2.2%	6.9%	28.3%	26.9%	23.0%	21.2%	22.0%
Other Bonds & Notes	47.6	62.0	51.7	42.1	19.1	20.1	24.0	22.7	22.7
Preferred Stock.	5.5	5.5	8.2	11.5	10.0	7.5	6.2	5.8	5.3
Common Stock .	25.1	12.4	30.7	34.7	41.0	43.8	45.5	49.1	49.0
Real Estate & Mortgages . .	12.8	13.9	7.2	4.8	1.6	1.7	1.3	1.2	1.0
Rate of Return, average* . . .			4.84			4.55	5.07	5.08	5.05

*Including capital gains realized.

Analysis of the 1953 portfolio shows that less than half of the government bond money was held in cash, commercial paper and maturities of five years or less. Within common stock holdings, continued increases in holdings of utilities, railroads, bank, and oil shares occurred in 1953. Reductions were made in holdings of automotive, food, beverage, retail store, and telephone stocks. The tendency to consolidate holdings into fewer, but larger, commitments was continued. At June 30, 1952, there were 174 common stock holdings averaging $870,000 each, compared with 187 holdings averaging $460,000 each in June of 1948.

Yale University follows a formula plan of investment as a policy adopted in 1938. The formula calls for 70 per cent of the portfolio to be devoted to fixed income securities and 30 per cent in equities. If the equity proportion rises to 40 per cent, enough equities are sold to reduce the ratio to 35 per cent; conversely, if equities fall to 20 per cent of the total, enough equities are purchased to restore the ratio to 25 per cent. This calls for rather wide equity price fluctuations before shifts become necessary.

The investment policy of the Massachusetts Institute of Technology merely designates a desired percentage of the fund, as set by the Finance Committee, to be devoted to stocks. From 1935 to 1940, the proportion ranged from 35 per cent to 40 per cent, and from 1940 to 1945 was built up to 45 per cent. In 1945 it was reduced to 30 per cent, but never fully attained because of the rising equity funds since that date.

The experience of the larger colleges and universities has attested the soundness of their investment policies. It is to be admitted that common stock investment values fluctuate more widely than those of fixed-income issues. If common stocks held in fair proportion rise in the market, it would appear that policy would dictate selling equities in order (1) to provide a reserve against unwise selections or buying at too high prices, (2) to set up a surplus of capital gains that can be used to maintain annual distributions from the fund to the university or college, and (3) to permit some element of growth from the accumulation of gains. This is a very wise policy since no taxation liability is incurred. The manner in which the policy is set, the limits established, and the timing of the moves appear to be integrated with the problems of security selection.

1. Which classification of securities appears better for investment

purposes: (a) bonds, preferred stocks and common stocks, as determined by the legal provisions of the issues, or (b) fixed income securities, including all bonds and preferred stocks in good standing, and equities, consisting of defaulted bonds, preferred stocks not paying dividends, and common stocks? Would you suggest any alternative classification?

2. What are the principal merits of establishing a policy for institutional investment? When is such a policy statement not needed?

3. What is the apparent quality of the security issues included in endowment funds?

4. If the Finance Committee has maintained for a period of years a 4½ per cent distribution to the university for meeting operating expenses, but the rate of return on the fund falls to 4 per cent, should the distribution be reduced or maintained at the expense of capital? Does the same answer hold true for an individual's investment program? For a pension trust?

5. If distributions are made in part from realized capital gains, what would happen in the event of a drastic, say 50 per cent or more, drop in the prices of equities? Would it be better to forego paying out realized capital gains, and retain them as a reserve against possible capital losses?

6. Within the policy adopted, should the endowment fund be invested wholly in readily marketable issues or large corporations, or may sizable blocks of issues of smaller firms, relatively nonmarketable, be included?

7. Would the situation in any of the above questions vary for a foundation established for charitable purposes?

37.   Investing for a Church Endowment

As another example of institutional investing, but on a modest scale, this problem involves a review of the basic policy decisions in investment.

Early in 1952 an investment house was asked by the chairman of the board of trustees of a small church in a suburban community for some suggestions concerning the investment of a $25,000 fund that had been left the church by a deceased member. The trustee stated that the objective of the fund, in the minds of the board and of the pastor, was stability of principal, but with emphasis on a relatively good rate of income to maintain the vestry, the original intention of the donor.

The securities markets in early 1952 saw common stock prices at relatively high levels, particularly for growth industry issues such as oils and chemicals. Believing that this type of issue could better be bought on a lower basis at some future time, the manager of the investment house suggested that some convertible preferred stocks be bought instead of growth issues. He therefore prepared and submitted his suggestion for investment of a $25,000 fund which would give an income of $1,310 at the then prevailing dividend rates, or an average yield of 5.22 per cent. The list included:

    40 shares Air Reduction convertible preferred
    40 shares Granite City Steel convertible preferred
    40 shares American Telephone and Telegraph common
    50 shares Brown Shoe common
    100 Quaker Oats common
    100 shares Champion Paper common
    40 shares Sinclair Oil common

1. Are common stocks suitable media of investment for a church endowment? A complete portfolio of common stocks? Do these answers always hold?

2. Analyze the portfolio recommended at current prices and dividend rates. How have the objectives of stability of both principal and income held up? Is any variance due to poor diversification or to a general change in the securities markets? Would you recommend any changes in the portfolio at this time to make sure that an income of at least $1,200 a year is achieved while the $25,000 principal is rebuilt or maintained?

38.   An Appraisal of Mutual Fund Investment Policies

Because of the importance of mutual funds as investment media, two problems on the methods used are included. This abstract of an authoritative article,[1] written by an investment officer of a fund, deals principally with the supervision given to the investments made in the light of changing conditions.

Operated primarily as an institutionalized service, a mutual fund provides two basically important things. The first is investment in a carefully diversified group of securities of many companies and, with the exception of the "industry" funds, in most major U.S. industries. The number of securities held by the average fund is about 50. It may run from 30 to 100 for different funds. Thus, the investor who holds shares in several funds may have a pro rata interest in the securities of several hundred corporations in all major industries. The second is the continuous supervision of the investment—the thing with which we are concerned here.

The base mechanics of mutual fund operation are, of course, familiar. Worth noting is that, although they all operate along the same lines and with the same general intent, their investment approach, policies, and record of results vary widely. Thus, although the investor is provided with a number of readily identifiable advantages no matter what fund he acquires, he will not necessarily obtain the same investment results.

The hard stone and mortar foundation on which mutual fund security selection and supervision rests is no different from that for any informed investing. This is the gathering and evaluation of all statistical data and information about a security and its issuing company from all available printed matter. The security's historical record as to price movement, earnings, and dividends is first tabulated and studied. Attention next shifts to the broad economic factors that have a bearing on the company's position in its own industry, and to the outlook for that industry and for business in general. Greater emphasis is placed on relative analysis. The larger mutual funds, at least, are in a position to probe deeper for facts and information. It is not uncommon for a fund to have several full-time, trained field investigators on its supervisory staff. Managerial and administrative personnel come in for close scrutiny.

As the mutual funds have access to pretty much the same base statistical and factual information, why will investment results vary

[1] William D. Carter, "The Quality of Mutual Fund Portfolio Supervision," *The Analysts Journal*, published by the N. Y. Society of Security Analysts, Vol. 6 (Fourth Quarter, 1950), pp. 32–36.

so greatly for identical market periods? In the answer to this question lies, in a large measure, the answer to why those who are becoming increasingly interested in mutual funds' investment activities frequently misinterpret information about them. And if such misinformation is applied to their own investment problems, the results can be unfortunate.

Differences almost immediately show up with any detailed inspection of the processes and policies of the individual funds. The size of a fund, and, hence, the money it has available for investment supervision, is a factor. This, in part of course, dictates the size of their staffs and, hence, the extent to which information may be gathered and appraised. However, it by no means may necessarily determine the quality of such supervision. Of prime importance is the ability of the men who exercise the final say on which securities should be added or eliminated from the fund portfolio, and in what dollar amounts. This is the last but most important step in portfolio supervision, and the success of it depends in large measure on whether those responsible are able to render seasoned judgment.

The principal differences in investment results lie almost entirely in the varied characteristics of the funds themselves. It is at once apparent that each of the four broad differences in objectives must lead to marked differences in investment approach. The common stock funds are concerned only with one broad classification of securities, and their entire supervisory processes are geared to this end. Thus, they do not have to deal with more than 50 per cent of the estimated 3,500 listed securities. (Mutual funds, generally, confine themselves primarily to the major listed markets.) As a practical matter, many stocks can automatically be eliminated from consideration, and so common stock funds probably concern themselves with considerably fewer than 1,750 issues. The "balanced" fund's supervisory staff must be equipped to select securities it seeks for its portfolio from a wider field of choice. It is concerned not only with the relative values of individual securities but also with determining the balance to be held at any one time between defense-type and aggressive-type securities.

The multiple "class of security" funds are even more obligated to keep most listed issues under continuous, detailed analysis. This calls for a larger supervisory staff than usual. The "class of security" analysts maintain, however, that, although their processes require more attention to detail, they offer the advantage of positive yard-sticks that show them at any time how a security is doing in relation to the average of all others of the same class and that offer a continuous check on investment results. The individual "industry" funds, with their attention centered in one direction, are able readily to corral and brand the specific securities that are of interest to them.

Realizing this, it is immediately more apparent why mutual fund investment results differ so greatly. This can, of course, be traced almost entirely to the funds' varying investment objectives which, in turn, govern their over-all supervisory policy.

Let's see how this works out in practice. The management policy of some mutual funds is to seek conservative income. Their supervisory processes are geared to that end. Others strive for generous income, others for both income and appreciation. Still others are strictly appreciation or growth funds, and income is of decidedly secondary consideration. These policies range from mildly speculative to quite speculative. Thus, a prospective investor may unknowingly find himself studying the performance record of several conservative income and several speculative growth funds during a period of sharply rising market prices. One or more of the growth funds will almost certainly attract his attention because they have, in terms of price, far outperformed the income funds. Income earned during the period will, in all likelihood, not be considered. Nor will the investor be aware that the growth fund, which by policy is not interested in income, is designed to achieve as much capital gain as possible in rising markets but will also depreciate as rapidly in value, on the average, in declining markets. He almost certainly will come to the erroneous conclusion that one of the growth funds is the far superior investment. Mutual fund comparison tables, which appear as regular features in some financial publications, may, and probably quite often do, mislead the investor for the reasons stated.

Mutual fund portfolio changes are being increasingly studied by the investment fraternity. Information of value may frequently be gained from them because, of course, they offer a broad sampling of seasoned investment judgment. However, the informed securities man knows that changes in portfolio securities may also be misinterpreted if the intent behind the fund's supervisory processes is not understood. The annual report of a "balanced" fund, for instance, might reveal that 20 securities had been added to or dropped from the fund portfolio. Some of these changes could have been made with long-term income in mind, others to effect a rebalance between defensive and aggressive portions of the portfolio. The latter might involve securities of a more speculative nature which were acquired for their near-term prospects. A study of the 20 listed in the fund's report would not, therefore, necessarily reveal which ones were of good investment calibre. A "class of security" fund's portfolio changes would be particularly misleading if it were not understood that each such fund is confined to one class of securities and that its basic purpose is to provide the investor with the investment characteristics of only that class of securities.

1. What publications give periodic comparative analyses of the investment performance of mutual funds?
2. Define each of the four types of mutual funds mentioned.
3. Must growth funds be considered speculative?
4. From the listings given in the *Wall Street Journal, Journal of Commerce,* or a similar periodical, prepare a grouping of funds according to objectives. For a statement of the objectives of the funds, consult either Weisenberger's annuals or *Moody's Banks.*

39.   Investment Methods of Mutual Funds

The articles included in this problem comprise a valuable addition to investment literature, for they differentiate the principles underlying security selection as practiced by some of the leading mutual funds. It is important to discern the variance in viewpoints that may be associated with the objectives of the fund being managed.

Beginning on July 28, 1953, Shelly Pierce, a member of the financial staff of the *Journal of Commerce,* wrote a series of articles which sought to give the answers to two questions: How does a mutual fund go about picking out the securities that make up its investment portfolio? and in weighing two securities, why does it select one instead of the other? He canvassed leading officials of open-end investment companies and presented the results in weekly articles, from which the following were taken. All the articles in this problem deal with individual funds, rather than the views of managers of more than one fund.

MASSACHUSETTS INVESTORS TRUST [1]

Mutual funds are always making changes in their investment portfolio. Changes in portfolios are made for any number of reasons, two of the most obvious of which follow: a stock may no longer fit in with the objectives of a fund, and prospects for the particular company or industry involved may have turned downward.

Merril Griswold, chairman of Massachusetts Investors Trust, in discussing how this stock fund picks securities, observes that "in twenty-nine years of operation, through depression and post-war economic periods, we have learned that there is no stock which should be regarded as sacrosanct. Consequently, there is no stock held which is not for sale provided there is a more attractive stock available to replace it. Our investment work is by no means confined to a process of selection from stocks of well-known and well-established companies. There is a constant looking to the future—a continuing survey of enterprises that will be 'blue chips' of some later year due to developments in such fields as science and technology or for reasons of other sorts."

How does M.I.T., the largest open-end trust in the business, make selections and changes? Mr. Griswold cites the oil industry as an example. "We may favor company A over company B or C for the following reasons: while the earnings of all three at a given time may be equally good or nearly so, our preference for A over B or C may be based on its better long-term prospects, or its more solid position in the industry and the quality and depth of its management. We pay particular attention to management ability and capacity."

In making selections or changes of stocks, Mr. Griswold points out that one of the first considerations "is the broad economic outlook, since certain kinds of stocks are better to own under some economic conditions than others. In considering individual companies, besides management ability, we must look at the company's competitive position, including all aspects of the company's operations and such financial factors as capital structure, future money requirements, dividend policy and the like. Another important factor is the current relative market position of the stock in the light of past performance and future probabilities.

"Again, 'probable safety of capital and probable income' come into the picture. When we have added up all the factors to be considered we expect to achieve these investment objectives. And in this connec-

[1] *Journal of Commerce,* July 28, 1953.

tion it may be pertinent to observe that almost 100 per cent in market value of the stocks now owned by the Massachusetts Investors Trust paid dividends in 1952, and over 87 per cent of them have paid dividends consecutively for the last ten years or longer."

WELLINGTON FUND [2]

Flexibility is an important element in mutual fund investment policy and is followed by Wellington Fund, one of the largest balanced funds. According to A. Moyer Kulp, vice president and executive director of Wellington's investment committee, it "is well adapted to meet changes in business and market trends, whether they be minor or major in degree. It is equally effective in a major market swing or in the selective two-way markets which characterize the broad trading range of a transition period such as 1946-49 and the current market situation."

As additional fund shares are purchased, there is a steady stream of cash coming in which must be invested. "Under normal conditions," says Mr. Kulp, "these incoming funds would be placed in selected common stocks and senior securities. In a depressed market the investment might be made entirely in common stocks, whereas during an uncertain period it might be placed in bonds or kept as a cash reserve."

Mr. Kulp points out that a conservative balanced fund, such as Wellington, will usually activate a change in investment policy in a series of steps. When markets become depressed and the fund adopts an aggressive investment program, common stock holdings are increased first selectively as outstanding values begin to appear and finally, on a broad scale, if the market decline becomes severe and prolonged. "On the other hand," he notes, "when security markets are booming and excessive optimism becomes prevalent, a series of defensive steps are taken beginning with the elimination of high-priced, volatile securities, and if the boom becomes extravagant, representative common stocks are reduced on a broad scale."

Among the factors taken into consideration by this fund's investment management in the selection of stocks are: current and prospective business trends; money supply; wholesale commodity prices; influences of factors peculiar to this decade, such as population increase, new family formation, strategic bargaining power of labor, high and widely distributed spendable income, rapid technological developments, large defense and foreign-aid expenditures; positions of individual industries; awareness of, and ability of managements to meet changing conditions; financial, earnings and dividend record — historical, current and prospective; and market price.

"This comprehensive approach," explains Mr. Kulp, "is in the nature of a screening process which first points out the industries most favorably situated at a given moment, singles out the companies which appear

---

[2] *Ibid.*, August 18, 1953.

to be the most promising for the common stock investor based on demonstrated record and future prospects provided that purchase is made at a reasonable price."

INCORPORATED INVESTORS [3]

Diversification of security investments is one of the advantages of mutual funds, but the extent to which it is pursued varies greatly with different funds. One fund may have its assets invested in several hundred stocks while another may only own a fourth as many. Incorporated Investors is probably the least diversified of any of the common stock funds, according to Amory Parker, vice-president, in discussing that fund's method of selecting stocks. As of June 30 it had 44 stocks in its portfolio. Almost 50 per cent of the portfolio, as of June 30, was invested in two industries — natural gas and oils, and the railroad industry. Natural gas and oils accounted for 25.7 per cent while 23.6 per cent of assets were invested in railroad securities, of which 22.9 per cent was represented by stocks.

"Wherever possible," explains Mr. Parker, "the fund makes its heaviest investments in those industries which it believes offer the best chance of capital appreciation." For this reason the management's decision on what industries to concentrate in obviously has more influence over the fund's performance than the selection of the individual companies. "For example, in the case of the rubber industry, we currently own stock in all four of the major tire and rubber companies. As another extreme, in the case of public utilities, we own only one company and led the management to sell out all public utility stocks some time ago."

The management, he explained, would decide to make an investment in a certain industry only if it believed that the industry had great growth ahead of it and if the stocks of the industry were selling at great discounts from their true worth.

"If it was because of the growth potential," Mr. Parker continued, "the management would seek out the company or companies which appeared to derive the greatest benefit from the growth. Was the company management aggressive and capable? Did the company plan to expand out of its own earnings, through borrowed funds, or by diluting its equity with common stock financing? Did it have inherently greater growth potentials by starting from a smaller base? Does the company have an aggressive research program, likely to produce new products over the future?"

Initial investigations are carried out by men in investment houses "whose judgment and accuracy the management has learned to respect over a period of years," he said. This phase has followed talks with the company management by officers of the fund. When the fund officers feel that they have enough information to judge the company, the next

---

[3] *Ibid.*, September 29, 1953.

step is a consideration of its comparative value. "By that we mean is it sufficiently more attractive to warrant the elimination or reduction of our holdings in any other company. Is an investment in this company likely to be more profitable than an additional investment in a security already owned by the fund? We try to keep the number of securities in the portfolio as low as possible consistent with prudence."

COMMONWEALTH INVESTMENT CO.[4]

Diversification, one of the features of mutual funds which makes them attractive to many uninformed investors, is practiced in some degree by all funds, but in the case of Commonwealth Investment Co. it is a fundamental principle in the selection of securities for its portfolio. The extent to which it adheres to the principle of diversifying its investments is shown by the fact that it owned 328 different securities, as of Sept. 1. The types of issues in its portfolio included 222 common stocks, 74 preferred stocks and 32 bonds, debentures, or notes. Furthermore, these securities, other than Government bonds, represented investment in 36 broad industrial classifications. "This wide degree of diversification is favored for reasons of risk spreading, liquidity, and opportunity," explains Douglas R. Johnston, vice president.

The other main principle followed by Commonwealth in its portfolio management is its policy of gradually buying and selling of the individual securities making up the portfolio. "The purpose of this policy," says Mr. Johnston, "is to secure a satisfactory average cost on the one hand and a satisfactory average selling price, on the other hand. Theoretically, maximum benefits would be obtained by filling entire security positions at lowest prices followed by complete eliminations at top prices. Commonwealth's management, however, is skeptical of the ability of investment management to perform in this manner with profitable consistency. Instead, it believes that the most satisfactory over-all results will be secured by buying on several occasions in a low or reasonable price area and by selling several times at price levels that seem to represent rather full to excessive valuation."

Selection of securities by this balanced fund focuses upon value "which has both quantitative and qualitative features." Potential investments are checked from such standpoints as financial strength and earning power, trend of growth, response to movements in the business cycle and quality of the management of the company whose securities are under consideration.

"Favorable conjunction of these factors with an attractive price level is rare," says Mr. Johnston. "Thus, a stock may qualify admirably on all counts, except that its price may seem too high in relation to its appraised value. Another stock may qualify for purchase consideration on the bases of excellent current earnings and dividends relative to

---

[4] *Ibid.*, October 27, 1953.

price, yet its great vulnerability to cyclical business conditions may make it an unduly risky investment at an advanced stage of business prosperity. In short, it is up to the managers to secure the facts concerning a security; verify their opinions as to qualitative considerations; place a sound value on the issue and relate value to prices at which the security is available."

Of course, choice of individual issues and types of securities must be in line with the objective of the fund. This goal is reasonable income along with protection and long-term growth of principal, subject to the risks involved. Essentially, according to Mr. Johnston, the management followed an aggressive policy which is geared to the satisfaction of longer-term investment objectives. Thus, the fund's common stock position has been a median of 63.9 per cent. It touched 71.5 per cent at the end of 1948 and is now around 61.5 per cent.

In order to accomplish its objective, the management has always sought above average return from the preferred stocks and bonds which make up the fixed income part of the portfolio, according to Mr. Johnston. "Generally, therefore," he continues, "such investments have been acquired with consideration for yield return and some degree of appreciation. At times the opportunities in this field appear to be limited. Under these conditions the management places funds in highly-liquid, prime-quality, short-term U.S. Governments and corporate obligations, awaiting the return of more inviting conditions. This is considered preferable to the possible risk of carrying low-yield preferred stocks and low-yield, long-term bonds for an extended period of time."

In its research activity the Commonwealth organization utilizes, of course, annual reports, statistical services and institutional and government reports, as well as field reports and contacts with specific managements, and other outside sources of information. Primary emphasis is placed upon the generally available factual material. Field reports and actual management contact are used largely to verify questionable data or to amplify information considered incomplete.

Fidelity Fund [5]

Underlying the selection of stocks by Fidelity Fund, Inc. is a constant search for a security which is undervalued, both in relation to the market and to its particular group. In looking for undervalued securities, the fund first makes a statistical comparison and analysis of the industry groups to determine which appears the most attractive in this respect, according to Lawrence A. Sykes, vice-president. Weight is given to such factors as market price, yield, intrinsic worth and future potential. After it has been determined which industry group or groups are most undervalued, a careful statistical analysis of stocks within the group is made. From this study, one or more stocks which appear most attractive are selected.

---

[5] *Ibid.*, December 1, 1953.

Fidelity makes several technical tests to determine whether the price of a particular stock is attractive or not at the moment. After this is done the fund analysts attempt to tie this in with the general market outlook. "For example," explains Mr. Sykes, "we use what we call an index of confidence, which is the ratio of high-grade to secondary stocks. In the past this relationship has proved to be a good barometer of speculation. Other technical tools would include, among others, odd lot transactions and short sales. This technical approach, together with an analysis of general business conditions strengthens our final conclusions on the overall market outlook."

Actual field checks are made with the management of companies whose stocks are under consideration for purchase. Then there are cross-checks which are also an important factor, says Mr. Sykes, in determining why the fund buys or sells a particular stock. For instance, if it is determined that a particular situation is a buy as the result of conclusions reached by way of the fundamental and technical approaches, another cross-check is then obtained through contacts with investment and market specialists who, it is felt, are especially close to this particular situation and whose judgment the fund has come to rely on after long experience. "All these cross-checks, when added together, we hope, give us a solid foundation on which to base our final decision," observes Mr. Sykes.

Fidelity's research staff is broken down by the allocation of certain industry groups to each member so that each staff member in effect becomes a specialist in his particular field. "On the other hand, through group discussion, he doesn't lose his broad perspective and relation of this group to the market as a whole," he adds. "Of course, a good deal of judgment, based on long individual investment experience, plays an important part in our final decision."

1. Does the fact that these funds are varied in type, e.g., stock funds, balanced funds, and also in objective, e.g., appreciation, income, etc., account fully for the different approaches to investment selection? Are there similarities in approach, regardless of the type of fund or objective?

2. Can the individual investor use the methods of investment fund management in selecting securities? How would you go about doing this, if it is possible?

3. How do stock funds vary their commitments? Do they change according to the cycle, or other factors, or are their holdings more or less permanent? How do balanced funds change with the business cycle?

4. From the data given in *Moody's Banks* or Weisenberger's *Investment Companies* (annual) compare the overall results of the

companies covered in this case for a period of at least ten years. Which company has the best record for both income and gain or loss? Is the result attributable to the form of the investment company, its objective, or the management?

40.   A Criticism of Investing Policies

The article that constitutes this problem was written by a well-known, experienced investment personality who has for many years served on boards of large financial institutions.[1] Although he wrote, in other parts of this article, about institutional investing policies, these sections deal very well with attitudes adopted by many individuals. It would be well to look up the history of the man whose name is used as a pseudonym.

. . . I have listed below and discussed some attitudes that I have frequently encountered in . . . investing and that are handicaps or worse to achieving better results. These can be identified by common stereotype phrases.

If we are wrong, let's be in good company. There is a tendency to select issues on the basis of their popularity or because they have been purchased by large and well-known institutions. This policy causes excessive competition for certain securities and unjustifiably neglects others. The fact that this practice is widespread tends to render even more profitable its direct opposite: namely, a deliberate seeking to be in the minority. The phenomenon of seeking "to be in good company," I consider to be a survival of personal trust practice, a kind of substitute legal list. This leads to a preoccupation with quality at any price, to the neglect of value. But emphasis on value is basic to good investment results.

(a) Let's sell before they go still lower.

(b) Buy 'em before they run away.

The above represents in shorthand form what I call the amateur psychology of buying and selling things with changing values. What I think may fairly be called the professional point of view is very largely opposite. This tends to be profitable possibly because it is inherently more sound, but certainly because the amateur attitude is vastly more widespread, and in dealing with men and markets it is profitable to be what might be called an early minority. The question may logically be raised, "What if everybody tries to do this? Would it not be a self-defeating process?" No, I believe not, because the result would be fundamentally that future developments would be discounted further

---

[1] "Menippus," "Some Self-Criticism of Institutional Investing," *Analysts Journal*, Vol. 6, No. 4 (Fourth Quarter 1950), pp. 29–31.

and more adequately in advance of their happening. If the classical economists were correct, as I believe they were, in their belief that the social and economic value of speculation is to discount the future and thus minimize the shock waves of time and events, then the more adequately we all can perform this function, the better it is for our society and our economy. To do that presupposes that there will be an early minority.

Why, THAT couldn't POSSIBLY happen! This phrase is graven on the tombstone of innumerable investment hopes. It is the instinctive, almost reflex reaction to the disturbing possibility that something may turn out to be unpleasantly different from what it is now or from what we have expected it to be. The "something" may, of course, in particular cases, be anything that affects investment values, earnings per share, interest rates, Government competition, labor costs, or what you will.

It is valuable to cultivate an awareness of one's own innate reluctance to visualize drastic changes, to visualize them as an imminent reality. To be aware of it is not the same as doing nothing about it. On the contrary, we have to be aware of our unimaginativeness, to combat it. We do not like to think and we do not care to adapt ourselves to change, still less to meet the change halfway by adapting to it in advance of imperative necessity. But to be a competent investor requires that we look forward to change and step forward with zest to meet it. It matters not that we claim to see the shadow of coming events, if we do not act as though we saw them, for in that event it makes no practical difference. Surveying past important events, putting oneself in the position of an investor at the time, is considerably less fatuous than it appears at first glance.

The market is always right. In the sense that the market knows more about any given situation than any one of us does, this is obviously true — also trite. Less true and positively misleading is the connotation that no one else knows less about the future security than we do. Only on this supposition can the statement mean that there is no use in our trying to forecast the future of the situation, and acting on that forecast. The practical application, however, is all too frequently just that: What's the use of trying to outguess the future? Essentially, the catchword "the market is always right" is merely another rationalization for inaction.

Let's not act until we are certain. This is another of the stereotypes widely encountered as a kind of Fabian tactic, in accordance with our instinctive desire to avoid thinking, making decisions, and taking responsibility. There are several unrealities here. First, the word "action" is algebraic — it can be either positive or negative, with "action" including also "inaction." Second, the tacit — and unreal — assumption is present that information that is so confirmed as to be a certainty is nevertheless known to so few other persons as to be still undiscounted in the price of a security. The corollary of this seems to be better known to stock speculators than to bond investors. It is simply that investing is a series of decisions based on calculated risks. After all, to be a successful investor on the basis of the actuarial viewpoint requires merely that our securities at all times be subject to a higher proportion of favorable than of unfavorable contingencies.

Don't worry, the pendulum always swings back. This is the comforting afterthought that time will save us from the consequences of our investing sins. It is closely related to the statement: "Let's hold it until we can get out even." The trouble with both is that the whole pendulum is moving, quite apart from its swings. So, cyclical movements, when superimposed on a trend line, do not necessarily bring one back to any prior point. . . .

1. Are any of the above viewpoints valuable for the institutional, as contrasted with the individual, investor?

2. Does "Menippus" advocate an overthrow of diversification in the interest of a more positive approach to security movements? How?

41. Costs of Life Insurance

The individual seldom has too great an accurate knowledge of the pattern and relation of the premium rates on various types of insurance. All the data for this problem can be obtained from any life insurance agent.

1. Complete the following table of life insurance premiums and other data for $1,000 policies, assuming that dividends are left to accumulate at interest:

Type of Policy	Age at which policy is written				Cash Value*
	25	35	45	55	
Renewable 5-yr. term					
Term to 65					
Whole life					
20-pay life					
Life to 65					
20-yr. endowment					
Endowment to 65					

*For policies taken out at age 45 only.

2. What is the difference between participating and non-participating policies of stock life insurance companies?

3. Can premiums be paid in advance? If so, at what rate of discount?

4. Comment briefly on the pattern of differences in premiums by age at which the policy is written and by type of policy.

5. Assume that the whole life, limited-payment life, and endowment policies carry a 2½ per cent guaranteed rate of compounding. What would be the cash surrender value for each type of policy at age 65 for policies taken out at age 45? Can you now compute the net cost of the various types of insurance? Are there any differences in net cost? Does net cost afford a better method of comparing rates for different companies?

6. Assume you are age 25 and are considering purchase of $5,000 of 20-year endowment insurance with (a) annual premiums of $50.32 per $1,000 which can be prepaid for a lump payment of $822.93 per $1,000, or (b) single premium payment of $720.28 per $1,000. What are the factors to consider in deciding between the two methods of payment?

7. Assume you are age 25 and are considering purchase of (a) $1,000 in Series E Savings Bonds, costing $750.00 and maturing in 9 years, 8 months, with an option of leaving the bond for extended maturity of an equal length of time, or (b) single premium 20-year endowment insurance at a cost of $720.28. Which would prove the better investment over the twenty-year period? Is this all you should consider?

42. Home Ownership Versus Rental

Since many people have little idea of the costs of housing, this problem is of special value in dealing with the question of home ownership versus rental.

1. From real estate agency advertisements in your local paper, select what you consider to be a modest but adequate house for a family with two children. From the agent find out the age, location and condition of the home, its approximate initial cost,

its approximate value in 1950, and the tax bill on the property last year.

2. Inquire as to the approximate costs of closing the sale of the home, including such things as bringing the abstract up to date or securing title insurance, transfer taxes, and so forth. Then inquire as to the costs of recording the new deed. To the seller and the buyer add a minimum cost of $20 for completing the transaction. Such legal costs are not always necessary, but are a safety precaution.

3. What would the cost of buying this house have been in 1950? Considering real estate brokerage fees at a 5 per cent minimum, what would be the approximate net proceeds of the sale at the present time? Had you bought the house in 1950 and sold it now, would you have gained or lost? How much? Compare the percentage of gain or loss with the relative change in the consumer price index from 1950 to date. Did home ownership afford any protection against price level hazards to the principal invested?

4. Estimate the real cost of housing to the owner of the house, including maintenance, depreciation, and other costs. How does this compare with the rental value of the property? Would it be more profitable to buy the house for rental or residence purposes?

5. Assume that your family income amounts to $500 a month. The usual measure applied in real estate transactions is that total costs should not exceed 250 per cent of the buyer's annual income. This would mean that a $15,000 house is just within the range of possible purchase. What added costs must be taken into account to get a more accurate figure on the total cost of the purchase of a house?

43.   Determination of Investment Policy for an Individual

The following article [1] *highlights the problem of the individual*

[1] *Moody's Stock Survey* (May 11, 1953), pp. 486-7.

in his attempt to determine the amounts of stocks and bonds to
hold in a portfolio. Its inclusion here affords a good introduction
to the problems faced by the individual in determining a suitable
investment policy.

In former years it was common practice to plan individual portfolios
in so-called balanced proportions, say half stock funds and half bond
funds, keeping to these ratios year after year. But the inflation of war
and post-war years changed many investors' concept of the correct
portfolio arrangement, bringing them strongly over to the idea of having
the biggest part of total funds, sometimes all, available to put into
commons, leaving little or nothing for bonds.

Behind the trend just mentioned is the fact that for 10 years or
more in this country we have been passing through an era that was dis-
couraging to bond investment and encouraging to stock investment. Bond
investment was made unfavorable because of the inflation (which cheats
the fixed-income investor by cutting his purchasing power) and by the
starvation rates of interest (2½% on long Governments was offered during the war, versus 4% or 5% in the 1920's). At the same time, the inflation tended to raise both dividends and market prices of stocks,
especially of stocks of favorably situated companies, when taxes did not
offset that effect.

The experience of most stock investors was, of course, good over the
past 10 pears. And if you had overshifted to stocks compared with your
fundamental objectives, no harm was done, provided you held good
stocks.

At this time, however, the inflation is ending and the yield on bonds
has been rising. The last long-term Government bonds bore a 3¼%
coupon. The two kinds of investment are now more nearly equal in
attractiveness. Temporarily, that is, in the course of the next year or so,
bonds may even move up and stocks may react — assuming a letdown in
business.

The chief question which this prospect puts up to the investor, it seems
to us, is the second one stated above — whether the lure of stocks under
conditions of recent years has had a greater influence on his policies
than he should have permitted. Did you allow yourself to become, say,
an all-out stock investor, alloting all your funds to the stock field, when
in more normal times your proportions had been, say, half in stock and
half in bond funds?

There is, of course, no "textbook" rule which will settle this question
for you. You will have to judge it mostly for yourself or in consultation
with others.

Some Specific Suggestions

(1) We believe thoroughly in a program which allots the greater part
of one's total funds permanently to "stock funds," i.e., funds available
for common stocks. The shift in conditions which now is taking place

does not in the least threaten the long-run qualities and potentialities of stocks. The growth trends in the country are still persisting. But we would say that it requires certain psychological qualities to be a long-term stock investor of this kind. You must have the temperament for it, which means chiefly that you must be prepared to absorb some fluctuations in both capital and income, as between good times and poor times.

And, as of the present moment, we would repeat two features of such a policy: (a) You should continue to hold some sizable part of your stock funds temporarily out of the stock market as a buying reserve, to be ready for stock-buying opportunities that may develop selectively over a period of months. A third of your total stock funds might logically be so alloted under present conditions. (b) The balance of your stock funds should logically continue only in stocks of strong character and generally high quality. Accent quality and stability; avoid cyclical, unstable situations unless you have a specially positive, not a mere casual, reason for being in certain issues.

This continues the same policy we have recently been recommending. We see no reason to change it at this point if you are a "convinced" long-term stock investor. We think the long-run results will be profitable.

(2) On the other hand, if you are temperamentally or otherwise a person who should in normal times have a "balanced fund," illustrated by the idea of half your total investment capital in stock funds and half in bond funds, and if you find you have strayed from such a basic arrangement so that you have much more than half in stock funds, the present offers a favorable chance to begin moving back toward your originally intended position.

If you do conclude that you are too far over into the stock side and plan a correctional adjustment, we would point out these two considerations in respect to bonds: (a) It generally pays to buy only high-grade bonds, regardless of whether they are corporate or some other type of obligation. (b) It may pay you, if you are one of those who feels he should return to a more balanced portfolio position, to look into tax-exempt bonds as the medium for your bond funds. (Relatively high taxes will probably prevail for a considerable time, even after tax cuts.) Whether tax exempts will actually be attractive to you will depend on your tax bracket, of course.

Meanwhile, in the case of a balanced portfolio, the stock money should be treated the same way as in the case of the more "all-out" stock investor. We mean that an important proportion of the stock money should now be in a buying reserve, while the stocks that are held should be in strong issues.

1. Does this commentary implicitly follow the concept of diversification? Does diversification mean an unbending following of one plan of investment, say of half stocks and half bond values?

2. Does this commentary appear to imply that at one time a 100 per cent common stock position might be followed? A 100 per

cent bond position? Why? Is this variation of proportions consistent with the concept of a single plan of investment?

44. Objectives of Individual Investment Policies

This problem is intended to highlight the necessity for establishing objectives of investment for each individual, with differing circumstances dictating different policies.

One of the leading investment services has clearly stated the need for clear determination of investment objectives. The article is here given in full.[1]

In considering what stocks to hold and buy, it is of course not only wise but necessary to know your own objectives. What am I investing for? is the question everyone should refer back to in each step as he goes along. . . . To illustrate how that question determines the kind of stocks for you, we report below two cases. Both are strictly investment problems; that is, neither is concerned with short-term operations. Yet they are sharply different, as you can see.

(1) Couple Needing Income

John and Mary Harle, husband and wife, are recently retired middle-class people who have moved to Florida. They have neither dependents nor other reasons for trying to make their capital grow. Almost their sole investment problem is to generate as much income as they prudently can. They have investment capital of $80,000 and he receives a (taxable) pension of $3,000 a year. Both are over 65.

The proposal to reduce taxation of dividends is right down their alley, of course. A quarter of their money is at present in Treasury bonds, the rest in good stocks. They figure now that if the proposal goes through and if they should put all their capital into stocks at 5½%, not only would their gross income increase by some $600 a year, but their total tax after the dividends credit would be down $630 (they are counting the 1954 tax rate reduction in figuring this, of course).

They'd be better off, in short, by over $1,200 in "take home" income three years from now. Their tax position last year and, prospectively, in 1957, they figure as follows:

Sources of Income	1953	1957
Pension	$3,000	$3,000
Dividends	3,300	4,400
Interest	500	
	$6,800	$7,400*

---

[1] *Moody's Stock Survey* (February 8, 1954), p. 634.

Exemptions and Deductions	3,080	3,120
Taxable Income	$3,720	$4,080
Approx. Fed. Tax	818	188
"Take Home" Income	$5,982	$7,212

° Includes $100 dividend income excluded from taxation for each person.

Their watchword has been prudence, however, and to move completely into stocks seemed to them to border on imprudence.

Actually, in our view, it depends on the circumstances and on which stocks. Income stocks of the type of high stability in dividends seem most unlikely to lead them into trouble. And, since yield is very important to them, the electric power group as a whole could be considered. There they can average nearly 5½ per cent at this time by picking and choosing. . . . Here, then, is a case where no straining to over-reach on speculative lines is involved, where liquid funds are not needed, and where income is the goal. We would advise them to go ahead with their idea of moving entirely into conservative stocks.

(2) Quest for an Estate

Arthur Schultz is facing nearly the opposite investment problem. He is younger, earns a large salary, calculates 20 years ahead of him before retirement, and wants to build as big an estate as possible so that if he dies first his wife will be comfortably off and in any case his children will have no financial worries. His investment object is thus not current income, but to make his capital grow. It will, he hopes, be taxed as an estate; he doesn't want to take capital gains as he goes along.

The proposal to reduce taxes on dividends thus doesn't interest him directly (though it probably should). He invests only in "growth" issues, often with a very low current yield, and holds a substantial buying reserve, since he is always on the lookout for cheap stocks and wants to be able to act quickly.

Further, the growth stocks he needs are of a particular kind. For instance, he is not interested in utility stocks of the type carried in our growth list because they are either too slow in pace or too limited in potential. His eyes are on issues whose long-term possibilities are not limited by anything visible. He takes to the Aluminiums, the American Cyanamids and the Pfizers. He holds duPont and General Electric and Aluminum Co. of America. He also buys long-range stocks that many would call speculations — but he terms them "ultimate" investments.

• • •

In between the two cases are many investors who seek capital gains on a basis that is not so long as Mr. Schultz's and who strive for dividend income, too. To them the lists of liberal yield and of growth issues will appeal.

1. In what type of investment situation would each of the follow-

ing investment objectives apply: dependable income of a given minimum amount; nontaxable income; preservation of funds; maximum income plus safety of principal?

2. What criticisms can be raised against the implicit advice that both investors mentioned put all their holdings in common stocks?

3. Under what assumptions can growth issues be held for periods of upwards of twenty years?

45. A Portfolio for Recession Times

The selection of a portfolio of common stocks designed to meet with the perils of a recession is a rather difficult task. The following problem presents one attempt at solving the requirements of price stability and income.

A stock portfolio for a $20,000 investor confronted by recession was presented by *Moody's Stock Survey*, September 14, 1953. The accompanying comment affords an important view.

Many stocks would fit the requirements of a typical long-term stock investor at this time — as you can see from reviews of stocks to hold and to buy as published weekly in Stock Survey. The portfolio below differs somewhat from the "typical" in that, since it is for a medium or small-size investor, we have emphasized low price, relatively high yield and pretty sober stocks. This doesn't mean, however, that stocks such as General Motors, Atchison, International Paper, Westinghouse, etc., which we have recommended for holding or buying, should not continue to be held in proper amounts by the typical investor.

In commenting on the portfolio, an accompanying article stated:

The concepts behind these ideas have been:
That the economy was due for a period of pause, nonstimulation and recession, but that a depression or deep deflation was not probable;
That the change from boom to recession would take place gradually, not with a sudden break;
That in such a trend there would have to occur a moderate decline in average earnings and dividends, though cushioned by tax reductions;
That the market (if we may speak of it as though it were a person) was already thinking of all these possibilities or even more serious ones, and that its valuations of current earnings and dividends had thus re-

TABLE IV-3

	Recent Price	Indicated Dividend	Indicated Yield	Cost	Cash Income
Stocks for High Income Stability:					
35 American Gas & Electric	30	$1.64	5.47%	$ 1,050	$ 57.40
40 Irving Trust Company	22	1.10	5.00	880	44.00
21 Ohio Edison	37	2.20	5.95	777	46.20
60 Northern States Power	13	0.70	5.38	780	42.00
60 San Diego Gas & Electric	14	0.80	5.71	840	48.00
				$ 4,327	$237.60
Stocks for Long-Term Growth:					
25 Aluminum Co. of America	45	$1.60	3.56%	$ 1,125	$ 40.00
25 American Cyanamid	44	2.00	4.55	1,100	50.00
35 Libbey-Owens-Ford	34	2.00	5.88	1,190	70.00
50 Lone Star Gas	24	1.40	5.83	1,200	70.00
80 Southern Company	14	0.80	5.71	1,120	64.00
				$ 5,735	$294.00
Other Stocks for More Liberal Income:					
30 Atlantic Refining	27 1/2	$2.00	7.27%	$ 825	$ 60.00
30 C. I. T. Financial	26 1/2	1.80	6.79	795	54.00
30 General Public Utilities	25	1.60	6.40	750	48.00
20 McKesson & Robbins	35 1/2	2.50	7.04	710	50.00
45 Wisconsin Public Service	17 1/2	1.10	6.29	788	49.50
				$ 3,868	$261.50
Stock Totals				$13,930	$793.10
Current Yield from Stocks					5.69%
Temporary Buying Reserve:					
$6,000 in savings banks at 2 1/2%				$ 6,000	$150.00
Grand Total				$19,930	$943.10

mained sober, and in fact were becoming more restrained as the months went along;

That the future market consequences of such developments would be an irregular declining tendency in stock prices, but of moderate rather than severe proportions and made up of highly selective net changes;

And finally, that beyond the time when a recession might come, bringing lower average stock prices and dividends, with average dividends and prices rising and easily reaching new peaks. . . .

It is a fact that some investors think of themselves as long-term holders of stocks when everything is going well, but wish they were out of them when the trend is the other way. Such people suffer acutely in a market decline and seem constitutionally incapable of standing firm on a policy that calls for keeping invested.

In respect to such an investor, we would say that his present position is like that of the air traveler about to board the plane. If he is afraid of the journey, he had better call it off now, for once aboard, the plane's doors will close and the flight will start. He can't change his mind then.

1. Explain why each of the issues in the first two groups meets the requirements set forth. Are not the long-term growth issues subject to sizable cyclical risk? How is this consistent with the objectives of investing during a recession?

2. If a much-advertised recession did not occur, how would an investor with the suggested portfolio fare? Is this of significance in handling the problem of investing?

46. Investing for a Widow

The following problem is based on a variation of a classical problem first posed in 1925. Although some repeat contests on this theme have been held, the problem below poses the question more thoroughly and represents a real situation.

In August 1950 the editor of the Investment Department of the late *Chicago Journal of Commerce* received the following letter:

Gentlemen:

One of our most valued employes was killed in an automobile accident Friday, June 16, 1950.

His widow will receive some insurance money aggregating approximately $30,000. We will appreciate your furnishing us your recommendation for sound investments in which her insurance money can be invested to give her the maximum amount of safe return.

At the annual return of government bonds the investment of all this money in government bonds would only pay her about 2½ per cent return, or a total of $750. She can invest approximately $9,000 of this money with the insurance company by leaving it on deposit and get a return of 3 per cent, which I think she should do. This would be practically as safe as government bonds and pay her ½ per cent more return.

If she can average 4 per cent return on the balance of $21,000 she would have a return of $840 on her other investments, plus the $270 on the $9,000 or a total of $1,100.

Thanking you to furnish us your definite recommendation in regard to this at your earliest convenience and by return mail if possible, we are,

Yours sincerely,
"Secretary"

Upon inquiry, the editor found that the widow, who was 64 years of age, had one year to go before receiving benefits of $45 a month from social security. In the meantime, she would receive from workmen's compensation the sum of $24 a week for nine years. The problem was thus posed: security plus income!

In giving this problem to its readers, the *Chicago Journal of Commerce* stated that it would publish the most interesting replies as chosen by three financial institutions in Chicago. Altogether 27 replies were printed during the following month. The financial staff of the paper were impressed by two main points common to many of the replies received. First was the heavy reliance placed on the dividend outlook for equity investments, including recommendations for investing a substantial portion of the $30,000 in common stocks. Reasons advanced for these views included: a desire to invest money in something "solid," such as companies owning minerals, land, or the like, as an "inflation hedge" type of thinking; evidence that the purchase of common stocks was forced by the "cheap money" policy of the incumbent administration in order to get a return of 5 or 6 per cent, and a continuity of dividends. The second main point of the letters was the Christian neighborliness expressed in the letters, evidenced by "may she rest well nights with her financial problems solved" and other words of good will.

Early in October 1950 the paper published the actual plan used in solving this problem (Table IV–4).

The following comment was made by the financial editor: "At the maximum, income on present dividend bases will be $69.19 a week. It will fall off at the end of the workmen's compensation payment period by $24, amounting to $45.19 a week. The investments made by the widow were about the mean of those suggested by all those writing in. There was considerable emphasis upon sound equities, many recommended that she keep the $9,000 at interest

TABLE IV-4

Number of Shares		Total	Est. Annual Income
100	Commonwealth Edison Co.	$ 2,912	$ 160
50	E. I. duPont de Nemours & Co.	3,306	170
50	General Motors Corporation	3,863	400
50	Phillips Petroleum	3,095	200
50	F. W. Woolworth Co.	2,238	125
30	U. S. Gypsum Co.	3,094	270
35	Massachusetts Investors Fund shares	1,019	50
50	Parke Davis Co.	1,950	90
		$21,477	$1,465
	Insurance (Equitable) @ 3%	9,000	270
		$30,477	$1,735
	Workmen's Compensation Insurance from 6/16/50, 400 weeks to 2/18/58		1,248
	Total until May 3, 1951		$2,983
	Social Security after 5/3/51, $51.25 a month . .		615
	Total after May 3, 1951		$3,598

with the insurance company and there were many recommendations for investment in trust funds."

1. Value the portfolio as of a recent date, using the estimated annual dividend rates for the current year. Have the objectives of "safety plus income" been achieved? How? Did the portfolio have sufficient diversification to take care of all risks?
2. How would you readjust the portfolio under current conditions, assuming no subsequent change were to be made for approximately three to five years? Write a short summary of not more than 300 words (the contest limit) to explain your changes.
3. Could the widow's objectives have been achieved as well by use of investment fund shares alone as by the portfolio actually chosen?

47.   Financial Planning for a Widow

This problem involves the formulation of a financial plan and an investment program for a widow. Included is the question of handling a block of stock in a small, closed corporation.

Charles Robbins just died and his widow comes to you as an old family friend, and as a trust officer at the First National Bank of a medium-sized city. She asks for your advice and guidance in the handling of her financial affairs. Since you have lived in the same neighborhood with the family for over ten years, you know them quite well.

Mrs. Robbins is now 40 years old and has two small children of primary grade age. She has for some time been quite active in the social and community affairs of the city in addition to being a regular member of her neighborhood church.

The estate of Mr. Robbins includes:

(a) A residence appraised at $25,000 with a mortgage due to be paid up within five years at a 4 per cent rate. Payments on the mortgage, taxes, and insurance amount to $128.35 a month.

(b) A checking account balance at your bank, $20,000.

(c) Several life insurance policies, totaling $80,000, payable to Mrs. Robbins with several settlement options of the ordinary type included in straight-life policies.

(d) A thousand shares, or half-interest, in a small, local machinery company in which Mr. Robbins was an active officer. The tax authorities value the stock at $20 a share for inheritance purposes, but there is no active market for the stock. In the four past years an annual dividend of $1 a share has been paid; Mr. Robbins had been drawing a salary of $10,000 a year. The book value of the stock is about $24 a share.

1. How would you advise Mrs. Robbins about the insurance settlement options?

2. What would you advise her to do about the stock?

3. Formulate a financial plan for this family to cover the next 15 years. What investment policy would you suggest?

48.   Investing for a Retired Businessman

This problem concerns the adequacy of investment income to meet living expenses of a retired man and wife. The alternatives are rather clearly drawn for simplicity.

Mr. Fulton, age 60, has been a successful businessman in a small community for the past 30 years. He has raised a family of three daughters who are now married to successful husbands. He and Mrs. Fulton have decided that after a rather restrictive life they should now retire and travel. Mrs. Fulton's health has not been good and the family doctor has advised winter vacations in the Southwest for her and Mr. Fulton. If a buyer can be found for the business, it should bring about $50,000. If not, a manager can be hired, but the net drawing Mr. Fulton can expect will be reduced to about $300 a month. This is drastically below the current income of over $7,500 a year he is now receiving while expanding and modernizing the business location.

At the present time Mr. Fulton has a business checking account of $10,000 of which he uses about half for seasonal business needs. His insurance policies are paid and amount to $30,000. He also has a portfolio of securities purchased through the years.

		Cost	Market*	Income*
$5,000	Atchison Top. & S. F. Ry. 4s, '95	$ 5,600	$ 5,150	$200
3,000	Canadian Natl. Rys. 5s, '54	3,120	3,180	150
5,000	Southern Pacific Co. 4 1/2s, '69	3,350	5,050	225
100 sh.	Am. Tel. & Tel. common	15,400	15,938	900
100 sh.	Consol. Edison common	2,000	3,862	200
100 sh.	General Electric common	3,600	7,275	300
50 sh.	U. S. Steel common	2,500	4,238	150

*Assumed to be current prices and yields.

The Fultons currently spend about $400 a month in living expenses. They do not intend to abandon their home, for they hope to return to the Northern climate during the summers. However, the added costs of traveling and of living in rented quarters will lift their expenses in the coming years to about $650 a month. These changes arouse Mr. Fulton's anxiety about the prospects of preserving some estate to pass on to his grandchildren.

1. What should be Mr. Fulton's primary investment objective? What factors must be considered in attaining this objective?
2. Should Mr. Fulton attempt to make up the deficiency in his income by trying to increase the yield from his portfolio or should he "live up his principal?" If the latter, how would you plan for a liquidation of his holdings commensurate with his needs for cash? Would commissions and odd-lots be a factor to consider?
3. Would you consider using up the cash surrender value of the life insurance as a form of annuity? Assuming this would provide an income for Mr. Fulton's life of $135 a month, what type of conversion of the life insurance policy would you suggest?
4. Would you suggest any changes be made in Mr. Fulton's portfolio? Should he "cash in" on any of his gains? How should he reinvest?
5. How can Mr. Fulton protect his wife's future in the event of his own death, should it occur within the next year or two?

49.   Investing for a Businessman

This rather comprehensive problem is taken from life, and poses a combination of policy and selection.

Mr. Sherburn Shaw graduated from engineering school in 1935. He went to work for a large manufacturing company as a designer of electrical equipment. Because of his industry and ambition he advanced quickly to become head of the design section. Early in 1940 he was shifted to the purchasing department to replace an executive who was retiring. Here again he showed considerable ability.

In 1938 Mr. Shaw was married. He bought an old house in the suburbs of the large community in which he worked. By 1943 his family had grown to include three daughters and a son and he had built a new home suitable to his newly acquired executive status. This was financed by a $15,000 mortgage at 4 per cent, taken out from a local savings and loan association. Monthly payments amounted to around $100 to cover interest, taxes, insurance, and repayments.

Throughout the war Mr. Shaw continued at his job, although he was becoming restive. Early in 1945 he was approached by a fellow executive about the chances of forming a small new company to engage in manufacturing electrical systems for aircraft. Because of his contacts Mr. Shaw was in a position to know all the details of subcontracting, and thus could contribute greatly to the administration of the firm. His associate had engineering experience and was to direct the manufacturing side of the firm while Shaw handled the office.

After some thought Mr. Shaw decided to take up the new challenge. His savings at the time amounted to about $40,000 of which he put $25,000 into the new venture. His salary with the new firm was set at $6,000 plus a bonus of 10 per cent of all net profits after taxes. The first few years were the usual experience for a new firm. The losses in the first year, while set-up expenses were high, were cancelled by the profits of the second year when a large contract from a major aircraft manufacturer was received. In the third year, 1948, another substantial gain was achieved, and Mr. Shaw's bonus alone amounted to over $15,000.

It was at this time that Mr. Shaw began to think of the securities markets. He saw that prices had fallen from their postwar highs and reasoned that this might be the time to step in and form the basis of a retirement fund. His insurance needs were taken care of by a policy for $60,000 held by the company, the proceeds to be used to repurchase Mr. Shaw's interest in the firm. Mr. Shaw went to the local office of an investment house and brokerage firm for advice.

The president of the firm was interested in Mr. Shaw's plight. He had seen the new firm progress and thought that perhaps at some future date there might be a need for further financing. Accordingly, he determined to give Mr. Shaw the best advice possible. He wrote to a large New York brokerage firm with which he placed orders for New York Stock Exchange trades and received the following suggestion.

A suggested portfolio for a businessman who seeks to invest $25,000 at a modest yield but with opportunities for eventual appreciation, particularly from growth issues, might well consist of:

United States Savings Bonds, Series G .... $ 5,000

20 shares Allis Chalmers $3.25 convertible preferred
20 shares $3.50 American Cyanamid conv. preferred
20 shares Kimberly Clark $4 second conv. preferred
20 shares Parafinne $4 convertible preferred

$8,120

50 International Harvester common
30 General Motors common
50 National Lead common
50 General Electric common
20 Atchison, Topeka & Santa Fe common
50 Inland Steel common

$12,030

Mr. Shaw received the reply and consulted with the local investment man. He was rather perturbed at the low return of 4 per cent, but agreed that if this could be compensated by growth over the next ten or more years, he would be entirely satisfied. If the new firm were to need new funds, however, he could not add to the portfolio for perhaps another five years. He promised to let the investment firm know when such new financing would be forthcoming.

1. Was the investment man ethical in turning over the inquiry to his New York correspondent?
2. Appraise the portfolio suggestions in the light of current conditions. What has happened to the principal? To income?
3. Should the investment firm have included Mr. Shaw's common stock holdings in its analysis? Why or why not?
4. Would the situation have been any different had Mr. Shaw been an executive of the larger firm rather than one of the principal stockholders of the smaller firm?

50.   Individual Portfolios of Varying Size

This is one of the more comprehensive, yet simple problems on the question of policy for individual investors. The variety of objectives presented and the means of attaining results offers much room for intelligent discussion.

In December 1947 Merrill Lynch, Pierce, Fenner & Beane, one of the largest investment and brokerage houses in the country, published a number of sample portfolios for varying amounts of investment: $2,500, $5,000, $10,000, $25,000, and $50,000. These portfolios were intended to serve as guides for both employees of the firm and for customer use. For each amount three plans were presented: one of high grade, low yield securities for a fund in which safety was held most important, a second combining liberal income with appreciation possibilities, but with a corresponding risk element, and a third, designed principally for appreciation. The plans for funds of $2,500, $10,000, and $50,000 are presented in Table IV-5.

1. Why do not the second portfolios equal the first multiplied by four? Why is the third group not the second multiplied by five?
2. Noting that the values devoted to each issue are held to be about constant within any one group of security types, is this any improvement over a practice of rounding out lots into 100 or 50 shares? Would the cost of odd-lot buying be considerable in these portfolios? Would the brokerage firm be interested in making odd-lot transactions?
3. Note that in some cases the identical issue is used in both the plan involving liberal income and appreciation possibilities and the plan involving only appreciation. Is there any inconsistency in this practice? Can an issue be bought for both purposes?
4. Using the portfolios for one amount, bring the valuation and income data up to the present. Use a bond guide and a stock guide, or statistical manuals where the companies have changed through merger or sale. Compare the relative changes in values with those for the general stock price index of the S.E.C. as

given in the Appendix. Have these portfolios done as well as or better than the general market? Which plan has actually proved the best in achieving its intended end? Which has given the best income? Which the best appreciation? Could this have been opposite to the results had the market been declining from 1948 to the present time?

TABLE IV-5
INVESTING $2,500

Plan "A" for Safety of Principal:	Value	Income
$1,000 U.S. Treasury 2 1/2%, 12/15/67-72	$1,010	$25.00
200 U.S. Savings Bonds, 2 1/2%, 12 yr. Series G. .	200	5.00
20 shares General Electric common.	700	32.00
10 shares Monsanto Chemical Co. common	580	20.00
Total.	$2,490	$82.00
Plan "B" for Liberal Income:		
10 shares Allis-Chalmers 3 1/4% cum. conv. pfd.	$ 940	$32.50
10 shares Libbey-Owens-Ford common.	560	30.00
25 shares National Distillers common	525	50.00
15 shares Westinghouse Air Brake common . . .	525	45.00
Total.	$2,550	$157.50
Plan "C" for Appreciation:		
20 shares Crane Company common	$ 720	$52.00
20 shares Westinghouse Electric common	560	25.00
40 shares Eastern Airlines common.	680	10.00
45 shares International Telephone & Telegraph . .	585	nil
Total.	$2,545	$87.00

TABLE IV-5 (Continued)
INVESTING $10,000

	Value	Income
Plan "A" for Safety of Principal:		
$2,000 U. S. Treasury 2 1/2%, 12/15/67-72	$ 2,020	$ 50.00
2,000 Consol. Edison 1st & Ref. 3%, 1972.	2,025	60.00
1,000 Pere Marquette 1st Ser. "D" 3 3/8%, 1980 . .	1,015	33.75
30 shares Chase National Bank common.	1,050	48.00
40 shares Commonwealth Edison Co. common .	1,040	56.00
25 shares Dow Chemical Co. common	1,000	21.88
10 shares Fireman's Fund Insurance Co.	940	30.00
20 shares Minneapolis-Honeywell Regulator . .	1,140	40.00
Total	$10,230	$339.63
Plan "B" for Liberal Income:		
70 shares American Airlines 3 1/2% cum. conv.	$ 4,130	$245.00
20 shares American Tobacco "B"	1,380	70.00
50 shares Bendix Aviation	1,600	100.00
125 shares Columbia Gas & Electric	1,500	93.75
30 shares Timken Roller Bearing	1,560	90.00
Total	$10,170	$598.75
Plan "C" for Appreciation:		
25 shares Chrysler Corporation	$ 1,525	$ 71.88
60 shares Home Insurance Co.	1,440	72.00
60 shares Southern Natural Gas Co.	1,440	90.00
25 shares Texas Company	1,450	75.00
80 shares Eastern Air Lines	1,360	20.00
30 shares Ex-Cell-O Corporation	1,380	78.00
100 shares International Telephone & Telegraph .	1,300	nil
Total	$ 9,895	$406.88

TABLE IV-5 (Concluded)
INVESTING $50,000

	Value	Income
Plan "A" for Safety of Principal:		
$10,000 U. S. Treasury 2-1/2%, 12/15/67-72.	$10,100	$ 250.00
5,000 Ches. & Ohio Ref. & Imp. Ser. "E" 3-1/2%, '96	5,150	175.00
5,000 Consol. Edison 1st & Ref. 3%, 1972	5,063	150.00
5,000 Municipals — 20 year.	5,119	112.50
15 shares Allied Chemical & Dye Corp.	3,015	135.00
35 shares Corn Products Refining Co.	2,345	105.00
70 shares General Electric Company	2,450	112.00
35 shares Gulf Oil Corporation	2,485	96.25
50 shares Manufacturers Trust Co. (N. Y.). . . .	2,550	120.00
40 shares Monsanto Chemical Co.	2,320	80.00
100 shares Philadelphia Electric Co.	2,300	120.00
70 shares Pittsburgh Plate Glass Co.	2,660	119.00
35 shares St. Paul Fire & Marine Insurance Co. .	2,450	70.00
50 shares F. W. Woolworth Company	2,300	125.00
Total.	$50,307	$1,769.75
Plan "B" for Liberal Income:		
55 shares Allis-Chalmers 3-1/4% cum. conv. . .	$ 5,170	$ 187.75
85 shares American Airlines 3-1/2% cum. conv..	5,015	297.50
45 shares Armour & Co. $6 cum. conv. pr. . . .	4,905	270.00
50 shares United Aircraft 5% cum. conv.	5,300	250.00
90 shares Ex-Cell-O Corporation	4,140	234.00
75 shares Libbey-Owens-Ford Glass	4,200	225.00
60 shares Lone Star Cement.	4,140	255.00
120 shares Pacific Gas & Electric	4,320	240.00
80 shares Panhandle Eastern Pipe Line	4,240	240.00
75 shares Texas Company.	4,350	225.00
85 shares Timken Roller Bearing.	4,420	255.00
Total.	$50,200	$2,670.25
Plan "C" for Appreciation:		
70 shares Chrysler Corporation	$ 4,270	$ 201.25
115 shares Crane Company.	4,140	299.00
170 shares Home Insurance Co.	4,080	204.00
75 shares Libbey-Owens-Ford Glass	4,200	225.00
200 shares Public Service Elec. & Gas (N. J.). . .	4,200	280.00
120 shares Westinghouse Air Brake	4,200	360.00
250 shares Eastern Airlines	4,250	62.50
90 shares Ex-Cell-O Corporation	4,140	234.00
325 shares International Telephone & Telegraph. .	4,225	nil
200 shares National Gypsum Co.	4,200	150.00
450 shares Niagara Hudson*	4,050	nil
175 shares United Aircraft	4,025	218.75
Total.	$49,980	$2,234.50

*Exchanged in 1950 for Niagara Mohawk Power Corp. on basis of 78/100 share
of Niagara Mohawk common for each Niagara Hudson common share, plus a
small payment in cash if exchange were made in 1950.

51.   Dollar Averaging in a Single Issue

Dollar averaging is one of the more simple methods of investing according to a formula and one which should be considered by all students of the subject because of its new importance lent by the Monthly Investment Plan.

Using one common stock of the ten included in table A-2 in the Appendix, prepare a dollar averaging program for a designated period of not less than ten years since 1939 for an investment of $150 quarterly. Do not calculate actual brokerage or taxes involved but assume the 6 per cent rate applicable to the Monthly Investment Plan to be in force.

In similar manner assume that an average stock might be bought at prices equal to the S. E. C. general stock price index, with the index representing the cost of ten shares. Prepare a dollar-averaging program for the same ten year period, again assuming $150 invested quarterly and commissions of 6 per cent.

1. What average rate of appreciation was achieved in the individual issue for the period studied? What was the rate of appreciation for the general stock index issue bought as directed?
2. Does it make any difference whether a dollar averaging program is begun under depression or prosperity conditions? What psychological factors must be considered? What principle does dollar averaging bring out? Is it wiser to average purchases or try to follow a cyclical plan of investing?

52.   Investing According to a Constant Amount Formula

This realistic problem is designed to show the difficulties involved in applying a formula plan to specific circumstances.

Mr. Wealthy accumulated a sum of $15,000 in his bank account as a result of operating a grocery store in a medium-sized city in the western states. He owned his home and the building in which the business was housed. His children were all away from home, some married, others working in industrial plants. As he realized that he had only about ten more years of active business life, Mr. Wealthy decided to consult an investment dealer in his city about the ways in which an estate might be built up. The dealer had read widely in periodicals on investments and securities and suggested that Mr. Wealthy establish a formula plan of investment which could show potential gains for the future.

To illustrate what could be done under a formula plan of one type, the dealer prepared a sample of the results which could have been obtained during the period 1939 to 1949, inclusive. He took a sample fund of $10,000 to be invested in equities and cash. The plan called for holding approximately equal amounts in each of four stocks at the beginning of the plan in June, 1939, with a total equity holding of $5,000. The other $5,000 was to be placed in a savings account. For illustrative purposes the dealer held the investment in the same four issues, but the portfolio was to be readjusted at the end of each June to make the equity portion equal to approximately $5,000; all adjustments were to be made in equal amounts among the four issues.

1. Using table A-2 given in the Appendix, set up the formula plan for four selected issues. Work out valuations each June, and make the proper adjustments. Assume average brokerage costs of 5 per cent are charged to the cash section; dividends are credited to cash, half of the preceding year and half of the current year amounts.

2. Compare the results of following the constant amount formula plan of Question 1 with that of leaving the original 1939 investment intact. Consider brokerage costs and dividends in your answer.

Upon receiving the second exhibit, Mr. Wealthy was of the opinion that favorable changes in results might have been achieved by shifting the portfolio from four issues held throughout the plan to an alternation of issues. Some would be held only when equities were rising, others when equities were falling. The dealer agreed that results would be better or worse depending on the issues chosen, but also pointed out that higher brokerage costs would have been incurred as well as differences in the dividends received.

3. Comment on the difficulties involved in working out a formula plan according to Mr. Wealthy's suggestion.

Starting in June 1949, Mr. Wealthy adopted a portfolio consisting of General Motors, U. S. Steel, Union Carbide and General Foods common stocks. He has followed this plan with annual adjustments to bring the equity portion back to about $5,000 at the start of each July.

4. What is the value of Mr. Wealthy's portfolio at the present time? Assume the same brokerage and dividend charges as in Question 1. Compare this result with those obtained from a larger portfolio represented by the S.E.C. general stock price index for the same period.

5. Would it be better to readjust on the basis of selling when the equity portion exceeds $6,000, and buying only when it falls below $4,000? What do such delaying provisions accomplish?

53. Investing in a Constant Ratio Formula Plan

This problem affords an interesting contrast to the problem which precedes. The principles of formula plan operation can be learned from many sources, but the results of this plan are often called the best from a theoretical point of view.

Mr. Rich, a neighbor of Mr. Wealthy, was the owner of an automobile sales company. He became interested in formula plan investment through talking to Mr. Wealthy. Mr. Rich approached the investment dealer and asked about other forms of formula plans. The dealer told Mr. Rich of the constant ratio plan which was considered by many as theoretically better than the constant amount plan. To afford a comparison, the dealer worked out a constant ratio plan for the period 1939-49, on the supposition that at the end of each June the fund would be balanced between equities and cash. Four selected issues were taken for the initial portfolio, to be held in approximately equal dollar amounts, with brokerage costs of 5 per cent and dividends received both to be charged to the cash account. No shifts in the stocks in the fund were to be made in the example.

1. Work out the results of the constant ratio plan for the period, June 1939-June 1949, according to the details listed above. Use data in Table A-2 of the Appendix.

Mr. Rich examined the exhibit prepared by the dealer with interest. He began to read investment literature and, from one source, found that it might be a good policy to sell those issues which did poorly in the market. He asked the dealer what changes in results might be obtained from following such a course of action in the constant ratio formula.

2. What would you reply to Mr. Rich?

Mr. Rich also noted that changes in the portfolio might be made more frequently than once a year, quarterly, for example, but he then decided that since he was in the automobile business active trading in securities might not be very feasible for him. He decided on a plan of establishing a constant ratio plan for $10,000, using equal portions in equities and in cash, as advised by the investment dealer. The four stocks which Mr. Rich decided to hold were: Bethlehem Steel, National Biscuit, Air Reduction, and Celanese. Accordingly, approximately equal amounts were invested in each of these issues at July 1, 1949.

3. Using the method of question 1, work out the results of Mr. Rich's portfolio to date. Also calculate the dividend returns.
4. Compare the results of this portfolio with that for an "ideal" general stock portfolio, represented by the S.E.C. index for the same period since 1949. Why is there a decided difference in results?

Part V

54. An Introduction to Security Analysis

One of the most logical and frequently used methods of analyzing securities is described in this problem by an eminent analyst and educator. Careful consideration will be rewarding, for many of the techniques used by analysts are studied.

The following summary of an article, "Techniques of Investment Management," by William F. Edwards affords a practical approach to the problems of security analysis.[1]

How can a practical research organization convert general ideas about the outlook for business and the security markets, and the findings of field research, into the selection of specific securities? This discussion will attempt an answer. It is impossible to know for a certainty what will happen in the future. This is true of general business. It is equally true of individual companies. It is even more true, if possible, of the security markets. Investment probabilities are never so one-sided that they equal a certainty. Thus, we make decisions that are relative and not absolute. The only thing absolute in investing money is risk. Cash is subject to change in its real value. Government securities and high-grade corporate bonds can change both in real value and in dollar value. Equity securities are exposed to every kind of risk from the quirks of nature to emotional outbursts of individuals. Therefore, the objective is to develop a procedure with a maximum of probabilities on your side. One must strive for proper decisions and at the same time, hold within reasonable bounds the consequences of errors of judgment.

The investment approach must be soundly conceived. And it must be workable in practice. The logic of one's reasoning is adequate in some

---

[1] *Proceedings of the National Federation of Financial Analysts Societies,* 1948, pp. 83–88.

places, but it is the profitableness of decisions that counts in the investment of money. It is always a matter of judgment, but a sound and practical approach can contribute greatly to, if not control, the dollar and cents quality of judgment.

There are individual investors and investment fund managers who overlook the economic hills and valleys. These people pay little attention to the general business situation and the outlook for security markets. They thus appropriately limit their research to industries and individual companies.

On the other hand, for investment funds that are mobile and that aim for the best practical results considering risk, the appraisal of general business and the outlook for security markets is of first importance. The price trends of investment grade long-term bonds and preferred stocks (excluding the relatively small number of issues that have special features, such as a high coupon rate with the market price held down by call price, valuable conversion privilege or a large sinking fund) are almost entirely controlled by changes in interest rates and their effect upon security prices. Specific security research is necessary to be sure that they remain of investment grade, or are sold unless it is decided to downgrade the portfolio. Otherwise the studies should be directed toward the outlook for bond and preferred stock prices generally.

The price trends of reasonably well-selected common stocks are probably controlled to the extent of at least two-thirds by the general movement of stock prices. This observation is not made to lessen the importance of industry and individual company research. The many outstandingly good selections that are made fire the zeal of the skillful security analyst. But this should not cause one to lose his perspective. We should give the various considerations their proper weight in developing an investment approach that is fundamentally sound and workable.

The building up of a general business forecast should always be done with the objective of looking ahead. The Chinese proverb, "Dig a well before you are thirsty," is good investment philosophy. It it necessary to consider to the extent possible all of the influences that will have an important bearing upon the future. These are everchanging. Today they would include such factors as:

1. Industry's capital expenditures
2. Inventories
3. Agricultural prospects, domestic and foreign
4. The international situation
5. Employment conditions
6. Government budget and prospective tax legislation
7. Credit conditions
8. Consumer buying power
9. Prospective demands relative to capacity to produce
10. Political developments during 1948 and their effect upon general conditions

11. The condition of the security markets, including the supply of and demand for new capital.

Another approach that helps in building up a general forecast is to consider the trends of economic data and what they afford in one's effort to measure probable adjustments and maladjustments in business. An example is the relationship of new orders to sales and production. Another is the working capital position of industry relative to current volume of activity. A period of extremely active capital goods expenditures can lead into over-expansion with culminating depression effects. Disproportionate rises in various prices and wage rates disrupt the ability to exchange goods and services.

The investment manager must weave together the various influences until he has a worthwhile concept of (1) the probable trend of business during a reasonable period ahead, (2) the probable level of business, and (3) how long it may be before there will be an important change in the business background. We give this analysis concrete expression by making estimates, say for 1948, of personal income payments, the Federal Reserve Board Index of Production, general price level, total retail sales, etc.

Before going further with the use of this data, it is prudent to mellow one's conclusion by recognition of the current phase of the business cycle. This is one way of holding within reasonable bonds the consequences when in error. . . .

We are now prepared to appraise carefully the outlook for individual industries. I have selected the automobile industry for this purpose but others would have served as well. It is only logical that there exists a relationship between individuals' income and the amounts spent for automobiles. For each $1,000 of personal income, about $22.75 was spent for cars and trucks at wholesale value during the acute depression years. This figure declined to less than $12.00 during the war years. However, during the prewar years of fair business when the people employed felt prosperous and business managers were looking ahead, $37.50 was spent for automobiles at wholesale value for each $1,000 of personal income.

We see this relationship very clearly — albeit in another way — in the relation of personal incomes to the factory sales at wholesale value of cars and trucks, expressed through a correlation graph. We may also compare total retail sales of durable goods with factory sales at wholesale value of cars and trucks, again through a correlation graph.

Similar studies can be made of each of the major industries and throw a great deal of light upon their relative positions with regard to the demand for the products.

The next logical step in our analysis is to translate industry estimates into individual company sales estimates. This can again be done by a correlation graph between factory sales at wholesale value of cars and trucks to the sales of a particular company, say General Motors.

Translating an estimate of sales into profits is the next step. This can be done by relating General Motors' sales to its operating profits. It is to be observed that during the war, reconversion and depression years, the company's profit margin was abnormally low. In the other of the more recent years, however, the company generally carried through to operating profits about 15 per cent to 17½ per cent of sales. The forward looking security analyst wants to know the reasons why profit margins in the future might be more or less than this amount.

Great care must be taken in comparing profit margins of different companies even within the same industry. For instance, Chrysler Corporation's profit margin has generally averaged 8 per cent, about half that of General Motors. This is not necessarily unfavorable. It reflects a difference in the operations of the two companies which would be known to a careful analyst. It shows that companies have personal traits as distinctive as those of individuals, and this needs to be allowed for in our research work.

These statistical studies leading up to an appraisal of past progress and future prospects of individual companies plus a study of the financial position of the companies provide most of the information to determine if the investment status of bonds and preferred stock is being maintained or changed.

When it comes to the final selection of common stocks, however, only the basic background has been laid up to this point. Another field of study needs to be pursued with equal care in order to build up maximum probabilities of good investment judgment. I can little more than suggest the scope of such research in this discussion.

There are three approaches that supplement each other and can be used concurrently:

(1) The first approach is the trend of general business, of activity in the industry, of company sales and earnings and of security prices. If all of these factors are in a favorable trend and are likely to continue favorable for a reasonable period ahead, the probabilities are good that the company's stock will do relatively well.

(2) The second approach is to evaluate probable earnings and dividends. This must be done on a relative basis and not by the use of historical figures for a particular company. The analyst must be ever-aware of possible changes in the rate of valuation (price-earnings ratio) for an individual security. Companies may keep the same name but change their business considerably which may influence the valuation of earnings. It is clear that a substantial improvement in a company's financial position would improve the quality of its common stock. At this particular time, careful attention must be given to the possible need of additional capital. We have found that during the past year, the announcement of new equity financing reduced the market value of the company's common stock about 20 per cent on average. This development alone could be of dominating importance and make unattractive,

at least temporarily, what otherwise would have been a relatively attractive selection.

(3) The third approach is the market position of individual securities. Any security is a bad purchase at a price. It is desirable to invest in the securities of sound companies but this should not cause one to forget that at a price its stock could be a bad risk. Price tags are often more important than name tags. It is also important to consider the volatility of securities. To own a list of highly volatile securities in a declining market is like trying to swim upstream. A good man might not be able even to hold his own, whereas even a poor swimmer could make good progress when going with the stream.

Having followed through all of the steps from the appraisal of the outlook for general business, security markets, individual industries and specific companies, to the relative position of individual companies, the investment manager is prepared to select the proper securities. The most attractive of the stocks affording a high yield are the securities best suited for a fund interested primarily in income. The most attractive of the stocks with above average volatility meet the requirements of funds seeking capital gains when the outlook favors an aggressive policy. On the other hand, most attractive of the stocks with low volatility are desirable when the outlook calls for caution.

The investment nuggets for which we are searching are the stocks which appear relatively the most attractive in view of the outlook and are also good values on the basis of individual appraisal. The procedure outlined is aimed at marshalling maximum probabilities on the investor's side and at the same time holding within reasonable bounds, the adverse consequences of erroneous judgments.

1. Using the period 1929 to date, prepare correlation graphs as indicated in the article for one of the companies whose data is presented in the Appendix. For industry data it is suggested that industry indexes prepared by the Federal Reserve Board be used, together with personal income and expenditures figures prepared by the Department of Commerce. From a careful examination of the graphs, establish a probable range of common stock prices within which fluctuations should hold at the current level of business activity.

55. Market Analysis and Security Analysis

Since many people are confused as to the proper spheres of different types of analysis, this problem is included. The authorita-

tive statements clearly define the place of each in the world of securities policy.

The following summary of two addresses given at the 1948 annual conference of the National Federation of Security Analysts reveals the differences between market analysis and security analysis. The first talk was given by Harold M. Gartley, the second by Benjamin Graham, both authorities in their respective fields and both have attracted considerable attention in the securities markets.[1]

I

There are three approaches to stock market study — value analysis, economic analysis, and market analysis. The first two are classified as fundamental, studies of causes, while the last is technical, a study of effects. Only the price trend and the variations in transactions on the exchange truly reflect all of the causes. Because of a missing factor, there is always a lag or lead between the results of value or economic research and actual price trends, even when the results are quite correct. The missing element, the interplay of confidence and fear — the psychological factor which has an important part in making every price trend — is included in market analysis. Therefore, it is the most comprehensive of the three approaches.

There are four specific divisions of stock market analysis which can be recommended as the most likely fields for serious efforts. All of them have been researched extensively by a number of capable analysts intent on finding means to supplement the fundamental approach in stock market forecasting. No doubt there are other productive avenues, and it may be that the most outstanding work has never been publicized. The four which have long since proved their worth in practical forecasting are briefly:

1. *Price Ratio Data*, including:
   (a) Prices of individual stocks versus composite or other averages. The results show the relative performance against the market. Changes in relative trends, as expressed by ratios of both volume and price, provide reliable evidence of trend reversals.
   (b) Prices of minor groups (steels, oils, chemicals, etc.) versus the general market average. When a key group ratio shows a turn, along with others, it is likely to be of great importance. These studies are very valuable for both timing and selection.

---

[1] Harold M. Gartley, "Modern Approaches to Stock Market Analysis" and Benjamin Graham, "Two Ways of Making (and Losing) Money in Securities." *Proceedings of the National Federation of Financial Analysts Societies,* 1948, pp. 3–7, 88–94. Also see: D. H. Kerchner, "Possibilities and Limitations of Investors' Services," *Journal of Business of the University of Chicago,* Oct. 1937, Jan. 1938.

(c) Low-priced aggregates versus high-priced aggregates. These ratios can be interpreted to understand the internal structure of the market, which is constantly reflecting the impact of psychological as well as fundamental forces.

(d) Relative Velocity Ratings. The relative gain of the individual stock compared to the gain of the general market is computed, with these averaged for a period of five years or more, with separate average ratios computed for both advances and declines.

2. *Volume Ratio Data,* including:

(a) Volume for an individual stock versus its group, a sample average, or the market as a whole. This indicates turnover.

(b) Volume of low-priced marginal or "hope" shares versus volume of high-priced shares. This presumably shows speculative versus investment activity.

3. *Breadth of the Market Data.* The data include daily advances, declines and total issues traded. A seven-day moving average of the ratios of advances and of declines to the issues traded shows conditions of over-optimism or over-pessimism.

4. *Segregation of Trading Ratio Data.* The data used include the shares traded, number of transactions, both divided into long and short positions for both round-lot and odd-lot transactions.

This is a basic outline of the present-day approaches. In the end the success of modern stock market analysis depends upon combining a number of meritorious studies which reflect the principal internal market factors. As a preponderance of evidence develops in one direction or the other, rational and unemotional conclusions can be drawn. It is improbable that these studies can be molded into a single index which will automatically signal every important trend reversal — instead the labor of thoughtful observation has to be applied day by day to a number of series.

II

If an investor were to ask if 52 is a good price for buying General Motors common stock the answer would be "yes." It would be the same if the question were to ask the reasonableness of expecting General Motors to sell as low as 40 in the next few years. The process of determining a security value depends on averaging the widely fluctuating values. Intrinsic value bears an organic relationship to market prices, with sound valuations those which on the whole tend to pass over into and be vindicated by average market prices. There is no similar relationship between the low and high prices created by the vagaries of the market and the analyst's conception and technique of appraisal. The market fluctuations are clearly the field of the stock-market analyst. This neatly apportions the field. The security analyst determines the approximate central value for a security; the market analyst determines the approximate range of price fluctuation about this central value which is to be expected in the current stock-market cycle.

The only trouble with this idyllic concept is that it bears no recognizable resemblance to current practice. With the notable exception of the public-utility field, comparatively little work of the security analysts is specifically directed to finding a central or appraisal value of the subject issue. Their chief interest remains, as ever, in studying long-term or nearer term prospects of a company, and then concluding with a qualitative and largely subjective verdict, which rarely seems to take the existing selling price into careful account. And as you know the market analyst then concerns himself typically with the timing, rather than the amplitude of market fluctuations. There can be no real community of interest, or collaboration, between market analysis and security analysis except in terms of price rather than of time.

Good timing is important to the investor only as a means of buying at a lower price and selling at a higher price than would otherwise occur. The wide-awake investor looks at stock quotations not for peace of mind, but for sound buying and selling opportunities. His mental tranquility comes from his knowledge that he owns a diversified list of securities yielding a satisfactory income, and which competent analysis indicates to be worth at least as much as he paid for them. He knows by experience that the more disheartened the speculators become, the more promising are his own opportunities and prospects.

I am convinced that there are no a priori and immutable stock-market relationships with high forecasting value. One of the great drawbacks of market forecasting techniques is that by the time adequate preliminary or pilot tests of their efficiency have been made, and when real money is about to be staked on them, they may already have lost a good part of their virtue. The typical security analyst will always start with the past record, and he may often be controlled by it; yet he is free to take an entirely independent view of prospective earnings, provided he has substantial reasons for the change. He may even emphasize assets more than earnings if the special conditions apply.

Security analysis must depend on an unequal distribution of wisdom among the great mass of security-holders and their advisors. But the field is wide. The market analysts must depend on uninformed security holders or buyers.

If we assume a possibility of all investors following one or the other types of analysis we should find that following security analysis would tend to establish full values without excesses and irrationalities. But the farther we carry the prevailing techniques of market analysis and the more widely we spread their influence, the greater the danger that we may be intensifying the irresponsible and destructive price fluctuations of Wall Street.

1. Are market and security analysis two methods of approaching

the same risk? Show how both must necessarily assume the presence of a third alternative method of approaching the same risk.

2. Comment on the effectiveness of each of the three methods (a) as a device for continuous investment, (b) as a device for continuous speculation, (c) as devices for periodic holdings of securities.

56. Analytical Methods of Mutual Funds

To show the practical application of the theories and methods of security analysis by mutual funds, this problem is continuing a series of articles on "How Mutual Funds Pick Stocks" which began in an earlier problem.

The following articles appeared in the *Journal of Commerce* series on mutual fund investment methods written by Shelley Pierce. These articles are particularly complete summaries of various approaches and methods of security analysis; hence, they are deserving of rather careful study as to variant opinions.

LORD, ABBETT & CO.[1]

Investment researchers of Lord, Abbett & Co., sponsors of affiliated Fund and American Business Shares, work up a list of 400 to 500 companies from which are picked common stocks for its portfolio.

Major considerations in picking a company to be studied are its size and its competitive position. Other factors are a balanced capital structure suitable to the nature of the concern's business and it must be in sound financial condition. To win a place on this list a stock must be sufficiently marketable that its purchase or sale can be accomplished readily without undue effect on the stock's market price.

"Adequate marketability allows comparative investment research to produce results because it places the management in a position to make the changes which its studies indicate to be desirable," an official of the firm explained.

When stocks have assumed investment characteristics and an earnings outlook which makes them likely candidates for portfolios of either of the two funds sponsored by Lord, Abbett, they are added to the list from time to time. On the other hand, if the position of a company deteriorates, its stock is taken off the list.

---

[1] *Journal of Commerce*, August 25, 1953.

After the list of stocks is selected it is under continuous analysis and study. In this process an effort is made not only to indicate the desirability of each security as an investment at current market prices, but also to give an accurate description of its investment characteristics. When the analysis has been completed, the stocks are placed in several categories, including growth stocks, stable stocks, income-producing stocks or cyclical stocks.

"It is the availability of background information of this type, continuously brought up to date, which enables our management to adjust its holdings quickly and with confidence as market prices or economic conditions change," the Lord, Abbett executive stated.

Appraisal of the market prospects of the stock of two companies in different industries, such as, for example, a railroad stock and the stock of a drug company, is difficult without a yardstick for measurement which applies equally to both of them, it is pointed out.

"We believe that investment in a common stock should be made on the basis of its value," says the company executive. "The investor should pay for the company's ability to make profits and pay dividends, how much he should pay depends upon the general investment characteristics of the company, for these determine the rate of capitalization of earnings and dividends. Since all common stocks have these characteristics, stocks of dissimilar companies can be compared to determine their relative investment merit."

Among the things studied in determining a stock's earning power are an estimate of the demand for the company's products and an examination of the company's productive capacity, including an analysis of technological improvements, an investigation of prices and costs, and an indication of the company's earning power at various levels of operation. The study should also show the company's maximum earning power as well as the probable minimum earnings under conditions of recession in its industry.

"We make such estimates and check them against the company's results under various circumstances in the past, analyzing separately the various components of the balance sheet and income statements. With these studies in hand, we can capitalize the earning power of a stock in a manner consistent with the characteristics of the company in order to determine its value."

These general characteristics upon which the rate of capitalization of earnings and dividends depend are listed as follows:

"1. Secular growth prospects. We are willing to pay more for a company with unusual growth prospects than for a company with average growth prospects.

"2. The stability of earning power. Other things being equal, we are willing to pay more for a company while earnings fluctuate in a narrow range through the business cycle than we would for a company whose earnings fluctuate widely.

"3. The risk element. The higher the risk the less we feel justified in paying for the company's earnings."

BROAD STREET GROUP [2]

The quality of the management is an important factor considered by mutual funds when they are picking stocks for their portfolios. The Broad Street group of funds, which includes Broad Street Investing, National Investors, and Whitehall Fund, is no exception to this rule.

Fred E. Brown, vice president, insists that behind stocks bought by Broad Street must be capable management in whom we have confidence and can place the trust that is inherent when an investment is made. "We lay great stress on management because we believe that in the long run, more than any other factor, the quality of management will determine the success or failure of any individual management," he said.

But Broad Street goes even further. "We want a management that is approachable and will give us honest answers to honest questions," Mr. Brown added. Broad Street, he said, also stresses "strength and adequacy of financial strength not only in relation to current needs but also to future requirements. We want marketability for an investment."

"There are changing likes and dislikes in investments just as in clothes or any other thing that the public buys," he continued. "Unless investment choices are in step with this style factor they may fall disappointingly short of the results expected for them."

Each choice of a stock made by Broad Street "is based on detailed analysis and research which includes ordinary armchair statistical methods and extensive field investigation using company, industrial, financial, and other sources." The funds look for a stock with a price-earnings ratio that is reasonable or low in relation to the ratios for comparable stocks and that returns "a reasonable to high relative yield."

"We also look for an anticipated future trend of earnings that may preserve or improve their comparable relationships for price-earnings ratio and yield with favorable effect on the market price of the stock. When we are considering stocks of chemical companies, we place great stress on research activities and production know-how. We look for a record of product improvements and new products that has paid off and for evidence of developments under way that promise good results in the future. But, we are less interested in the distribution and sales organization of a chemical company than that of a kindred company in the drug field where these activities are of permanent significance.

"In the case of a machinery company, its backlog of orders and the book value behind the stock may be of prime consideration. In the case of a soft drink manufacturer or a cigarette company, however, sales promotion ability and brand names are of much more importance.

"In the oil industry a company's discovery and production record may

---

[2] *Ibid.*, September 1, 1953.

rank high on the list of considerations, whereas in the case of a railroad the prospects for traffic in its established territory and the opportunities for internal operating as well as financial improvements may rank first."

In explaining why Broad Street chooses one stock over another, Mr. Brown used one group of stocks, the electric utilities, as an example.

"In the electric utility field, we look first at the price-earnings ratio. There is sufficient similarity between the utility operating companies so that this ratio may be regarded as the investing public's fair measure of the value of a company's current and prospective earnings. We know that the more marginal, less adequately financed and less well-managed companies sell at the lowest price-earnings ratio. If we can find an exception to this rule, in all probability we have found good value.

"We look at prospective growth in per share earnings and the influence that this growth may have on market price over a period of time. We look at the level of earnings of a particular company in relation to the allowable rate of return. We look at capital structure and the adequacy of the equity ratio in relation not only to current but also to future business. We know that if this ratio is low and new capital is needed, equity financing and diluted per share earnings are a probability. We look at the solidity of earnings which includes an examination of the sources of demand — residential versus industrial — reasonableness of depreciation charges and the extent of amortization and special charges of all types.

"We look at the policy of the company in respect to interest charged on construction and the effect that this may have on its ability to earn a reasonable rate of return on new facilities. We look at hydro conditions to determine whether earnings are inflated or deflated by favorable or unfavorable water power conditions. We look for non-recruiting tax savings and for vulnerability to tax increases. We look at the territory in which a company operates not only in respect to its growth and the nature of this growth, but also in order to determine the political climate in which the company is operating. We examine the attitude of public regulatory bodies.

"Current yield and management's attitude toward future dividend payments are other factors weighed. The general position of electric utility company stocks as it may be affected by market sentiment is a further consideration.

"Our purpose in an investment is not restricted to the over-all objectives of the investment company but more often is the specific purpose to be served by a stock as one of the many stepping stones toward such objectives. Thus, within the same portfolio, at any given time, the purpose of one stock may be to provide a high rate of current income while another will be chosen for its promise of future income or capital appreciation and still another will be selected to provide stability of income or capital value."

CALVIN BULLOCK [3]

In selecting securities for the six investment companies which it manages, the Calvin Bullock organization sets up every month an approved list which is described as "our theoretical ideal portfolio" and which serves as a guide to security transactions and investment planning. The list contains all classes of securities, according to Harold E. Aul, vice president in charge of the management department. The common stock portion is set up on a percentage basis, taking that portion of the portfolio invested in such issues as 100 per cent, with a percentage allocated to each industry group. As of Aug. 31, leading categories in this portfolio were 16 per cent utilities, 9 per cent oils and 5 per cent steel stocks. Each industry group is further broken down by percentages as to individual companies within the industries favored for investment.

One of the first steps taken by Bullock analysts in making investments is to determine just where the economy is in the business cycle. If a recession is on the horizon, there would be no point in even considering purchase of a highly cyclical stock, regardless of its apparent statistical merit, points out Joseph H. Humphrey, assistant vice president. Instead, efforts at such a point should be concentrated on increasing the proportion of defensive type securities in portfolios.

A projection is made a year ahead on a quarterly basis of the gross national product and its important components so that the proper economic background is provided on which to base investment policy. Course of activity of the important parts of the economy are projected and the total is added up to get the figure for gross inational product.

When gross national product has been determined, the analysts relate projections for their respective industries to this total or its components. For example, Mr. Humphrey notes that retail trade might be expected to move in line with consumer disposable income. Any deviation from this relationship, such as occurred in the wave of buying which followed the outbreak of hostilities in Korea, when consumer purchases outstripped income, "carries the implication of a subsequent downward swing until normal relationships with consumer income are re-established," he adds.

Aware of the fact that this projection, like any other economic forecast, is not infallible, a new one is made every quarter, taking into consideration conditions as they then exist. Projections are also checked against the actual trend of economic developments in the interim period.

An example of the practical application of this data to the various Bullock portfolios is cited by Mr. Aul.

"The research staff was asked to make projections about security values on the basis of certain assumptions," he says. "It was assumed that there might be a decline of 20 per cent in the Federal Reserve Board index of industrial production in 1954. It was further assumed that 1954 would bring a much tighter price competition with resulting lower

---

[3] *Ibid.*, October 13, 1953.

profit margins. Finally it was assumed that that year would bring the elimination of the excess profits tax. The research department then projected a rate of earnings on the basis of these assumptions and applied them to the industries and corporations represented in or which were potential investments for the company's portfolio. The over-all result of this projection indicated that present prices of quality common stocks seemed to make reasonable allowance for the degree of earnings decline which might lie ahead under the foregoing circumstances.

"However, it appeared necessary to make extensive portfolio revisions reflecting the impact on different industries and companies of the assumed conditions. As a specific example, in Dividend Shares, which is the largest fund, cyclical stocks were reduced much as holdings of railroads and steels. Oil stocks were also reduced as a percentage of total assets. The proceeds of such sales were ultilized to increase commitments in industries having defensive or strong growth characteristics such as the electric utilities and the chemicals."

VALUE LINE [4]

Selection of stocks for the two Value Line funds is accomplished through ratings which are a mathematic construction based upon years of actual market history, according to Arnold Bernhard, president. . . . The method developed by this organization, Mr. Bernhard explains, is to correlate statistically the prices of a stock over the past twenty years to its dividend-paying ability and its long-term growth over the same period, and then to project the correlation into the future.

"These ratings being mathematical and objective," he says, "the recommendations that follow from them are not influenced by emotionalism. In general, when stock prices fluctuate below the normal value rating, stocks are cheap, and when they fluctuate above the rating, stocks are dear."

The level of gross national product is set by the organization's top investment committee and all earnings and dividend estimates made by the analysts must be geared to this. A particular company's sales for the past twenty years are correlated to the national gross product by the analysts. Then given a future level of gross national product, a rough estimate can be made of the specific company's future sales.

This marks the start of a detailed projection of future sales and profits. From the initial estimate adjustments are made for such factors as price changes, loss or gain of competitive position, plant additions, acquisitions or sales of subsidiaries, technological changes and other factors. After reaching a sales estimate, the other items in the projected income account are worked out.

Also undertaken at the same time are independent correlation analyses to determine the percentage of the particular industry's sales to the pro-

---

[4] *Ibid.*, November 17, 1953.

jected gross national product, the percentage of the individual company's sales to those of the industry in which it operates, and the range of profit margins. The two independent approaches are then synthesized after comparison and discussion.

Specific per share dividend estimates are also worked out. While dividends are a matter of discretion with corporate directors, Mr. Bernhard observes that "it is surprising how consistent dividend policies of a particular corporation are. For example," he adds, "it is found that over the years, in most cases directors will have a fixed policy with respect to the percentage of earnings that are paid out in dividends. Thus, dividends usually show a constant relationship to earnings."

But this is only the initial step. The analyst must make adjustments for capital needs, including plant expansion and debt retirement. In addition, working capital requirements are correlated to sales. After these steps a specific estimate of per-share dividends is reached.

After this the analyst starts his field work, going to the corporate executive with his organization's estimate of future earnings and dividends. "In recent years there has been a tendency to make a fetish of field work," says Mr. Bernhard. "We have seen many instances where field work was more misleading than it was helpful. The value of field work depends in large measure upon the approach and ability of the individual analyst. However, a necessary requisite is that the analyst can offer the corporation executive a well-thought-out estimate of future conditions."

The organization also makes long-term predictions and is now working on estimates for the period 1956-58.

HUGH W. LONG & CO.[5]

It is the view of the research department of Hugh W. Long & Co., that the investment of funds "is an art, not a science, or, at best, a very inexact science," according to Thomas J. Herbert, vice-president and investment officer of the company. The Long organization is the manager of Diversified Funds, Inc., which includes three general management funds, and Manhattan Bond Fund, Inc.

The difficulty in investing, Mr. Herbert points out, "naturally lies in human inability to foresee the future clearly in conflicting interpretations of past and present events as indexes of future happenings, as to both general economic conditions and specific situations.

"No one has yet been able to develop successfully a technique that will consistently identify the tops and bottoms or movements of security markets at the time they occur. Alert management must have an appropriate philosophy and supporting techniques to guard itself against any fatal delusion that it can accurately predict either the future or the epidemics of mass moods."

---

[5] *Ibid.*, December 8, 1953.

In appraising the relative attractiveness of common stocks, the Long organization uses the basic technique sometimes described as the "sound-value approach," according to Mr. Herbert. "This is a tool, not an end-all answer to the problem of investing," he explains. "The premise is very much the same as an individual would use in determining what represents a fair price to pay for a small business. What we are interested in is a sound value, not based upon the results of the last year or quarter or the outlook for the next six months, but based upon what the results may reasonably be expected to be over a period of years.

"There are four primary questions to be answered: What is the normal future earning power of the company? What is the normal future dividend paying capacity of the company? How should such values be translated into dollar price per share for the stock? What is the current and prospective asset value of the stock? The fourth question is pertinent only for certain companies. The first three are applicable to all.

"The sound-value approach is a long range approach. An undervalued stock may remain underpriced for some substantial period of time and an overvalued stock may go even higher eventually but if good judgment has been used in determining the sound value, price will adjust itself to value. There is nothing mechanical in this approach, judgment is used all along the line, and judgment must be applied to the decision of when to buy or sell individual securities and shift emphasis between different industries and classes of securities."

Considerable use is made of correlation charts in appraising future earning power and dividend paying capacity, Mr. Herbert stated. In studying a food chain stock, for instance, industry sales would be correlated with total U. S. disposable income. The sales of the company under consideration would be correlated with industry sales and directly with disposable income.

"Such correlations," he continued, "show trends which provide a basis for making projections into the future. Judgment is required all along the line in making the appraisals. For example, in projecting future sales volume for a food chain company, assumptions must be made as to the future level of disposable income under varying economic conditions. When ranges of future sales have been set, the next step is to correlate the company's sales with profits before Federal taxes. The trend of profit margins shown from such a correlation forms a basis for applying profit margins to future sales estimates. An assumed level of future corporate taxes is then applied to determine estimates of earning power."

"In determining dividend-paying capacity, the past relationship between earnings and dividend payments is studied. Many companies show a consistent correlation or a trend which may be applied to future earnings estimates. Wherever possible, such estimates of future sales volume, profit margins, earning power and dividend-paying capacity are checked with the management of the company as to the reasonableness of assumptions made or the existence of factors which might be expected to substantially change the trends shown by the correlation studies.

"The next step is to translate the estimates of earnings power and dividend paying capacity into dollar value per share of stock. Here again, past relationship between earnings and market prices are of considerable value. Detailed comparisons of price times earnings ratios and deviations from the price times earnings ratio of the Dow-Jones industrial stock average are studied for clues to possible future relationships. If a growth stock is being appraised, the heart of the problem is to determine both how liberal the appraisal can be and how cautious the appraisal should be in order to determine what market decline might be anticipated if growth should suddenly cease and current earnings should be appraised at a much lower multiple.

"From this sound-value approach, price areas are determined. They are areas of potential value serving as a guidepost in estimating relative attractiveness of a stock for future appreciation. It is a technique that helps management find securities with a major potential for future market enhancement, and is also a warning sign to prevent the purchase or retention of securities at too high a price when mass psychology often fails to differentiate in a rising market between the basic value of individual securities."

1. Classify the above organizational methods into those which emphasize market approach, economic approach, security value approach.

2. Does the introduction of statistical methodology tend to improve or harm the determination of when to buy and sell what issues?

3. Can the individual use the methods of the mutual funds or do they merely represent the efforts of sophisticated investors? Can the mutual funds do better than the individual who concentrates his research and holdings in a relatively few industries (say four or six) and the major companies within each industry?

57. Industrial Survey—Farm Equipment

This problem introduces an example of the type of industrial survey that is often advised as a preliminary step to selection of individual issues.

Moody's Stock Survey, February 9, 1953,[1] featured a three page

---

[1] Pp. 634, 636.

survey of the farm equipment industry and the companies engaged in this line of activity. The following text is a fine illustration of the essential factors to be considered in an industrial study as a background for choosing issues of companies in a particular field.

The industry is now facing the first really competitive market since before the war. The sellers' market has disappeared and from here on merchandising will be the primary factor affecting earnings and dividends. We see no grounds for expecting any strong growth in the demand for farm implements, but stability may be reasonably expected. . . .

Sales of farm equipment bear a fairly close relationship to the net income of farmers. This is not to say that farmers buy implements strictly out of income. But the degree of prosperity has been the major determining factor. Before the war farmers spent on the average around 7 per cent of their net incomes on new farm machinery. During the war, when such production of machinery gave way to more direct war production, and when farm income rose sharply, this ratio fell off. And, conversely, since the war farmers have bought relatively more machinery to make up for the war shortage and to help meet the growing world demand.

We believe some decline in the proportion of farm income being spent for new tools is likely in the period ahead. In Table V-1 we summarize this relationship in recent years, with a projection for this year.

Note in Table V-1 that net farm income is expected to decline somewhat further this year. Thus two factors will tend to bring about lower sales of farm equipment. It appears, therefore, that manufacturers' shipments may run in the neighborhood of $1.8 to $1.85 billion this year, or roughly 15 per cent under the 1952 level. This assumes steady prices on finished equipment, which is optimistic, if anything. Already some types of farm equipment are selling well below authorized ceiling prices.

At the same time that sales of farm equipment are trending lower, the companies' operating costs are likely to be rising moderately further. Certain raw materials—aluminum, possibly steel and copper—may be more costly. Wage costs are still rising. And selling costs may go up substantially. Operating profit margins seem sure to be under pressure compared to pre-steel-strike operations last year.

Only one of the major companies, Allis-Chalmers, stands to gain importantly from eventual elimination of excess profits taxes. It reported nine-month earnings (through September, 1952) of $5.99 a share after an estimated accrual of $2.65 a share for excess profits tax.

If the nearer-term outlook for profits is not particularly rosy, holders of farm equipment stocks can take heart from the longer-term view. Continued population growth, along with near (if not complete) exhaustion of possibilities of bringing new land into cultivation, add up to one important conclusion—that from this time forward every acre in cultivation is going to have to feed or clothe more people. And increasing use of farm equipment, germicides, insecticides, plant foods and improved

TABLE V-1
FARM INCOME AND IMPLEMENT EXPENDITURES

	Gross Farm Income	Production Expenses	Net Income	Manuf. Shipments	Per Cent of Net Income
	(Billions)			(Millions)	
1935	$ 9.6	$ 5.1	$ 4.5	$ 235	5.2%
1936	10.6	5.6	5.1	319	6.3
1937	11.2	6.1	5.1	412	8.1
1938	10.0	5.8	4.2	343	8.2
1939	10.4	6.2	4.3	329	7.7
1935–39 Average. .	10.4	5.8	4.6	328	7.1
1940	10.9	6.6	4.3	393	9.1
1941	13.7	7.7	6.1	543	8.9
1942	18.6	9.7	8.8	530	6.0
1943	22.9	11.3	11.5	344	3.0
1944	24.1	12.1	12.0	617	5.1
1945	25.3	13.0	12.3	700	5.7
1946	29.0	14.8	14.2	851	6.0
1942–46 Average. .	24.0	12.2	11.8	608	5.2
1947	34.0	17.2	16.8	1,295	7.7
1948	34.5	18.9	15.6	1,734	11.1
1949	31.8	18.2	13.6	1,813	13.3
1950	32.1	19.7	12.3	1,792	14.6
1951	36.7	22.4	14.3	2,205	15.4
*1952	36.9	23.4	13.5	2,150	15.9
*1953	36.3	23.6	12.7	1,800	14.2

*Estimated

irrigation will play a critical role in this quest for higher productivity per acre.

In Table V-2 we show certain data relating to land use in the United States. This table clearly shows that further growth in farm utilization of land will be limited.

In Table V-3 we show certain other data bearing on long-term demand for farm equipment.

This table shows how farms are tending to be bigger and how population is growing relative to land used in farms. At the same time the farm labor supply is slowly but steadily diminishing, which means the individual farmers' productivity must also increase. Thus, inadequate labor power must be compensated for by larger capital outlays.

These trends indicate the favorable long-term background for farm equipment makers.

TABLE V-2
LAND UTILIZATION IN THE UNITED STATES*

Year	Grand Total Land Area	Total Land in Farms	Pasture and Grazing Land	Timber Land	‡Other
	Millions of acres				
1880	1,905	536	883	368	118
1890	1,905	623	818	344	120
1900	1,905	839	625	318	123
1910	1,905	879	600	301	125
1920	1,905	956	502	319	128
1930	1,905	987	437	349	132
1940	1,905	1,061	382	325	137
1950	1,905	1,142	292	322	149

*Source: Bureau of Agricultural Economics.
‡Includes urban areas, parks, wildlife refuges, military land,
roads, railroads and other uncultivated and waste lands.

TABLE V-3
FARM LAND UTILIZATION

Year	Total Land in Farms (millions of acres)	Number of Farms (millions)	Average Acreage Per Farm	U. S. Population (millions)	Total Land in Farms Per Unit of Population (acres)
1880	536	4.0	134	50.2	10.7
1890	623	4.6	135	62.9	9.9
1900	839	5.7	147	76.0	11.0
1910	879	6.4	137	92.0	9.6
1920	956	6.4	149	105.7	9.0
1930	987	6.3	157	122.8	8.0
1940	1,061	6.1	174	131.7	8.1
1945	1,142	5.9	195	138.9	8.2
1950	1,159	5.4	215	151.7	7.6

As far as farmers' ability to buy equipment goes, there is no indication of serious shortage of purchasing power. Farm income is not likely to drop drastically, and farmers' credit standing is strong compared to pre-war.

1. Appraise this summary forecast of the sales prospects for agricultural equipment for (a) the near-term, and (b) the longer-term. Are there any factors left out in this analysis?

2. To what extent can an industry survey of this type be used in appraising the earnings prospects of individual companies engaged in whole or in part in the farm equipment manufacturing business? Would the effects of these prospects weigh more heavily on some companies concentrating on certain types of equipment more than on manufacturers of more general lines? Would the export market be of any importance to certain companies?

3. Look up the relative importance of farm machinery to the major firms in this field: Allis-Chalmers, J. I. Case, Deere, International Harvester, Minneapolis-Moline, and Oliver. To what extent would a survey of this type be valuable in appraising the prospects for these companies?

4. The following analysis was made by a leading brokerage house in February, 1953. How does it differ from the Moody analysis? In which type of analysis would the amateur investor be more interested? Why?

Near term industry and earnings prospects suggest this group may continue to have difficulty acting in line with the market although these equities have already had a considerable period of sub-average relative price performance.

While gross farm income attained a record high in 1952, net cash income declined moderately under pressure of rising production costs. Lower commodity prices are apt to continue as a factor in 1953 but the farmers' spending ability is not expected to be very materially lessened. Production of farm equipment should be on a more normal basis since last year's drought as well as material and labor problems are not likely to be duplicated. These factors affected profit margins unfavorably. While the industry gross output may be lower than in recent peak years, continuous operations should prove more conducive to satisfactory profit margins. War scare buying has run its course and normal seasonal buying trends should become more evident. (Merrill, Lynch, Pierce, Fenner & Beane, "Security and Industry Survey," February, 1953, p. 43.)

58.   Tools for the Analyst

A knowledge of source materials is an important part of the equipment that a security analyst and market analyst must possess.

This problem will bring many of these tools into the attention of the student of investments.

Security Prices and Yields

1. Where can the following indexes of common stock prices be found? How frequently are they computed? How do they differ?
   (a) Dow-Jones Averages
   (b) New York Times Stock Price Averages
   (c) Associated Press Stock Price Averages
   (d) Standard & Poors' Stock Prices Index
   (e) National Quotations Bureau Indexes
   (f) Securities and Exchange Commission Indexes
   (g) Moody's Stock Price Averages
2. How do the following bond price indexes differ?
   (a) Moody's Bond Price Averages
   (b) Standard & Poors' Bond Price Averages
3. Compare the usefulness of bond yield averages with bond price averages. What are the most significant bond yield averages?
4. Where can you find daily stock price indexes or averages for foreign securities? Monthly averages?
5. Where can you find comparisons of yields on long-term government bonds for the United States and foreign countries?

Money Supply

1. Of what significance is a study of monetary factors to the investor?
2. Where can important data on the holdings of various types of investors in U. S. Treasury securities be found?
3. Name at least two sources of data on the supply of currency and deposit money in the United States and foreign countries.

Wholesale Prices

1. Of what significance is data on wholesale prices to the investor?
2. What type of commodities are included in wholesale price indexes?
3. Name at least two sources of data on wholesale price fluctuations in the United States and foreign countries.

Industrial Production

1. Is an overall index of industrial production more desirable for the investor than separate indexes for specific industries, such as mining, manufacturing, construction, public utility activity, and the like?
2. Where would you find desirable indexes of production for the United States? Do they cover all desirable fields of activity?
3. Where would you look for indexes of industrial production in foreign countries? Of what significance would they be to an American investor?
4. What type of information for specific industries might be of value to the investment analyst? Where can such data be found?
5. Where would you look for specific information on the following industries:
   (a) Steel and iron
   (b) Railway traffic
   (c) Electric power production and use
   (d) Petroleum production and use
   (e) Textile production
   (f) Automobile production and sales
   (g) Building construction
   (h) Food and meat production and consumption

Company Data

1. Compare the data given in a company annual report with that presented in an investment statistical manual. What differences do you find? What is the apparent reason for any changes?
2. What are the differences between the annual reports of a corporation and the reports made to the Securities and Exchange Commission? What companies must make S.E.C. reports? Of what significance are these to the investor?
3. Examine a prospectus and then see how a statistical service handles the same materials. What differences have you found? Which is the better source for the investor?
4. Where can reports on the holdings of large investors be found? Can "insider" buying and selling ever be discovered?

59. Content of Financial Statements

The adequacy and quality of financial statements available in corporate reports is of significance to security analysts. This problem offers a rather comprehensive study of the main facets of reports which are necessary for satisfactory analysis.

The quality of corporate reports has improved measurably in the past two decades, but the investor is interested in much more than a glossy-paper booklet replete with pictures and glowing words of praise for the previous year's achievements. The security analyst, in particular, is interested in extracting a maximum of information from an authoritative release of the corporation. Hence, he desires accuracy and completeness, above all, so that proper evaluation of securities can be made.

In the following summary of an important article written in 1947 by a prominent analyst and former president of the New York Society of Security Analysts,[1] the attitudes of professional analysts toward financial reports are revealed in considerable degree. Although some accounting knowledge is required for full comprehension of the requirements of analysts as here stated, even the amateur investor can better appreciate the type and scope of information which, by rights, is due to him from the management of any corporation.

According to some cynic, "politics is concerned with who gets what, how much, and when." This definition might apply equally well – and possibly with greater accuracy–to security analysis. It too is concerned with who buys (gets), holds, or sells what securities, how much, and when.

The function of the security analyst as an appraiser of securities for present as well as potential owners calls for careful study of securities for facts (quantitative analysis) such as earnings and assets, and also of a host of other factors, management, outlook, and the like (qualitative analysis). The examination of corporate income accounts and balance sheets (preferably certified) sent to stockholders is a basic requirement in quantitative analysis and logically precedes the qualitative phase.

---

[1] J. M. Galanis, "Shortcomings of Financial Statements from the Security Analyst's Viewpoint," *Analysts Journal*, vol. 3, no. 4 (fourth quarter, 1947), pp. 35–50.

From the figures supplied in these statements, it is possible for the analyst to apply various initial tests to the adequacy of earnings coverage of fixed charges and of asset values in the case of fixed value investments, that is, "straight" or nonprivileged bonds and preferred stocks. These tests alone can normally provide the basis for a decision to select or reject a given security—without further extended investigation of the qualitative factors.

The quality of financial statements has improved steadily in the past decade, doubtless through the efforts of the SEC and the NYSE as well as through corporate management. "Many companies have experimented with the publication of simplified forms of income accounts and balance sheets using nontechnical terminology, primarily aimed at employees and small shareholders. Although he appreciates the commendable motives behind these simplified reports, the analyst (who is presumed to possess a good working knowledge of accounting) still prefers the detailed or technical statements. He regrets the lack of consistency of detailed information supplied by some large corporations. For example, after the stockholder has been provided for two or three years with considerable detail on sales, earnings, and the like, only the briefest kind of detail—with no explanation for the change—may be forthcoming in the third or fourth year."

A policy of overconservative accounting is viewed as equally undesirable as underconservative accounting. The failure of industrial companies to show income accounts and balance sheets on a two-year comparable basis is widespread. It is especially important, where significant changes in methods of accounting procedure have been made since the previous annual report, that explanatory footnotes to the income account be provided. Chief criticism of industrial company financial statements is less of actual methods of presentation of items in income accounts and balance sheets than of the omissions of information highly important to sound analysis, especially for making comparisons with companies in similar fields. Reports to stockholders usually omit mention of many significant detailed items revealed in 10-K reports, which are filed some time after stockholders' reports are released.

In order of general importance, details on such important items as sales, cost of sales, rental costs (retail stores), depreciation, reserves, miscellaneous and nonrecurring income, foreign and domestic subsidiary income, and taxes, are considered too meagre. The calculated omission of sales, a key figure, is a source of major irritation. The telescoping of all operating revenues into a single figure, where the total includes royalty and licensee income, resale items, and important miscellaneous income items, can be definitely misleading and, in fact, detrimental to the company when compared with others in the same field.

At least the main items of cost, wages, materials, selling, distribution, and administrative expenses might well be listed separately in corporate annual reports. Treatment of development costs varies widely between companies. Despite the constant hammering at the necessity for showing depreciation, there are still a number of the smaller companies, particularly in the over-the-counter field, that continue to omit depreciation charges in income reports to stockholders. Where depreciation charges differ materially from the total allowed for tax purposes, footnote explanations would be helpful. The practice of combining all taxes into a single figure in annual reports serves to withhold from the analyst information on the amount of taxes paid to state and local authorities, foreign governments, and the Federal government. Where surplus adjustment items affect the tax charges as shown in the income account, such as profits made from the sale of a capital asset and cleared through surplus, an explanatory footnote should be forthcoming.

Where reserves are set up via charges through the income account, these should be clearly labeled. It would also be helpful if corporations were consistent in the treatment of such reserve charges against income, instead of charging the same type of reserves against earnings in one year and handling through surplus in other years. Although the analyst hardly expects and does not want annual reports of industrial corporations to show anywhere near the detail revealed in 10-K reports, he tends to view with a jaundiced eye the ostrich-like attitude of some managements in declining to show certain significant figures that are made available to the SEC.

In general, the analyst has no quarrel with the form of balance sheet presentation. Where marketable securities are held and shown at cost, the commendable practice is becoming increasingly prevalent of showing in parentheses the latest market value of such securities. The amount of reserves (for bad debts) should be revealed so that comparisons with similar reserves of other companies in the same field may be possible, providing some clue to (1) the relative adequacy of such reserves, or (2) the carefulness of credit policies. With respect to inventories, the analyst prefers this item to be shown broken down into the four major classifications: (1) raw materials, (2) work in process, (3) finished goods, and (4) supplies. Quite frequently property accounts as valued on balance sheets depart so far (either too high or too low) from present values as to be misleading. This problem of proper valuation is a difficult one, at best. One careful observer has suggested that a useful guide to true values of plant property would be the current insurance values shown in a footnote on the balance sheet. The coyness of some oil companies with respect to estimates of proved reserves is of little help to the analyst in appraising the value of oil equities. The practice of accelerated amortization of war-erected facilities has served further to distort property account valuations. Because balance sheet reserves are set up for many different reasons, financial reports should give sufficient detail to permit the analyst to: (1) identify surplus reserves, (2) to determine whether reserves set up represent reasonable estimates of expected future cash outlays, and (3) to identify arbitrary segregations of surplus aimed at such purposes as reducing reported earnings or holding down dividend disbursements.

In general, the annual reports filed by the railroads with the Interstate Commerce Commission (Form A) are considered entirely adequate. However, it is rarely possible to obtain copies of these reports direct from the company, and their purchase from one of the independent agencies in Washington specializing in such work involves considerable expense. There are a number of statistics revealed in annual reports to the ICC that are of vital interest to the security analyst, but which few if any companies include in their reports to stockholders. One of the most important omissions is in the passenger division. All roads show the revenue derived from passenger business, but none of them shows the costs allocable to this service. Another important omission in annual reports is in connection with wages. Many railroads also fail to show their fuel costs, although it is possible to compute this item where a breakdown of transportation costs is included in the report. Accounting treatment of "additions and betterments" lacks uniformity throughout the rail industry. It is of little advantage to the analyst to know how much money has been invested unless he also knows whether it has been spent on new rail, reduction of curves, new sidings, or any one of hundreds of other projects. In connection with new equipment purchases, it is important to know whether the money has been spent for new motive power or for new boxcars. Interest rates on conditional sales contracts for equipment purchases and the rate or term of amortization are also essential information to the responsible analyst. Very few roads reveal the age of their equipment in reports to shareholders. It would greatly aid the analyst to have the railroad company include in its annual report a statement of the annual rate of fixed charges at the end of the year. Probably the strangest omission is the failure to provide any breakdown of taxes, although they are usually grouped under "railway tax accruals," which may even include credits in one of the other tax accounts. Finally, there are still a few roads that omit tonnage figures for various commodities handled.

The recent trend toward oversimplification of utility annual reports does not meet with the favor of security analysts. All too many utility companies fail to show comparative income and balance sheets with the previous year. Few include more than a breakdown of their sales and revenues in their annual reports, although most companies have made information on sales and revenues broken down among the various classifications of customers, source of power, generating capacity, peak loads, and detailed operating costs available through "Institutional Utility Service." The wealth of statistical and financial information contained in the "report to Insurance Companies" might well be included between the covers of the annual report for the benefit of all investors, so that important trends and ratios can be determined.

The uniform system of accounts required by the Federal Power Commission and similar practices adopted by most local commissions are rapidly bringing a uniformity to public utility balance sheets and income statements. The dual regulatory authority, however, frequently presents problems that are difficult to resolve. Unless and until these regulatory bodies can agree, a company's accounting department can only follow the method it considers best and add a footnote explaining the controversy. Utility operating earnings should be shown before income taxes, with fixed charges then deducted, followed by income tax deductions. Many companies follow a helpful policy of deducting preferred dividends from the income account. In recent years, it has become common practice to include charges for "past service annuities" in operating expenses; they should be charges to surplus, and any tax benefits therefrom should be treated as a surplus credit. Interest credited to construction should be shown separately and not lumped with miscellaneous charges. The catch-all of "other income" should be broken down or at least commented on in a footnote when it represents an important portion of total income. The treatment of amortization of plant intangibles in the income accounts of utilities lacks uniformity. It should be stated as a deductible expense or a charge to surplus to aid the analyst in calculating the rate of return on invested capital. Utility balance sheets often still fail to show clearly the par value of the various stock issues; some even fail to segregate capital from earned surplus. One other defect that crops up from time to time is in the footnotes to the income accounts and balance sheets. The language used here is too legalistic, and, even for the experienced utility analyst, tends to be obscure.

To a large extent, the income reports of most over-the-counter companies are virtually worthless from the analyst's standpoint, primarily because of the meagerness of information. In addition to the brevity of income reports, financial statements of the majority reveal all the shortcomings previously noted in the reports of listed corporations. Adequate footnotes to the balance sheet are the exception rather than the rule.

Insurance company reports to stockholders (like some railroads and utilities) are notable chiefly for the absence of detailed information supplied to governmental authorities. The reports of fire insurance companies are viewed as especially deficient in information on such important groups of items as gross income, expenses by broad classifications, investment income, taxes, and net after taxes. It is especially difficult to ascertain from these reports alone the effects of the year's changes in the highly important item of unearned premium reserves.

Although financial statements published by banks have improved greatly during the past decade, too many banks still follow the old-fashioned policy of presenting only a brief "condition statement" (that is, balance sheet) that throws little light on results of operations. With respect to this statement, additional information on maturities of bond holdings and a simple breakdown of the loan portfolio would be helpful, as would a statement on the market value of holdings compared with book value. The bank income statement should have gross income broken down into (1) income from investments, (2) income from loans, (3) other income, from which would be deducted (a) salaries and wages, and (b) other expenses, and then taxes. This would give an indication of earning power. Additional data should include: (1) realized net profits or losses on security transactions, (2) net write-offs or recoveries on loans, and (3) other adjustments. This would lead to a final total showing net "indicated" earnings which would balance out the surplus and undivided profits accounts.

1. To whom must listed corporations make reports? Unlisted corporations?
2. For what reasons might management desire to withhold information from stockholders? From others? Is such a procedure ever good?
3. What is a 10-K report? Who must file such reports? How often?
4. Contrast the information an ordinary stockholder would want from an annual report with that desired by a security analyst.
5. Secure sample copies of annual reports of at least two companies and criticize them in the light of the comments made by Galanis. Has there been any improvement in annual reports since 1947?
6. See how the statistical services report the same information as is given in the annual reports examined. If there are any changes, why were they made?

60. Comparison of Accounting Reports

A knowledge of the similarities and differences in the financial reports of various types of corporations is necessary for a proper understanding of analytical methods. This assignment involves little effort but affords much food for thought.

The differences between financial statements published by industrial, mercantile, railroad, utility, bank and insurance companies are often confusing to the ordinary investor. Many new terms appear and the order of their presentation differs from one firm to the next. Although the financial statements of certain firms may vary from the usual types found in a particular category, there are advantages to making a rather extensive investigation of the various forms of financial statements.

1. You are asked to gather from a statistical source, such as *Moody's* or *Standard Corporation Records*, lists of the items which appear in the balance sheet and income statements of the following groups of firms:

    (a) a manufacturing firm, such as General Motors Corporation;

    (b) a merchandising firm, such as Federated Department Stores;

    (c) a railroad, such as Southern Railway;

    (d) a public utility, such as Connecticut Light & Power;

    (e) a bank, such as National City Bank of New York;

    (f) an insurance company, such as Fireman's Association of Philadelphia.

Do you notice any great differences in the order in which the balance sheet items appear for the various types of firms? in the income statements?

2. Now, in a columnar table, using one column for each type of firm, list the items which you would classfiy under the following headings:

ASSETS	LIABILITIES	NET WORTH	INCOME ACCOUNT
Current	Current	Reserves	Operating Income
Investments	Long-Term	Capital	Non-operating Income
Fixed		Surplus	Financial Charges
Deferred			Income Taxes
Intangible			Net Profits

Identify all of the items with which you are unfamiliar by referring to the analysis section of an investment text or a book on analysis of financial statements, such as written by Guthmann or Kennedy & MacMullen.

61. Fixed Charge and Preferred Dividend Coverage

The computation of fixed charge coverage and of a combined coverage is often found difficult to understand. This problem presents a short example of the various methods which have been proposed for measuring the earnings coverage of payment requirements.

As of December 31, 1952, the capitalization of El Paso Natural Gas Company consisted of a long list of issues with varying legal priorities.

$26,740,000	First pipe line 3s, 1966
12,000,000	First pipe line 3s, 2nd series, 1966
31,880,000	First mortgage line 3¼s, 1968
21,320,000	First mortgage line 3¼s, 1964
11,340,000	Pipe line 2nd series, 3¼s, 1964
28,000,000	First pipe line 3¼s, series due 1965
14,000,000	First pipe line 3⅝s, series due 1967
65,000,000	First pipe line 3¾s, series due 1968
16,000,000	Debenture 3¼s, 1957
8,000,000	Debenture 3s, 1958
73,500 shs.	4.10% cumulative preferred ($100 par)
25,000 shs.	4¼% cumulative preferred ($100 par)
100,000 shs.	5½% cumulative preferred ($100 par)
100,000 shs.	5.36% cumulative preferred ($100 par)
21,330 shs.	$4.25 conv. 2nd preferred, 1949 series (no par)
7,151 shs.	$4.25 conv. 2nd preferred, 1950 series (no par)
42,296 shs.	$4.40 conv. 2nd preferred, 1951 series (no par)
98,371 shs.	$4.40 conv. 2nd preferred, 1952 series (no par)
4,414,088 shs.	common ($3 par)

The income statement for the year 1952 ended with the following items:

Total income	$21,410,285
Amortization of debt discount & expense ⎱	23,962
Amortization of premium on debt ⎰	
Interest charged to construction ....cr.	1,910,855
Miscellaneous deductions	158,375
Federal income tax provision	4,445,000

Prior to the depression of 1929-1933 it was common to compute fixed charge coverage, or the number of times that earnings covered interest charge requirements by what has been called the "single issue" method. The earnings available for a particular issue, after deducting the charges for any issues which had priority, were divided by the interest charge requirements for the issue under study. Since income taxes were at low levels, it was not important to consider them. In more recent years, however, with the increased burden of income taxes it has become common for many analysts to compute interest coverage by using net income after Federal income taxes.

As one alternative to the "single issue" method it has been suggested that the coverage for any particular issue be computed by taking into consideration all of the interest charges of issues prior to the issue in question, plus the issue itself. This is a "prior deductions" method. A second alternative calls for computation on an "overall basis," with all interest charges bulked into a single computation that would apply to all issues.

Turning to the coverage of preferred stock dividends, a similar situation can be found. The earliest methods related earnings after taxes to preferred dividend requirements on a "single issue" pattern. Other analysts followed a "prior deductions" method, applying preferred stock dividend requirements to earnings after taxes, while a few used an "overall basis" for preferred stocks alone.

In more recent times the tendency of analysts has been to follow the procedure of relating earnings after taxes to fixed charges plus preferred dividend requirements to secure a "combined charges and dividends coverage."

The shifting of income tax rates to high levels caused the coverages after taxes in all cases to fall substantially lower than those experienced in the years before 1940. The lack of comparability of data over long periods of time disturbed many analysts. Bennett has suggested that preferred dividend requirements be altered to take into consideration not only the dividend, but the taxes which must be paid on the net income before the dividend can be considered covered.[1] His suggestion that preferred dividend requirements be divided by 100 per cent minus the effective tax rate to find the actual net earnings needed for coverage, and that this figure be added to the interest charges as the divisor for earnings before taxes appears a significant contribution.

1. Using the data for El Paso Natural Gas Company, look up the various priorities of issues, and for each group compute the coverages of the bond issues on the "single issues," "prior deductions," and "overall" methods. Do any inconsistencies appear which would lead you to a judgment as to the more pre-

---

[1] Bennett, Alden S., "Determining Combined Fixed Charge and Preferred Dividend Coverage," *The Analysts Journal*, published by N. Y. Society of Security Analysts, Vol. 3 (Fourth Quarter, 1947), pp. 63–66.

ferable method? Would it make any difference whether you used income before or after taxes? Which appears preferable from a logical point of view? From a practical point of view?

2. Using the data for El Paso Natural Gas Company, compute the coverage of the groups of preferred stock issues on the "single issue," "prior deductions," and "overall" methods, using the net income after taxes figure as the base. Do any inconsistencies appear? Is this a logical method to use?

3. Compute the combined charges and dividends coverage according to the two methods suggested above. Do Mr. Bennett's objections to the standard procedure appear logical?

4. Some analysts compute the dollars per share earned on preferred stock issues. Is this figure of any significance? To what method of coverage computation is this method similar?

5. Some analysts do not compute coverages of fixed charges, but prefer to compute a "factor of safety" on an overall basis. This "factor of safety" is computed by dividing the net income available after charges to the net income before charges, thus showing the per cent of decline in net income that could occur before hazarding the coverage of interest charges. Of what significance is this computation?

6. Investment texts usually give certain minimum coverages which are considered necessary before a security (bond or preferred stock) is to be considered of investment merit. Examine at least two texts and see the manner in which they compute coverages as well as the minimum coverages they advocate. Is this double distinction of great merit?

7. Look up Moody's and Standard & Poor's methods of computing coverages. Are these the best methods from both a logical and practical point of view?

62. Payout versus Retained Earnings as a Price Factor

Although the discussion of this problem is based on public utility common stocks, its scope might easily be extended to include other

*types of equity issues. The topic deserves serious consideration
by any student of security analysis.*

Since companies operating in the public utility field, especially
in the electric light and power industry, offer a fairly large sample
of homogeneous items, comparisons between common stocks of
these firms offer a very fertile field for analytical experimentation.
The following series of observations, taken in large measure from
Analysts Journal, offer some indications of the lines of analysis that
may fruitfully be pursued.

Writing on "Depreciation and Utility Security Analysis," A. W.
Hastings[1] summarizes the three schools of thought on depreciation
bases: that developed from periodical appraisal of the physical
plant, the straight-line method, and the sinking fund method, both
of the latter applied to original cost or prudent cost. It is held that
the sinking fund method is the soundest of the three from an economic point of view, yet often is of less practical value. Analysts in
the past have generally related depreciation charges annually to
gross revenues, and maintenance and depreciation charges to gross
revenues in their efforts to measure the adequacy of charges to real
plant operation. These ratios are held open to criticism when used
on an intercompany comparison basis because of the absence of
equal rates of change in plant and rates of change in gross revenues,
and also because they fail to reflect the relation of purchased power
to generated power. Yet the ratios are good when applied to the industry as a whole. Hastings holds that it would be better to apply
both charges to the gross plant figure on the balance sheet, but to
give some weight in analysis to the effects of growth, long-life
prospects, soil and disaster conditions, and the attitude of state regulatory authorities. He would accept depreciation and maintenance figures as given by the companies unless there is some good
reason to doubt their adequacy, rather than attempt to adjust them
to fit some chosen ratio to gross revenues. He thus would appear to
advocate taking reported company earnings in analysis rather than
attempt adjustments to secure comparability.

Once earnings for the utility have been established, it is a usual
second step to relate earnings to stock prices. H. H. Young, in one

---

[1] A. W. Hastings, "Depreciation and Utility Security Analysis," *Analysts
Journal*, vol. 1 (Oct. 1954), p. 3.

study,[2] found that company size was not important, nor was geographical location, except in New England where the local investment sentiment favored issues of these companies. In studying price-earnings ratios, he found that the ratios varied with the ratio of common stock and surplus to total capitalization. If the equity interest exceeded 50 per cent, the price-earnings ratio usually exceeded 15; correspondingly, if the equity interest were less than 15 per cent, the price-earnings ratio was 10 or less. A second observation showed that price-earnings ratios varied in direct relation to the percentage of gross revenues available for the common stock. A third relation of payout to price-earnings ratio was then examined. If the payout exceeded 85 per cent, the ratio generally exceeded 14; for a 70 per cent payout, the ratio was 12 or over; and for a 50 per cent to 60 per cent payout, the ratio was usually 8 to 10. The analysis was based on data for a large number of companies, and used 1943-1944 data.

H. Pastoriza[3] took issue with the third of these views. His studies showed that a dollar of retained earnings is given equal investment support as a dollar of dividends paid out. More specifically, the retained dollar was valued more highly by companies that had high credit outstanding, and less by companies with little debt outstanding. An average of 25 per cent of earnings was found retained by utility companies. Pastoriza then suggests that consistency might be achieved by adjusting earnings to a figure of dividends plus 25 per cent of retained earnings as a more meaningful figure by which to divide price to secure a comparable price-earnings ratio.

H. A. Diamant[4] took up Pastoriza's formula and claimed that it gave no weight to distortions in reported earnings nor to the factor of leverage in relation to operating revenues exerted by fixed and preferred charges. He concluded that the percentage of payout, as the relation of dividends to earnings available for dividends, has no meaning, for it is only an end result rather than being a real determinant of quality.

---

[2] H. H. Young, "A Study of Factors Influencing Price-Earnings Ratios of Utility Common Stocks," *Analysts Journal*, vol. 1 (Jan. 1945), p. 45.

[3] H. Pastoriza, "Valuing Utility Earnings, Distributed and Retained," *Analysts Journal*, vol. 1 (July 1945), p. 14.

[4] H. A. Diamant, "Public Utility Price-Earnings Ratios," *Analysts Journal*, vol. 2 (March 1946), p. 48.

Into this controversy stepped E. B. Barrett[5] some five years later. In a more exhaustive study than any of the practicing analysts was able to undertake, he examined the 1929-49 period and measured price movements against a battery of ten criteria ratios: payout, earnings over price, common equity to capital structure, operating ratios, percentage of operating revenues available for common, percent earned on total capital funds, rates of depreciation and maintenance to gross revenues, and the ratio of increases in revenues to increases in expenses. The sample covered 49 firms for the period 1937-1949 and a smaller number for earlier years.

Barrett found that firms with the lowest payout showed up the best in relation to price movements, but that the earnings/price ratio was a close second. He concluded that the low payout appeared to indicate a potential rise in dividends in the future and thus a future rise in market prices which could be favorable to an alert investor. It was found, however, that a low payout combined with a low ratio of common stock equity to total capitalization need not cause dividends to rise. It would appear better in Barrett's judgment to exclude payout as a measure affecting price unless the common stock equity exceed 20 per cent to 25 per cent of total capitalization. He concluded that his results were not fully conclusive, but might be of more value in years of declining stock prices than in all years.

1. Taking a list of at least 20 public utility companies of varying size and covering a period of at least five years, examine the ratios of depreciation and of depreciation plus maintenance to gross revenues and to gross plant. Which of the four ratios gives the more consistent results for each company? Are the arrays of rates relatively stable?

2. For the period 1949-1953 test out the various relations of stock prices described above. Does the market appear to give much weight to the payout of earnings?

3. E. L. Smith, in his "Common Stocks as Long-Term Investments," claimed that retained earnings were the source of long-term capital gains. It should logically follow that market prices would rise with book values. Examine the history of a number

[5] H. S. Schneider, "Two Formula Methods for Choosing Common Stocks," *Journal of Finance*, vol. 2 (June 1951), pp. 229-47, especially 234-7.

of industrial and railroad company common stocks to verify this conclusion. At the same time, calculate the payout percentages. Which appears to have the greater effect on industrials? On rails?

63. Book Values and Security Values

Since many persons interested in securities' markets look upon book value as a fair measure of intrinsic value, the following problem is included to clarify the issues involved.[1]

Book values, as a standard for measuring security values, is again attracting attention in financial quarters although its use has not proved as profitable as other standards such as dividend records and earnings.

Some investment firms have been calling attention to this factor as a method for determining undervalued situations. In some instances there have been modifications through use of working capital and eliminating fixed assets. From time to time there have been successful moves made to liquidate some companies to realize such values, although often the book value of a security may prove to be largely artificial.

Several years ago, prior to the start of the bull market, *Life* magazine (March 19, 1949) published an article entitled "The Strange Case of the Market," which contained a list of ten common stocks selling below book value. From time to time similar lists have been published in other publications, but investors looking for appreciation, with a few exceptions, could have done better by using other yard sticks.

Purchase of ten shares each of the issues listed by *Life* would have cost $3,900 in March, 1949, and today would be worth more than $5,200, an increase of about 35 per cent. The list at that time included Bigelow Sanford, E. W. Bliss, Cincinnati Milling, Douglas Aircraft, Foster Wheeler, Lee Rubber, Lima-Hamilton (now Baldwin-Lima-Hamilton), Montgomery Ward, New York Shipbuilding, and Pullman.

---

[1] *Journal of Commerce*, July 14, 1952, p. 3.

Capital would have been more than doubled in Douglas and Foster Wheeler while there would be small losses in Bigelow Sanford and New York Shipbuilding. Although the average value of the ten stocks was appreciating in value by 35 per cent since March 1949, the industrial stock average (Dow-Jones) gained 51 per cent and the railroad stock averages advanced 110 per cent.

Book value is defined as the value of the assets available for the common stocks after deducting all prior liabilities. The simple accepted practice excludes intangibles.

If a company can be liquidated and stockholders receive in cash or the equivalent the value at which various tangible assets are carried on the books, then book value is important. However, actual liquidation, it is pointed out, could result in a substantial discount. A sizable loss might result from sale of the inventory and a very substantial shrinkage could follow in liquidation of fixed assets except under certain favorable conditions.

Textbooks used by analysts point out that book value really measures not what the stockholders could get out of their business, but what they have put into the business, including undistributed earnings. Analysts point out that what appears to be a valuable asset today in the form of inventories might change considerably in a matter of months due to a sharp decline in commodity prices.

1. Re-examine the book values and market values of the securities named. Is there any evidence that at any time during the cycle of security prices market values might tend to approach book values?

64. Analysis for Institutional Investment

This simple problem offers some of the "screening devices" used by an institutional investor in selecting issues which will meet its requirements.

One sizable financial institution that deals principally in long-term debt issues and in equities uses the following income statement data as critical measures for preliminary analysis of issues in regard to their suitability for the investment portfolio.

1. Gross income.
2. Reported net income available for charges.
3. Available net income plus depreciation.
4. Times charges earned, actual.
5. Times charges earned, pro forma to include all debt plus any new financing being undertaken, with current yields applied to the whole debt.
6. Net income after taxes.
7. Dividends paid.
8. Dividends paid on senior equity issues, considering new financing, applying current dividend rate on all issues.

1. What is the objective of each of these measures of financial strength?

2. What benefit is derived from the fifth measure by considering total debt at current yields rather than on the basis of actual coupon rates for previously issued bonds? Would this be a good measure to use in cases of refunding only or for all new issues?

3. Should these data be computed for one year or for a series of recent years? Should norms be established for the ratios? What would be a minimum number of years to use in setting norms? What would you do for a borrower which could not furnish this data?

65.   Bond Quality Ratings[1]

The following article appeared in The Analysts Journal by special permission of Standard & Poor's Corporation. These letters provide an insight into the manner in which the S. & P. ratings are computed.

LETTER TO INSURANCE COMPANY
BY STANDARD & POOR'S CORPORATION

Mr. John H. Doe, Director of Research
Doeville Mutual Life Insurance Company
Doeville, New York
Dear Mr. Doe:

Our Mr. Foust has asked me to write to you about our bond quality

---

[1] *Analysts Journal*, published by N. Y. Society of Security Analysts, vol. 2, no. 1, pp. 9–17 (1946). Note that the figures in the exhibits would vary from year to year.

ratings. I welcome this opportunity to discuss the subject, for we at Standard are fully aware that these bond ratings have become highly important to the investing public and have been given a new meaning now that government authorities are using them to control institutional investments.

Before beginning this discussion, I want to point out that the Standard & Poor's organization had no part in having bond quality ratings used by public authorities in this manner. They did not ask our advice. The fact is they wanted a tool to control investments and they found a handy one in our ratings. Although we had no say in this matter, we have attempted to meet the responsibility to the best of our ability. We have been and will continue to be criticized, as would be expected since security appraisal is not an exact science.

The Standard & Poor's organization fully recognizes this new responsibility. The job of rating bonds is in the hands of three highly experienced men, who make up the Bond Policy Committee. Each member has 15 or more years' experience in this particularly specialized field. One of the members of this committee makes a study of all situations. Similar studies are made independently by our trade analysts. The reports are passed on by the committee.

In assigning ratings, particularly for new issues, we are always willing to discuss the matter at hand with any informed people outside our organization who desire to do so. I should say that in considering 90 per cent of all new issues we meet with company officials and/or bankers. Yesterday we met with the President and the Treasurer of Utah Power & Light, and last week we had a meeting with the President of Illinois Power Company.

The specific question put to us is: "What factors are used in determining a bond rating?" The answer is: Everything we can learn about the company and about the bond is given full consideration. Here is a list of the things we look for, though I am sure that all items are familiar to you and are used by your organization in your own work.

For an industrial issue we look at:

1. Earnings
   (a) Earnings prospects:
       (1) Immediate.
       (2) Long term.
   (b) Present earnings.
   (c) Past record.
   (d) Reputation of products and position of company in trade.
   (e) Character of the trade.
   (f) Quality of management by reputation and as depicted by:
       (1) Earnings record.
       (2) Sales trend.
       (3) Operating ratios.
       (4) Efficiency as indicated by amount of property to produce

a dollar of sales.
   (5) Depreciation practices.
   (6) Dividend policy.
2. Protection from fixed assets.
3. Protection from net current assets.
4. Protection from cash resources alone.
5. Adequacy of working capital for conducting the business and relationship between current assets and current liabilities.

For utility bonds we fill out a table similar to the following and compare with the average for all companies having exactly the same type of business. We can make such comparison for utilities because so many companies are similar. The table [V-4] shows the average for A1+ and A issues.

For a railroad bond it is our practice to rate the credit position of the road and assign that rating to the poorest bond of the system. We then rate upward for lien position. By lien position we don't mean merely whether it is a mortgage, but we are primarily interested in the earning power of the underlying lines and their strategic importance for (a) originating traffic, (b) terminating traffic, (c) for their connections with complementing lines, and (d) for their position in relation to the system as a whole.

The credit position is obtained by studying all factors obtainable and runs along these lines:

1. Earnings prospects:
   (a) Immediate.
   (b) Long term.
2. Present earning power.
3. Past earnings record.
4. Trend of company's freight volumes over a period of years compared with:
   (a) other roads in the region.
   (b) all Class I roads.
5. Potential competition.
6. Physical condition of the road as indicated by maintenance expenditures and efficiency.
7. Management as depicted by:
   (a) Earnings record.
   (b) Trend of freight volumes.
   (c) Efficiency as reflected by
      (1) Costs.
      (2) Gross ton miles per freight train hour.
   (d) Dividend payments
8. Finances.
9. Debt retirements in recent years.
10. Location of road, traffic composition and traffic originations.

TABLE V-4

	Average A1+	Average A
1. Funded and property ratios		
(a) Debt to net property (book value)		
(1) Mortgage		
(2) Total fixed debt		
(b) Percent Debt to original cost net property		
(1) Mortgage	43.8	61.1
(2) Total fixed debt	45.5	66.5
(c) Percent Depreciation reserve to gross property		
(1) Book figures	14.4	13.1
(d) Breakdown of total capitalization		
(1) Mortgage debt	39.4	49.4
(2) Junior debt	1.6	4.4
(3) Preferred stock	14.3	18.8
(4) Common stock and surplus	44.7	27.4
(e) Percent Gross property to gross revenue (original cost)		
2. Earnings		
(a) Rate of return on net property		
(1) On book values	6.0	6.3
(2) On original cost	6.4	7.2
(b) Mortgage interest coverage		
(1) Before federal taxes		
(2) After federal taxes	4.57	3.19
(c) Fixed charge coverage		
(1) Before federal taxes	5.76	3.49
(2) After federal taxes	4.20	2.56
(d) Earned on mortgage debt		
(1) Before federal taxes		
(2) After federal taxes	15.3	12.3
(e) Earned on total debt		
(1) Before federal taxes	20.4	15.3
(2) After federal taxes	14.7	11.1
(f) Percent Depreciation—Maintenance to gross revenue	15.2	15.6
(g) Percent Depreciation to gross property	15.2	15.6
(h) Percent Depreciation in operating income (1930—low point)	22.6	26.0
(i) Percent Breakdown of gross revenue		
(1) Electric		
(2) Manufactured gas or natural gas		
(3) Traction		
(4) Other		
(j) Operating ratio		
(k) Residential electric rates per 100 kwh. monthly		
(l) Average residential consumption		
(m) Percent Common stock earnings paid out		
3. Growth Factors		
(a) Percent Gain in population (1930-1940)		
(b) Percent Gain in kwh. sales		
(1) 1942 vs. 1932		
(2) 1942 vs. 1937		
(c) Percent Gain in gross revenue		
(1) 1942 vs. 1932		
(2) 1942 vs. 1937		
(d) Percent Gain in net operating income		
(1) 1942 vs. 1932		
(2) 1942 vs. 1937		
4. Intangibles		
(a) Territory		
(b) Regulation		
(c) Public ownership		
(d) Public power projects		
5. Indenture provisions		

I don't know whether I have mentioned everything we look for in rating bonds, but the foregoing, I am sure, will give you the idea that we are doing a thorough job.

Most of the criticism levelled at our ratings at the present time is in the railroad field. Too many people are carried away by the present huge earnings; they forget the past unsatisfactory trends in railroading, and apparently are willing to ignore the possibility of the resumption of the trend after the war. It is well to point out, therefore, as part of this review of our rating procedure, that some time ago we at Standard & Poor's decided that we would ignore war earnings as such in evaluating railroad bonds. We decided that we would, however, give full weight to the use of cash resulting from war-time operations either in building up working capital or for retiring debt.

As to the weight given debt retirement, our tests for higher ratings are: were the smaller charges earned in 1938, the last depression year, and by what margins were the smaller charges earned in 1936 and 1937, the last pre-war good periods? A few months ago we made a check of the effect of debt retirements and were impressed in some instances. We advanced ratings accordingly.

Very truly yours,
L. Brand
Secretary,
Bond Policy Committee

Letter to Standard & Poor's Corporation by Insurance Company

December 6, 1943.

Mr. L. Brand, Secretary,
Bond Policy Committee,
Standard & Poor's Corporation,
345 Hudson Street,
New York 14, New York.
Dear Mr. Brand:

Your letter of December 2nd describing the elements and manner by which your Corporation arrives at the bond quality ratings assigned to various types of securities is very much appreciated. It is the first time anyone has ever consented to put in writing any of the considerations given to this subject, although it is one of extreme importance and carries with it very great responsibility.

I expect to give your letter further study and hope to discuss it with my associates in the research division of this company's bond department. Meanwhile, however, one question presented itself to me which I think is of equal importance to the assignment of original ratings. I realize that the field covered is a very large one, but I am curious to know how and when reviews of existing ratings are carried on, and whether or not sudden changes in market prices of the security causes you to raise or lower any rating. Admitting that, over a period of time, markets will reflect the real credit picture, it would be of interest to me to know the extent to which you place weight on this factor. In considering this element, I am conscious of the fact (as I know you and your Corporation are also) of the vicious spiral which frequently results from the lowering of any rating below a minimum quality basis set up as a standard which apparently forces involuntary liquidation on the part of such holders who are subject to regulation. This necessitous liquidation, of course, carries with it other voluntary selling and can do untold harm to the credit of any company involved.

It seems to me that the timing of your rating changes is all important, and I will appreciate any information which you care to divulge on this question. I admit that I would not care to share your responsibility along these lines.

Again thanking you for your courtesy and looking forward to receiving your further reply, I am

Very truly yours,
John H. Doe

LETTER TO INSURANCE COMPANY
BY STANDARD & POOR'S CORPORATION

December 22, 1943

Mr. John H. Doe, Director of Research
Doeville Mutual Life Insurance Company
Doeville, New York
Dear Mr. Doe:

I can best answer the queries contained in your recent letter on bond quality ratings by telling you of our method of operation. I am glad that I have an opportunity of going into this, since we at Standard & Poor's believe we have an ideal arrangement. It is not foolproof, of course, but nothing is where the human element enters into the equation.

We have no set time for reviewing existing bond quality ratings. However, the members of our Bond Policy Committee are actively engaged in practical bond work and therefore must make frequent reviews.

Take my own position in the Standard organization. In addition to being the active head of the Bond Policy Committee, I am editor of our Bond Guide Reports. These reports cover about 1,000 situations — the active listed and unlisted bond issues. The reports are revised by our analytical division every three months, or more frequently if new developments warrant earlier consideration. As the reports are brought up-to-date they are submitted to me for approval, I should say at the rate of about 15 a day. Passing on these analyses gives me an opportunity for a quick, but still a close check of our quality ratings and our market ratings in the light of the new information developed. It is obvious that I must keep in touch with all new developments and must interpret these developments almost as soon as they take place.

Another member of our Committee is charged with the specific job of watching quality and market ratings, plus the preparation of daily bulletins for publication in the Bond Guide Reports—bulletins which cover and interpret all new developments affecting the bonds covered in the service.

The third member of our Committee has long experience in bond work, but his specific job, in addition to being a member of the Committee, is chief of the Bank Section of our Planned Investments Department. This division gives personal advice to banks and other institutions on investments and investment policy. The head of this department brings to the Committee his long experience on bonds, his studies on investment trends, and his opinions on interest rates.

And finally, the heads of our analytical units (rail, industrial and utility) make suggestions and participate in rating discussions on bond issues under their jurisdiction.

Any member of the Committee or any member of our analytical organization is privileged to bring before the full committee any suggestions for changes in bond quality ratings or in market ratings. Our organization is so flexible that we can discuss new developments in full committee at almost any time.

The charge that the ratings of the various agencies follow bond prices is flung out at will by our critics. They have no basis for this, but it sounds good from their angle.

Prices do not now, and never have had any part in our rating scheme. Our bond quality ratings are based purely on statistical, economic, and trade developments, as outlined in my last letter. We use bond prices in only one way so far as quality ratings are concerned, and that is as a check. After all, when we rate a bond we are matching our own knowledge against the ability of investors to gauge the situation. We believe we would be amiss in our job if we did not check our rating against the evaluation of other investors, as reflected in bond prices. We do this regularly and if we find that the two do not jibe, we immediately make a fresh study in the hope of finding out who is correct.

It is not unusual for the market to give weight to a temporary situation which does not fit in with the basic values as depicted by the quality rating. In such event we ignore it. On the other hand, the difference of opinion sets us off to a new study which may reveal some new basic development not yet generally available to the public. In such case, we give it full weight in our rating deliberations.

In recapitulation, we do not rate bonds on prices, but we do use prices as a clue to whether the situation requires a complete new study. We are not ashamed of using prices in this manner.

Very truly yours,
L. Brand
Secretary,
Bond Policy Committee

1. Some critics of ratings hold that no consideration should be given to the presence or absence of a specific lien on assets, that the earning power of the debtor is the sole criterion of sound investment. Appraise Standard & Poor's policy of lien provisions as a factor in determining bond ratings.

2. Since bond ratings are based upon comparisons with averages, which in turn change as time passes, does this not result in ratings based on past records rather than on prospects? Would this not then cause bond quality ratings to give a false impression of safety in the event of a sizable depression? Could not bond quality ratings deteriorate quickly under such circumstances?

66. Valuation of Listed Stocks by Formula Methods

This abstract of an article[1] by one of the leading exponents of the mathematical method of determining common stock valuations is very valuable in explaining the methods used by one prominent investment service and in showing its limitations.

Value and price are not necessarily the same thing. Yet the only determinant of value, which is something that cannot be defined, is price. We find a break in the circle of reasoning in the fact that prices are not the same at all times and that changes in certain variables, such as earnings, dividends, and assets are related to the corresponding changes in prices. If it can be found that a certain relationship between prices on the one hand and variables of earnings and dividends and assets on the other has been maintained for a long period of time, it might then rightly be concluded that at such moments, or even in such years, as the market deviates from this long held relationship, the distortion is a measure of the disparity between price and value. It can be said that, at such times when a given level of earnings, assets, and dividends fails to command the price that has been placed on it most of the time in the past, that is a time of overvaluation or undervaluation. And we can logically use this measure, not as a definition of value, but as a description of it, and as a method for determining the direction in which the market

---

[1] Arnold Bernhard, "The Valuation of Listed Stocks," *The Analysts Journal*, published by N. Y. Society of Security Analysts, vol. 5, (Second Quarter, 1949) pp. 20–24.

price will probably move by way of readjustment. It is the virtue of a normal relationship that it can be expected to prevail most of the time. What we wish to know is what will be the opinion, expressed in price, of all the buyers and sellers participating in a free market most of the time.

One cannot be perfectly sure that the variables of earnings and dividends and assets and habit of mind will actually determine the opinion of buyers and sellers. But one can make certain assumptions and then test them mathematically, to see whether or not a correlation exists between changes in the variables of earnings, dividends, and assets, and habit of mind on the one hand, and prices on the other, and, if such correlation is found to exist, whether the coefficient is so high as to be beyond the possibility of explanation by pure chance.

If a statistician were to correlate earnings, dividends, assets, and last year's average price of a given stock (last year's average price is the specific way of expressing "habit of mind"), he could do so through a computation known as a multiple variable correlation analysis. The Value Line rating, about which the reader may have heard, is a single line which expresses that correlation. In that line is expressed the price that the market over a 20-year span has placed on earnings, assets, and dividends at the various levels of experience most of the time.

In the absence of a commonly accepted definition of value, we must, to be practical, go on the assumption that value is in the long run the equivalent of price. But we may also proceed on the assumption that price at any given time is not always the same as value, because there is such a thing as a long term price appraisal which may differ from the current price appraisal. We find that the changes in price that occur from year to year can be ascribed in significantly high degree to corresponding changes in such variables as assets, earnings, and dividends, and habit of mind (price lag). We conclude, therefore, that the evolution of a standard of value, based on a correlation between changes in price and changes in factors of value, when found, should enable us to project the probable future of a stock, not with certainty, but with a sufficiently high degree of probability to validate the premise that such a projection is a practical standard by which to identify areas of undervaluation or overvaluation, not only in the stock market as a whole, but in the prices of individual stocks as well.

It is recognized that the practicality of such a rating depends on ability to forecast the future level of earnings and dividends with reasonable accuracy. There is evidence to prove that it can be and has been done. At the very least, the analysis proves that the normal capitalization of a given level of earnings and assets can be determined in advance and that, because the capitalization is normal, it will probably be realized. The inescapable hazard of projecting future earnings and dividends remains, of course. But the price that the market will probably place on a given level of earnings and dividends need no longer remain in the realm of pure guess.

If this method of evaluation is sound, then it follows that the stocks that are most deeply undervalued according to this standard should give the best account of themselves in the open market during a period of 6 months to 18 months, regardless of the trend of the market as a whole. This, as a matter of fact, is a result that has been proved in experience. That is to say, the stocks most deeply undervalued and therefore most strongly to be recommended have, as a class, outperformed in the market the stocks that, as a class, merit a lower recommendation, and those that merit the second best recommendation have out-performed as a class those that merited the third class recommendation, and so on. In short, it is possible by this method to separate the sheep from the goats in the market, according to value.

Differences between actual market price and the standard of value expressed in the Value Line rating can be very largely explained in terms of market sentiment. One good measure of market sentiment is the ratio of stock yields to bond yields. If such an average ratio is inserted into the equation as a fifth independent variable, the correlations emerge as almost perfect. This may mean, that if one can predict where the stock market averages and the interest rate will be next year, he can forecast pretty accurately where the price of a particular stock will be too, if he can forecast its earnings and dividends. Actually, though, the exercise is more promising than it first appears, because, for one thing, the stock-bond yield ratio lends itself to forecast better than the stock market averages alone, and, second, even if not forecastable, a stock-bond yield ratio, inserted into a multiple variable correlation analysis, gives a truer weighting to the other variables of earnings, assets, dividends, and price lag. The non-predictable variable (stock-bond yield ratio) can then be held constant, and a projection of the predictable variables in the equation can be made with greater assurance that they will reveal the true value of the stock, ex sentiment.

1. From data given in the Appendix, prepare correlation graphs comparing price with (a) earnings per share, (b) dividends per share, and (c) average price for the preceding year. Similarly, prepare a time chart of the four series. Which of the variables appears to have the greatest correlation with prices? Could a four-quarter moving total of earnings show greater correspondence with prices?

2. Work out average price-earnings ratios on the same firm for the years 1946-53, with both an average high and average low ratio. Apply these ratios to an earnings projection derived as in Problem 54. Compare these results with the Value Line approach.

3. Following the methods used by Mr. Bernhard, test out his theory. Take the period 1929-1939, for example, and see what

the price in 1940 should have been. Then, take the period 1939-1949, and compare the calculated value against actual price. If any error developed, in what factor can you find the explanation?

4. Are the assumptions stated in the excerpt valid? Can this theory be applied to determine cyclical turning points, or is it purely a method for long-run investment?

5. Consider the following statement on the bond-stock yield differential, written by Jules I. Bogen for the *Journal of Commerce*, June 9, 1953. What does this analysis add to Bernhard's contention that the ratio can be assumed to be constant for at least short-run purposes?

Yields offered by common stocks are still relatively attractive despite the sharp rise in bond yields, historical comparisons indicate. At the end of last week, according to Moody's Investors Service, the average yield on 200 common stocks was 5.62 per cent. This compared with an average yield of 3.59 per cent on corporate bonds on the same date.

Stock prices have been going up faster than dividend payments since 1950, so that yields on equities have declined. At the same time, bond yields have risen steadily. But the investor can still obtain 50 per cent more in current income from a representative group of common stocks than he can from a cross section of corporate bonds rated from Aaa to Baa.

The differential between bond and stock yields has been unusually wide in recent years. In 1950 and 1951, average dividend yields were more than twice bond yields. In the past 33 years, bond yields were actually higher than stock yields in 14 years. In five other years, the yield on equities was less than ½ of 1 per cent higher than that offered by corporate bonds. In only 8 years out of the 33 years since 1919 has the average yield on representative common stocks been 2 per cent or more above the corporate bond yield, as it is today. On the basis of historical comparisons, therefore, stock yields are still attractive, despite the fact that they have declined since 1950, while bond yields have risen simultaneously.

Very wide fluctuations in the bond-stock yield differential emphasize the dangers of using this figure as a sure clue to future stock price movements. Several factors influence the differential at any one time. More important among these are:

1. Investor appraisal of the trend of earnings and dividends. A wider differential will prevail when it is feared dividend rates may be reduced. This was the case in the early 1940's, and again after the stock market broke in 1946, when a postwar recession was anticipated. Conversely, stock yields ruled lower than bond yields throughout the 1920's and the early 1930's, when dividend increases were expected as a regular thing.

2. The breadth of the demand for common stocks. When individual

investors buy stocks freely for income, yields tend to decline, as in the 1920's. Reduced individual buying of stocks because of high personal income and capital gains taxes has tended to raise yields sharply in the past few years. It remains to be seen whether institutional buying of equities will narrow yields again, or whether this will occur only after personal income taxation has been brought down to make holding of stocks for income more attractive to middle and higher bracket investors.

3. Corporate dividend policy. This year, somewhat less than last year's amounts have been paid out in dividends. In the past, when the pay-out was higher, investors appeared satisfied with relatively lower yields. This anomaly reflected the belief that, with liberal dividend policies, larger earnings would be translated sooner into higher dividends.

Growing institutional interest in equity investment, and the prospect of lower personal income taxes and a dividend income credit, makes it likely that the yield differential will narrow further. Fears of a recession, however, tend to offset these influences. The bond-stock yield differential could narrow further, therefore, unless a downturn in earnings should undermine confidence in the maintenance of current dividend rates.

67. Valuation of Growth Stocks

The analysis of common stocks to determine their growth potentialities is an attractive occupation. Methods of approaching this problem vary, however, and you are here asked to appraise some of them rather critically.

Many investment writers have commented on the high price-earnings ratios at which growth securities sell relative to the price-earnings ratios for non-growth securities.[1] However, there is some disagreement about the influence of dividends on the price-earnings ratio. Some contend that the relative "pay-out" is of greater importance than the relative retained earnings, others hold opposite views. "Pay-out" is here defined as the proportion of earnings paid out as dividends. It might be well to look into some of the early studies in growth issues, particularly the writing of Laurence H.

---

[1] J. Grodinsky, *Investments*, Ronald Press, 1953, p. 384; D. F. Jordan and H. E. Dougall, *Investments*, Prentice-Hall, 1952, p. 109; R. E. Badger and H. G. Guthmann, *Investment Principles and Practice* (4th ed.), Prentice-Hall, 1952, p. 250; L. V. Plum and J. H. Humphrey, *Investment Analysis and Management*, Irwin, 1951, p. 536; D. H. Bellemore, *Investments Principles, Practices and Analysis*, Forbes, 1953, pp. 397–402.

Sloan, and the classical "Ebb and Flow of Investment Values" by Mead and Grodinsky.

The following excerpt, from "A Method of Valuing Growth Stocks," by George Mackintosh,[2] affords some light on one method of valuing growth stocks.

This study was undertaken to devise a method of checking the reasonableness of the apparently high price-earnings ratios of secular (long-term) growth stocks. We might define a secular growth stock as one whose earnings will probably persist upward in relation to average corporate earnings over a period of years. Demonstrated past growth is usually helpful in furnishing candidates for study.

This discussion is not concerned with non-secular growth of per share earnings, which can occur by (1) an upswing of the business cycle, (2) a reduction in tax rates, (3) a lowering of interest charges or preferred stock dividend requirements, (4) a betterment of the profit margin by reason of greater internal efficiency, (5) an individual company improving its competitive position, (6) purchase of another company on a favorable basis, (7) a special development of limited duration such as war, (8) a lowering of charges for depreciation or maintenance and repairs, or (9) a non-recurring type gain such as profits from sale of securities. We have in mind long term growth prospects which promise to extend well beyond the foreseeable future, which have a solid footing and which are based on industry trends. Almost always these are based on aggressive research for the development of new products and the extension of demand for existing ones. The latter is usually accomplished by quality improvement, price reduction, or both. Excellent examples of secular growth companies are International Business Machines, Scott Paper, duPont, Dow, Monsanto, Union Carbide and Coca Cola.

Investors are rightly bewildered by the varying price-earnings ratios of common stocks, particularly of the so-called secular growth stocks. Price-earnings ratios at any given time will differ from stock to stock because of many reasons, including (1) conservatism or lack of it in making charges against profits for depreciation, maintenance, repairs, inventory reserves, etc., (2) different types of capital structures which afford varying amounts of leverage to the common stock, (3) varying strength of working capital positions, (4) differing records of earning's stability, (5) proportion of earnings paid out in dividends, (6) yield afforded in relation to other stocks of similar quality, and (7) prospects for long term growth, stability, or retrogression of earnings. The last of these is usually by far the most important because the price-earnings ratio usually has as its largest component an estimate of the trend of earnings for some years ahead.

---

[2] *Analysts Journal*, published by N. Y. Society of Security Analysts, vol. 1, no. 1 (Jan. 1945), pp. 6–14.

For our analysis the years 1926 and 1936 were chosen, because in both years national income was close to $70 billion. Net profits of 888 industrial corporations were $2.8 billion in 1926 and $2.6 billion in 1936. In 1926 the federal tax rate was 13½%, in 1936 about 17½%. Both were periods of general market optimism. While earnings and dividends here examined are for 1926 and 1936, stock prices are as of August 1927 and February 1937, as in both these months the Dow-Jones Industrial Average made a high of 190 and enough time had elapsed to gauge the previous year's results.

In two tables Mackintosh presents his data. The first deals with eleven growth stocks: Dow, Coca Cola, Air Reduction, International Business Machines, duPont, Pennsylvania Salt, Hercules Powder, Union Carbide, American Can, Allied Chemical, and Sears Roebuck. Average net earnings per share in 1926 were $4.20, in 1936, $6.65; the annual growth rate of earnings on a compound basis was 4.8 per cent. The stock price was 62 in August 1927, and 148 in February 1937, after adjustment for stock splits and stock dividends, the annual growth rate of the stock price (average) was 9.1 per cent compounded. The price-earnings ratio average was 14.8 in 1926, and 22.2 in 1936. Cash dividends in 1926 averaged $2.39 and in 1936 $4.82, after adjustments. The yield in 1926 was thus 3.9 per cent, compared with 3.3 per cent in 1936. The dividend "payout" ratio in 1926 was 57 per cent, and 73 per cent in 1936.

The second table comprised data for ten non-growth stocks: Liggett & Myers, R. J. Reynolds, Burroughs Adding Machine, American Snuff, General Electric, Corn Products, Kresge, Timken Roller Bearing, Wrigley, and Eastman Kodak. The average net earnings were $3.97 in 1926, and $3.86 in 1936. The stock price average was 69 in 1927, and 76 in 1937. The price-earnings ratio in 1926 was 17.4, and in 1936, 19.7. Cash dividends averaged $2.60 in 1926, and $3.40 in 1936. The yield was 3.8 per cent in 1926, and 4.5 per cent in 1936. The "payout" ratio was 65 per cent in 1926, and 88 per cent in 1936.

If 1936 earnings had only been equal to those of 1926 such a result would have been superior to the results achieved by 888 industrials. . . . The higher price-earnings ratio reflected mainly the better esteem in which the shares were held as a result of proven growth, and to a lesser extent to the lash of the 1936 undistributed profits tax, which forced the group to pay out 73 per cent of earnings in the form of dividends versus 57 per cent in 1926 (66 per cent in 1935). Interest rates also played a minor role in the higher 1936 valuation as Baa bonds in February 1937 were yielding 4.5 per cent, against 5.5 per cent in August 1927.

The particular statistics given have shown the clear superiority of our growth stocks over non-growth. We recognize that these selections have been made by hindsight and thus presupposed a perfect segregation of stocks between the two groups in 1926. Perfection in such a task could not be expected, but a keen security analyst should have had a fair degree of success.

Study of the foregoing statistics has led to the preparation of Table V-5, which attempts to show a reasonable valuation for secular growth earnings in an environment of good business conditions and stock market prices such as in 1926-1927 and 1936-1937. Assuming certain annual growth rates and varying proportions of earnings paid out in dividends, the table gives what may be considered as reasonable price-earnings ratios. Growth beyond 10 per cent yearly tends to be unreal and may be capitalized at a low rate. Table V-5 shows the effects of dividend stringency on price-earnings ratios especially in the case of high growth rates where the ratios decline sharply with meagre dividends.

TABLE V-5

PRICE-EARNINGS RATIOS FOR PERIODS OF OPTIMISM

Percent Div. of Earnings	Annual Secular Growth Rate -- Percent										
	0	1	2	3	4	5	6	7	8	9	10
100	16	17	18								
90	16	17	18	18	20	20					
80	15	16	17	18	20	20	22	23	25	28	30
70	14	15	16	18	20	20	21	23	25	28	30
60			15	17	18	19	20	22	24	25	26
50						17	18	19	21	22	23
40									18	19	20

Note: No ratios are supplied for low growth companies not retaining a high portion of earnings or for high growth rate companies not paying out substantially all their earnings.

For those interested in the outcome over a period of years of applying the annual growth rates in Table V-5, the following compilation has been made. At the end of five and ten-year periods, assuming growth at varying rates from 1 per cent to 10 per cent (compounded annually) earnings would be higher by the percentages in Table V-6.

To illustrate the manner in which Table V-5 may be used, the stocks of International Business Machines and Allied Chemical are selected. Suppose that the security analyst in February 1937 was bearish and had to sell one of these stocks from a portfolio. I.B.M. earnings had grown at the rate of 7.4 per cent annually and 73 per cent of earnings were being paid out in cash dividends. After careful study it might have

TABLE V-6

Annual Growth Rate Percent	Gain in 5 Years Percent	Gain in 10 Years Percent
1	5	11
2	10	22
3	16	34
4	22	48
5	28	63
6	34	79
7	40	97
8	47	116
9	54	137
10	61	159

been possible to decide that future growth would probably continue at about this rate. Under such conditions Table V-5 would indicate a price-earnings ratio of about 25 times, or much above the prevailing ratio of 17.8 times. Giving effect to stock dividends, I.B.M. stock has done much better than the general market since February, 1937, despite impairment of its foreign operations by the war and the halting of secular earnings growth by excess profits taxes.

In 1936 Allied Chemical's earnings had grown at the rate of 2.3 per cent annually and 54 per cent of earnings were being paid in dividends. Moreover this growth was not of the secular type as it had been achieved in large part through using treasury funds to purchase common stock and retire preferred. But even admitting a 2 per cent secular growth trend for the future, Allied stock, according to the table, should be selling at 15 times earnings instead of the actual 21.6 times. Allied stock has done much poorer than the market since February 1937.

To demonstrate the reasonableness of Table V-5's contents, several examples are cited. From the column on the left it may be seen that a non-growth stock paying out 100 per cent of its earnings sells for 16 times profits. Under such conditions a yield of 6.2 per cent is returned, or a fairly generous return in relation to a yield of 4 per cent to 5 per cent on Baa bonds. But this higher return is offset to some extent in the possible deterioration of earnings by reason of a full payout.

Going now to the extreme right column, a stock with a yearly growth rate of 10 per cent annually and paying out 70 per cent of earnings should sell at 30 times. Price appreciation at the end of 5 years at a 10 per cent compound rate would be 61 per cent, and would reduce the price-earnings ratio to 18.7 times on the basis of the original price.

Again in the far right column, a stock with a yearly growth rate of 10 per cent and paying only 40 per cent out in dividends would be selling at 20 times earnings. This seemingly low ratio is due to the stock price being held back by the small dividend, as even at 20 times the yield is only 2 per cent. By the end of five years this stock would be selling at 12.4 times the original price.

The price-earnings ratio table is not only useful in appraising stock prices in a period of favorable stock market conditions, but is helpful now to one who has estimated future earnings of companies in such a postwar environment. It is thus possible to translate such estimated earnings into stock prices if the analyst also estimates the outlook for earnings' growth at that time. . . . Intimate knowledge of the subject company, its industry, and of course the forces behind future growth, are vital prerequisites. To estimate the future growth rate of Union Carbide, for example, each of its five divisions (ferro-alloys, industrial gases, carbon products, chemicals, and plastics) is studied from the angle of product trends into the future, and a growth rating of a certain per cent per annum is assigned. The composite growth rate is then computed by weighting the growth rates of the subdivisions according to their proportionate contributions to earnings. This composite growth rating is then checked with past growth performance of dollars sales, unit sales, operating profit and net income; the excess of plant additions over retirements; ratio of research expenses to sales and to operating income; working capital gains and debt reduction; maintenance of profit margins; ratio of earnings to net worth, and proportion of earnings retained in the business. It is necessary to check periodically on growth by these mechanical means in order to determine whether sufficient funds are being kept in the business to permit future growth, and to be sure that retained earnings are being profitably employed. This estimation of future growth trends depends in part on mechanical methods.

Certain companies have had solid growth during the war years which has not shown in net income because of the penalizing influence of excess profits taxes. This growth will be uncovered when the excess profits tax is removed. Profits of these particular companies will then be materially higher in relation to average corporate profits than at any time in the past. It is possible that worthwhile price appreciation may lie ahead for secular growth stocks, especially since the apparent lack of growth in earnings during the war period has put many such issues in public disfavor.

Stocks with good longer-term growth prospects warrant careful consideration by all investors but have particular appeal to those in the higher tax brackets. Such investors will gain more by price appreciation than they will lose from withheld dividends and they will pay only a 25 per cent tax on capital gains, when realized, against much higher rates on the dividends they might have realized.

1. Using the data for companies included in the Appendix, work out which ones exemplify growth situations according to the methods of Mackintosh. May a firm ever change its characteristics? What factors would cause such a situation?

2. Paradiso and Hirt in an article, "Growth Trends in the Economy" (*Survey of Current Business*, January 1953, pp. 5-10), present a long list of industries and their relative growth trends in unit production from 1940 to 1951. Would you expect all companies in the growth industries to share in the industry growth? Equally? What risks are present in selecting companies in a growth industry?

3. Examine Paradiso and Hirt's article (reprinted in D. H. Bellemore's *Investments*, pp. 411-413) and select companies which have major activities in specific growth industries. Look up their earnings data in a statistical manual and comment on the relation of unit volume growth to earnings growth for the period 1940-1951. In which is the investor primarily interested?

4. Some writers on investment analysis have said that growth should be measured by (a) total payments made to the public in the form of interest and dividends, (b) the trend of a five-year moving average of net earnings available for common stock, (c) the trend of return on total invested capital, including long-term debt and senior stock issues as well as common. Test out these measuring devices on the data secured for the preceding question and comment on which most fully reflected the changes in common stock prices. Is it possible to find an infallible measure of a growth situation?

5. Comment on the disagreement of Graham and Dodd (*Security Analysis*, 3d ed., pp. 396-400 and 708-9) with the growth theory of investment and its measurement.

68.   The Undervalued Issue Approach

The undervalued issue approach to security analysis is generally opposed to both the growth and cyclical methods. Even the amateur analyst should become familiar with some of its fundamentals, although it generally can be practiced only by an experienced hand.

Graham and Dodd advocate that the security analyst will achieve more satisfactory results by confining his work to four areas:

1. The selection of standard senior issues that meet exacting tests of

safety; also the selection of standard or primary common stocks which are not selling above the range of reasonable value.

2. The discovery of senior issues that merit an investment rating but that also have opportunities of an appreciable enhancement in value.

3. The discovery of common stocks, or speculative senior issues, that appear to be selling at far less than their intrinsic value.

4. The determination of definite price discrepancies existing between related securities, which situations may justify making exchanges or initiating hedging or arbitrage operations.[1]

In each of these areas emphasis is placed on the ability of the analyst to appraise securities and recommend for purchase those whose market values are not more than their appraisal values. This approach, in effect, becomes a search for undervalued issues, and is sometimes called a "bargain-hunter" concept.

Undervalued issues, according to these authors, appear most frequently in secondary issues, those of other than leading companies in the most prominent industry groups, and are more difficult to find only as a bull market reaches toward a climax.

In addition to various other types of special situations, undervalued issues can be divided into two groups: (a) senior securities, and (b) common stocks.

Undervalued senior securities are to be found in cases of companies whose earning power is temporarily, yet considerably, impaired with consequent unfavorable price action in the senior issues as a result of discontinuance of regular payments of interest or dividends. As a specific example of such a situation, reference can be made to the bonds and preferred stock of Gotham Silk Hosiery Company from 1937 to 1940. In both cases appreciation of upwards of 50 per cent could have been achieved within the period of about a year as the market again became aware of the firm's fundamental earning power and financial condition.

Common stock prices may fall far below their intrinsic values, as determined by conservative capitalization of earnings, and even below various liquidation values, including net current asset value, for a variety of reasons. General pessimism in the securities markets, such as occurred in 1932, certainly uncovered many undervalued situations. Refer to the average monthly prices of the issues

---

[1] B. Graham and D. L. Dodd, *Security Analysis,* third edition. McGraw-Hill Book Company, 1951, p. 659.

in the Appendix, then look at the financial statements. But even under more normal circumstances some industries fall into disfavor or even disgrace with the investing public only to rise again as their earnings stability or growth become apparent once more or some dramatic event occurs. One might look for such a resurgence of values in the drug company issues as a distinct possibility, following their decline in 1951-53.

The student of market price action for individual issues can find many examples of secondary stocks which lag behind general market rises for even lengthy periods and then suddenly soar to catch up with the more prominent issues. One has only to look at the record of Climax Molybdenum during war periods as a very exaggerated instance of this type of "lag" movement. Such occurrences are often due to investor unfamiliarity with the company, its products, or its earning potentials.

As a method of evaluating common stocks to find their "intrinsic value," Graham and Dodd recommend the equation: Value equals earnings multiplier times (expected dividend plus ⅓ expected earnings) plus or minus an adjustment for asset values.[2] Dividends and earnings are to be estimated as averages for a prospective five to seven year period. The multiplier should be based on normal market price-earnings relations under moderate circumstances. "For reasons difficult to defend in detail, we favor a range from 8 to 18, with a midpoint of 13."[3] Earning power value equal to twice asset values is held allowable, but anything above this should be reduced by 25 per cent of the excess.[4] On the other hand, if earning power values fall below net current asset values, they well may be raised to the latter figure.[5]

1. As an example of an undervalued stock, Graham and Dodd cite Bond Stores in 1949. Comment on the effectiveness of this appraisal, using the price ranges for 1950–52.
2. What reliance can the investor have that the market will recognize an undervalued security issue? When? Can a cyclical investment theory be used employing undervalued issues?

---

2 *Op. cit.,* p. 410, 454.
3 *Ibid.,* p. 458.
4 *Ibid.,* p. 482.
5 *Ibid.,* p. 485.

3. Trace the records of S. S. White Dental Supply Co. and of Philadelphia and Reading Coal and Iron Co. common stocks. Were or are these issues undervalued since 1948? Did they recover their full values?

4. Do you believe secondary issues include all obscure or small companies or can they be found in the less prominent, but large firms in most industries?

69. Comparative Analysis of Industrial Stocks

This problem states the methods employed by an institutional investment agency for comparing stocks in different industrial groupings. Since such comparisons are always desirable for the individual investor as well, the rationale warrants study.

The investment committee of a large institution employs a full-time counsel to aid them in the selection of securities for a sizable portfolio. Both bonds and stocks are included in the portfolio. Bonds are chosen according to statistical rating services. Preferred stocks of only the highest grade are considered. Since an important proportion of the fund can be invested in common stocks, the investment committee is quite properly concerned about the long-range prospects of equities.

To assist the committee in their selection of common stock issues, the counsel was asked to devise a statistical tabulation system by which intercompany and interindustry comparisons would be facilitated. The objective was to avoid industry prejudices which various members of the committee might have, and to present objectively data which could be used to attain the purposes of the portfolio, growth and income. Liquidity was to be achieved through investing only in issues which were listed on the New York Stock Exchange or the American Stock Exchange. Some stability of prices during cyclical swings could thus be established, according to the committee, through switching at proper intervals. Since the committee would meet monthly, it was felt desirable that the statistical tabulations be available at least quarterly, and more frequently if possible.

The counsel accordingly devised the following criteria for selection of securities. For each of the 29 criteria the medians of the arrayed data on all companies on the approved list of qualified common stocks for investment were computed. In general, one point was given to a security if its particular ratio were better than the median. Exceptions to this rule are noted in the tabulations.

Criteria for Investment of Fund

A. Balance sheet ratios:
  1. Funded debt, ten years ago. (Point only if none.)
  2. Funded debt, current year. (Point only if none.)
  3. Increase in total invested capital, last ten years.
  4. Increase in common equity, last ten years.
  5. Equity to total invested capital, current year.
  6. Increase in fixed assets, last ten years.
  7. Increase in net working capital, last ten years.
B. Income statement ratios:
  1. Operating profit margin, current year.
  2. Depreciation to sales, current year.
  3. Net income after taxes to sales, current year.
  4. Depreciation and net income to sales, current year.
  5. Net earned on net worth, current year.
  6. Net income to sales, ten year average.
  7. Net earned on net worth, ten year average.
  8. Net earned on total invested funds, ten year average.
C. Historical: Decrease from 1946-47 to lower of 1948 or 1949 in:
  1. Sales.
  2. Earnings.
  3. Dividends.
D. Growth over the last ten years (percent):
  1. Sales.
  2. Earnings.
  3. Dividends.
  4. Earnings per share.
  5. Dividends per share.
E. Dividends:
  1. Average payout percentage, ten years.
  2. Payout percentage, current year.
F. Prices:
  1. 1946-1947 high to current year high.
  2. Change over last five years.
G. Prospects for next year:
  1. Earnings compared to ten year average per share.
  2. Dividends compared to ten year average per share.

Of the ratios and percentages, seven were given double weight: A5, B6, C2, D2, D4, D5, and G1. The optimum number of credit points would thus total 36. The counsel determined that a score of 24 or better would be desirable to indicate potential purchases, while a score of 12 or less would indicate a potential sale.

1. State what each of the criteria was intended to measure. How did this contribute toward attaining the fund objectives of growth and income?

2. Would the use of medians as standards be dependent on the choice of companies and industries included in the list of qualified companies? How would you select companies for the qualified list to be subjected to analysis? Would it help to start with an array of industries, and a selection of above-average companies in above-average industries? What criteria of measuring "above-average" would you use?

3. Would this type of analysis be satisfactory for a fund which is to be adjusted cyclically? Is it satisfactory for a growth fund that is not to be adjusted cyclically? Or is it aimed more fundamentally toward a fund that desires income?

70. Comparative Analyses of Industrial Securities

This intermediate-level problem involves the use of data for two firms which are relatively closely allied, and brings into focus the relation of firm data to industry statistics as well as introducing the need for thorough analysis to find differences in earning and financial power.

The security analyst is usually asked to state a preference of one issue in an industry over all others, or to select the best of a group. This type of request often poses the question of digging into the data very closely to find the differences between firms as to their earning power and their financial strength, as well as setting out comparisons with industry averages.

The Appendix to this volume presents financial and price data for two firms in each of the following industry groups: chemicals, automobiles, steel and iron, foods, and textiles. The data were taken from *Moody's Industrials* and Standard and Poor's *Standard Corporation Records*. The data prior to 1934 reflect the annual reports of the firms and are relatively incomplete. Since 1934, however, the data are generally taken from the company reports to the Securities and Exchange Commission. The tabulations presented in the Appendix are abbreviated for convenience purposes and include most of the basic materials necessary for this type of comparative analysis.

1. Select one of the industries represented in the Appendix data and secure from various appropriate sources industry data needed to make company comparisons with industry. Then write a 250 word report on the industry economics.
2. Relate such items as earning power, sales, and prices to the industry data. Add a 100 word summary comparison of the two companies to the industry.
3. Calculate appropriate ratios and trend data, as well as other financial measures, which appear to show why one firm has a better earning power than the other. Using particularly a comparison of the 1935–1939 period with the 1946–1950 period, write a summary report of no more than 200 words telling why one company should do better than another in earning power over the next cycle.
4. Relate the earning power, financial strength, and dividend policy to the current market prices of the issues and select the one which appears to have the greater longer term merit. Be sure to tell, in no more than 150 words, whether you would select the particular issue (perhaps other than common stock) for income, for growth, or as an undervalued issue.

71. Analysis of a Merchandising Firm

One of the basic difficulties to proper analysis of merchandising securities is taken up in this problem.

Security analysts find that the problems involved in treating merchandising firms are not difficult nor are the methods far from those applicable to the analysis of manufacturing firms. True, the relative importance of current assets, particularly inventory and receivables, is greater, while the reliance on long-term debt is smaller.

The chief problems in analysis of merchandising firms, particularly those engaged in chain operations, are those of securing comparability of data over a period of time, and of getting proper inter-company comparisons of earning power.

Chain stores are constantly changing their number of stores, so it often becomes desirable to place both sales and operating income on a per store basis. In this way some ideas as to the relative growth of sales can be derived. For inter-company comparisons, however, the analyst must remember that stores need not cater to a general clientele; some deal principally with high income groups, others are specialty shops, and so on.

Another distortion of intercompany figures arises from the rental of premises by some firms while others tend to own their stores. It has been suggested that rentals be capitalized at a 5 per cent rate to give an equivalent asset value. Yet this does not take into consideration the problem of depreciating this equivalent asset value. Most rentals are on a net basis, with the tenant paying for maintenance, cost of operations, and taxes, in addition to a fixed payment to the owner. This rough adjustment can deal unfairly with firms, since it assumes no depreciation to the rented property occurs over the life of the lease. If a depreciation charge equal to half of the rental be included, a better basis for comparison might be possible.

1. Federated Department Stores, Inc. owns some of its principal stores and leases the rest under fairly long leases, whereas both Gimbel Brothers, Inc., and R. H. Macy & Company own their stores. Food Fair Stores, Inc. owns about one-third of its food stores, while Grand Union Company leases all of its food centers. Sears Roebuck & Company owned its stores for many years, but in the past decade or more has sold them under a "lease-back" arrangement; Montgomery Ward & Co. has operated on a lease basis. Compare the net profit margins and net

earned on invested capital for one of the above pairings, making sure to secure comparability to validate any conclusions as to relative earning power.

2. Compare the sales and net earnings of Great Atlantic & Pacific Tea Company, Kroger Company, Jewel Tea Company, Inc. (beware of the added sales source, here), and Safeway Stores, Inc., on a per store basis since 1945. Since Jewel and Safeway operate on a flat annual rental with a long-term lease, while A & P and Kroger favor short-term leases with renewal options, is there any inherent source of difficulty in times of depression? In times of inflation? Does this show up in the comparisons you make?

72. Analysis of Public Utility Bonds

The following short problem is interesting in presenting a challenge to standard methods of analyzing public utility bonds.

The usual standard ratios for analysis of public utility bonds are: (1) the ratio of debt principal value to the property securing the debt, and (2) the ratio of annual debt service requirements in the form of interest, discount amortization (if any), and sinking fund requirements to net earnings available for such charges.

C. Tatham, Jr., a New York security analyst, challenged these ratios and proposed that the ratio of debt service to the minimum property values of the company for rate-making purposes be used instead of the first of the standard ratios listed above.[1] His argument was that the proposed ratio was of particular value when it is advisable to relate gross income to the rate-making base. The new ratio would, in effect, measure the effect of operating costs and depreciation on the ability of the utility to meet its charges.

His second proposal was for an adjusted margin of safety, in which

---

[1] Charles Tatham, Jr., "Two Useful Ratios in Public Utility Bond Analysis," *The Analysts Journal*, published by the N. Y. Society of Security Analysts, vol. 1 (April, 1945), pp. 29–32.

net income after charges but before Federal taxes would be divided by operating revenues. This ratio would measure the amount of decline in operating revenues that could be withstood without danger to the payment of the charges.

1. Compute the standard and proposed ratios for two or more selected large public utility operating companies for the years 1937, 1940, 1945, 1948, and 1951. Do the proposals appear to have merit? Would you agree to displace the standard ratios with the new suggestions? Why?

73. Public Utility Securities and Depression

In view of the widespread opinion that public utilities securities are a depression-proof type of investment, this problem offers considerable material for thought by analysts and investors generally.

The electric utility industry is no longer depression proof, but could be vulnerable should a recession come along in a few years. This was indicated by Herbert J. Flagg, executive officer of the New Jersey Board of Public Utility Commissioners in a talk before the New York Society of Security Analysts.[1]

Mr. Flagg stated that the time has come for utility management in the interest of both customers and the industry, to meet new conditions by establishing realistic load factor type rates for residence service. In the alternative, a partial solution would be to increase the initial charge and the price for the first one or two blocks of the residential rate schedule in order to compensate more adequately for sharply increased customer and peak demand costs.

If this country has a recession, he pointed out, the portion of electric sales to be first and most drastically affected will be sales to the industrial power class. Experience also shows that while kilowatt-hour sales will go down, the kilowatt peak demand may go up.

The result, he stated, would be that the insufficient revenue from the under-priced demand (residential) portion of the service would

---

[1] *Journal of Commerce,* April 2, 1953, p. 4.

remain the same, but the more than sufficient revenue from the over-priced commodity (industrial) portion may be cut down by one-third or more.

It is obvious that the operating income from industrial sales will be reduced by a vastly greater percentage than the percent reduction in the operating revenue. Since in these days this class of service makes a relatively large contribution to utility operating income, it follows that any material decrease in such contribution will have a serious effect when carried down to net income.

He pointed out that in 1930 the operating income of the electric industry was about 65 per cent from residential sales and 35 per cent from industrial and commercial sales. When the depression was deepest about 50 per cent of the operating income from vulnerable sales had been lost but the over-all operating income that had been equivalent to an 8 per cent return on investment in 1930 was only reduced to about 7 per cent in 1934.

The percentages are reversed today, he said, and not less than 65 per cent of operating income is derived from vulnerable sales. Should the industry lose only 40 per cent of operating income from vulnerable sales in the event of recession in a few years, the rate of return would drop from 6 per cent to 3.7 per cent.

Assuming that the national average incremental revenue per kilowatt hour of consumption attributable to television does not exceed 2.5¢, Mr. Flagg computed that the average annual revenue per TV set is $6.25. This equates to an average annual operating revenue of $24.80 per kilowatt of diversified demand at the genera-tor.

This was contrasted to present revenue from the residential class of $80–$100 per kilowatt year. Even during the late depression the residential class was producing operating revenue of $120–$140 per kilowatt year of diversified demand.

The annual load factor of the TV load was estimated at probably not more than 12 per cent, and described as a dilution when com-pared with the recognized annual load factor of the residential class in the years before TV of 35 to 40 per cent.

At this point we should consider what it costs the industry to serve this load that produces a revenue of only $6.25 per year. A nominal estimate of additional plant investment responsibility is $64 for each

TV set. Five per cent rate of return on this investment would be $3.20. But it takes about $1.70 of operating revenue to produce $1 of operating income after taxes, allowable deductions, and so on. So the first $5.44 of TV revenue must be earmarked for a 5 per cent return on the $64 of additional investment responsibility. That leaves only 81¢ to offset the costs of operation and maintenance which are estimated to aggregate more than $7.

1. For a selected group of electric light and power companies, examine the decline in operating revenues experienced in the 1929–1932 period and in the 1937–1938 period, with separate data for residential and industrial and commercial classifications. Applying the percentages of decline to the revenues of the current year, what overall decline in operating revenues do you find possible? What would this mean to the net earnings of the various companies?

2. It has long been held that utility service charges decline with costs of raw materials, thus leading to reductions in rates. If Mr. Flagg's analysis is correct, what could be the prospects for residential service charges in the event of a recession of some size? What effect would this have on electric utility securities prices?

74. Detailed Analysis of an Electric Utility Company

This problem presents the data for detailed analysis of a well-known electric light and power company on a relatively thorough basis.

1. Compute the following measures: Times charges earned before taxes, times charges earned after taxes, times charges and preferred dividends earned after taxes, earned per share common, per cent of total capitalization, per cent debt of net plant, gross plant to gross revenues, per cent depreciation reserve of gross plant. How useful are these measures in analysis of the issues?

2. What rating would you give to the bonds? To the preferred stock? To the common stock?

TABLE V-7
MILLVILLE ELECTRIC LIGHT COMPANY
(All figures in millions)

Comparative Balance Sheets, 1948-1952

	1948	1949	1950	1951	1952
Assets:					
Electric plant	$45.62	$52.26	$56.80	$59.56	$64.08
Investment and funds	2.43	2.43	2.28	2.43	2.57
Cash items	5.76	9.24	4.79	1.52	9.11
Receivables	1.26	1.20	1.51	1.65	1.80
Materials & supplies	4.03	2.62	3.43	3.49	3.77
Other charges and accruals	0.08	0.07	0.07	0.03	0.38
Miscellaneous debits	0.12	0.10	0.21	0.14	0.11
Total	59.30	67.93	69.10	69.81	81.82
Liabilities & Capital:					
3.90% preferred ($50 par) .	---	8.00	8.00	8.00	8.00
Common stocks	21.00	21.10	21.10	21.10	21.10
Long term debt	18.20	18.02	17.85	17.67	27.24
Current liabilities	3.05	2.99	3.53	3.72	4.85
Deferred credits	---	---	---	---	0.16
Reserve for depreciation . .	11.12	11.46	12.08	12.70	13.80
Contribution for extension .	0.11	0.12	0.12	0.12	0.14
Earned surplus	5.79	6.20	6.39	6.47	6.52
Total	59.30	67.93	69.10	69.81	81.82

TABLE V-7 (Continued)
COMPARATIVE INCOME ACCOUNTS, 1948-1952

	1948	1949	1950	1951	1952
Total operating revenues	$16.36	$16.29	$16.71	$17.89	$19.37
Operating expenses	10.28	9.34	9.01	9.23	10.09
Maintenance.	0.73	0.84	0.80	0.95	1.08
Depreciation	0.24	0.86	0.94	0.97	1.30
Taxes, state & local	1.19	1.30	1.48	1.74	1.46
Federal income taxes	1.03	1.21	1.44	1.95	2.41
Total operating revenue deductions.	13.47	13.56	13.67	14.85	16.35
Net operating income	2.89	2.73	3.04	3.05	3.02
Other income	0.25	0.18	0.20	0.17	0.15
Gross income	3.14	2.91	3.24	3.22	3.18
Interest on long-term debt	0.51	0.51	0.50	0.50	0.50
Other interest.	---	---	---	---	0.03
Interest charged to construction (credit)	0.04	0.08	0.08	---	0.04
Total income deductions	0.48	0.44	0.43	0.50	0.49
Net income	2.65	2.48	2.81	2.71	2.68
Preferred dividends	---	0.06	0.31	0.31	0.31
Common dividends	2.30	2.31	2.32	2.32	2.32
Operating Statistics: Customers: (thousands)					
Residential	73.4	76.1	78.4	81.5	84.0
Commercial & industrial	11.6	12.0	12.5	12.7	13.0
Total (average).	84.9	88.0	90.9	94.2	97.0
Kwh. sales: (millions)					
Residential	136	147	165	183	206
Commercial & industrial	374	377	428	511	526
Other	512	553	480	330	335
Total	1,022	1,077	1,073	1,023	1,066
Revenues: (millions)					
Residential	$ 3.91	$ 4.20	$ 4.46	$ 4.84	$ 5.38
Commercial & industrial	7.82	7.95	8.33	9.43	10.04
Other	4.61	4.12	3.90	3.59	3.91
Total	16.34	16.27	16.69	17.86	19.33
Kwh. generated: (millions)					
Steam	1048	1113	1105	1200	1170
Hydro	8	8	9	10	10
Purchased.	9	3	8	5	5
Interchanges	--	--	--	6	22
System output.	1065	1124	1121	1221	1207
Peak load	0.183	0.192	0.227	0.230	0.267

TABLE V-7

	1948	1949	1950	1951	1952
Residential sale, percent total.	13.3%	13.7%	15.3%	17.9%	19.3%
Residential revenues, percent total	23.9%	25.8%	26.7%	27.1%	27.8%
Residential avg. rate per Kwh.	2.9¢	2.9¢	2.7¢	2.6¢	2.6¢
Residential average customer use, Kwh. .	1,860	1,935	2,099	2,248	2,447
Income Accounts:					
Percent depreciation to gross rev.	3.4%	5.3%	5.6%	5.4%	6.7%
Percent maintenance to gross rev.	4.5%	5.2%	4.8%	5.3%	5.6%
Percent depreciation to plant	1.23%	1.85%	1.65%	1.63%	2.0%
Operating ratio	76.0%	75.8%	73.2%	72.1%	72.0%
Preferred shares (thousand).	---	160	160	160	160
Common shares (thousand)	840	844	844	844	844
Financial Statistics:					
Price Ranges:					
Debenture 3-1/4s, 1971	105	105	108	106 1/4	106 3/4
	100	103	104	103	106
$3.90 preferred	---	51 3/4	53 3/8	53 1/4	49
	---	50	51 1/4	44	45 1/2
Common	56 3/4	50 1/4	53 1/2	49 1/4	53 3/4
	46	44 5/8	44 1/2	44 7/8	45 7/8

75.   Management Efficiency in Railroads

This problem presents the view of one of the foremost analysts. of railroad securities on a topic of vital interest to all investors. The comments on statistical measures is critical.

David A. Hill, one of the leading American analysts of railroads, participated in an investment seminar as part of the American Life

Convention, held in association with the University of Chicago School of Business, June 27, 1950.[1]

Management is a prime factor in the consideration of railway securities. Management is more important in the consideration of short term bonds than those due 40 to 50 years from now.

Of course, a road that has very able management at present will have to build up an organization that can carry on for some time after its president has retired, but long before 30 or 50 years have elapsed, its management may have degenerated and its competitors may then have aggressive leadership.

He suggested that if a particular road has superior management at present, it is well to decide whether its competitors are weak in that respect. "I raise that point, because I often wonder what would happen to the earning power of this railway or that, if its greatest competitor had a change in the operating head, resulting in severe competition not existing at the moment."

Discussing yardsticks for management efficiency, Hill listed the transportation ratio, the wage ratio, gross tons a train mile, and gross ton miles a train hour. The operating ratio is outmoded, he said, because it contains the maintenance ratio, which must be adjusted for possible distortion from 'skimping or splurging' in maintenance.

Gross ton miles a train hour is used widely, Hill said, but "in my opinion, is not as important as gross tons a train mile." He pointed out that the former contains the element of speed, which reflects good service, "but may or may not put money in the bank, depending largely on whether the train arrives at the terminal in time to save per diem, or perhaps the superior service may attract or retain some tonnage that would be lost under slower service."

It is "gross tons a train mile that rings the cash register," Hill declared, adding, "The objective of a good operator is to haul more ton miles with fewer train miles. If that cannot be done, the next best thing is to haul more ton miles with the same train miles, or if tonnage is not available, to haul the same tonnage, or even less, with decidedly fewer train miles. If you can combine these advantages and haul more ton miles with fewer train miles and do it faster, fine. But do not sacrifice tons a train mile for speed."

---

[1] *Chicago Journal of Commerce*, June 28, 1950.

Wage ratio is also important in this day of rising costs. "Any railway that can keep its wage ratio under control in years when wages are being increased obviously does have alert management, which has been mechanizing operations and using modern technique. But before we can lean on that for comfort we should separate wages spent on maintenance from total wage cost, for it is possible to keep the wage ratio under control by laying off maintenance gangs, closing down the shops, or postponing the painting of bridges and other structures. Unless you are prepared to make extensive statistical studies, or perhaps go out in the field and make personal inspection of the properties, the ratio of all wages to railway operating revenue is not dependable by itself. Moreover, one inspection of the property may mislead, unless you have some idea of its standards a few years before."

Hill placed the transportation ratio at the head of the list as the best single index of efficiency. It is little affected by maintenance policy. This ratio is the actual portion of the revenue dollar required to move passenger and freight traffic.

1. Define and describe the ratios mentioned by Mr. Hill.
2. Why were passenger service ratios not considered of major significance? What other ratios are used to appraise this type of service? What other services are omitted from this analysis?
3. What type of investor is able to make a physical check of the rail properties? Is this necessary for the individual investor?

76.   Yardsticks for Rating Railroad Bonds

The problem of rating bonds is one which confronts all investors, particularly those for whom fixed-interest obligations are an important part of the portfolio. Because of the unsatisfactory rating experience for railroad bonds during the 1930's, this problem presents a number of alternative solutions to the methods usually employed.

Railroad bonds have been accorded a favored position in the portfolios of mutual savings banks, insurance companies, and trusts for many years. It was only natural that states should legislate definite minimum standards of quality to be maintained by a rail bond in order to remain eligible for institutional investment. Experience with rigid standards during the depression years 1931–1934 was not satisfactory; many important and large bond issues were removed from the list of eligible securities because earnings fell or disappeared for a consecutive number of years. As a result the application of the statutes governing investment were suspended for a number of years by important states.

Attempts to remedy the situation were assayed many times. A thorough restudy of the problem of rating bonds was undertaken in New York. Other states approached the problem somewhat differently. New Jersey in 1946 adopted a new test for making railroad bonds legal for savings bank investment. Instead of requiring specified coverage of fixed charges, the new law permitted the purchase of rail bonds when reported fixed charge coverage was better than the average for the country over a three year period. In addition, a requirement was made that the percentage of operating revenue remaining after payment of fixed charges be greater than the national average for Class I roads.[1] This yardstick in effect merely compared individual roads with the national average for Class I rails with regard to fixed charge coverage and "safety factor."

The results of these tests are open to question on several scores. The effect of a large road having little funded debt, such as the Norfolk and Western, might cause sizeable unbalance in the national average. The term "average" may be taken to indicate either an arithmetic mean or a median. The safety factor may be large only as a result of favorable refunding of debt during the 1940's. These are merely a sample of criticisms that might be leveled against the New Jersey standards.

A second approach was made by Massachusetts in 1948. Abandoning its traditional prudent man approach, the Bay State radically revised its law governing savings bank investment to permit holding of bonds of railroads with better than average earnings under all types of business conditions. George M. Grinnell of a

---

[1] *Journal of Commerce,* May 8, 1946.

New York bond house developed a formula for the legislature under which only the bonds of those companies with a gross revenue of at least one-quarter of 1 per cent of the combined gross revenues of all Class I carriers could qualify under the new law. Furthermore, the portion of a road's revenue after paying fixed charges must be above the average, and the company must earn its fixed charges by at least as many times as the average of all Class I rails. The last provision carried a proviso that fixed charges must in all cases be earned at least one and a quarter times, even if the Class I average falls below that. [2]

Massachusetts thus adopted the New Jersey law in its substance, adding minimum size requirements and a rigid minimum coverage requirement. The common criticism for both laws might be that the appraisals could not be made until some time after all financial reports on Class I roads were made to the ICC and to the public. Little could be done until some time after the damage had been wrought. The yardsticks, however good, were not sensitive enough.

J. Walter Leason proposed an entirely new system of rating railroad bonds under a "Prior Lien Method of Rating Railroad Bonds." He noted the criticisms that gradations in quality are not sufficiently precise, that ratings are not reviewed often enough, that changes in ratings are slow to be made by rating agencies. He believed that under ideal conditions a rating system would change credit evaluations at relatively short intervals, preferably monthly, to show such changes in a numerical form. The necessary data for such a system would be available from the standardized monthly reports of earnings and working capital position required of the roads by the ICC. These could be used to give effect to the relative rank of each layer of debt, the relative amount outstanding and the relative interest charges applicable to each issue.

He defined his method as one "whereby a new numerical rating (with 100 as theoretical perfection) is given each month to individual railroad bond issues on the basis of the relative priority of the mortgage position in the case of blanket mortgages, cumulatively adding all prior liens and prior charges. In the case of divisional and leased line obligations, the same procedure is followed after

---

[2] *Ibid.*, April 16, 1948.

making studies segregating both revenues and earnings of the system. These basic figures are then related to selected performance ratios using present capitalization, historical and latest twelve months revenues and earnings (before income taxes), and the latest working capital position, each ratio being weighted proportionately with uniform standards, the total of the weighted component ratios each month being the numerical credit rating." [3]

Seven ratios were selected to determine the rating of a bond. The ratios and the weights assigned each are:

1. ten-year average fixed charge coverage, 10 points;
2. ten-year average margin of safety, 20 points;
3. latest 12-month fixed charge coverage, 10 points;
4. latest 12-month margin of safety, 20 points;
5. net liquid assets to debt, 15 points;
6. operating revenues to debt, 10 points;
7. transportation ratio, 15 points.

1. What are the difficulties attendant to revising standards of legal investment?
2. Should a standard rating measure for bonds be sensitive to changes in earnings, as Leason suggests? What logical difficulties arise from the use of an industry average as a standard?
3. Could measures as suggested above be found applicable to utility bonds? To industrial bonds?

77.   Detailed Analysis of a Railroad

The wealth of materials available for analysis of railroad securities is well illustrated in this problem.

The following information is available for analysis of the securities of the Oklahio Railway Company. You are asked to prepare a report commenting on the quality of the bonds, preferred stock and common stock, as of early 1953.

---

[3] *Ibid.*, August 9, 1949.

TABLE V-8
OKLAHIO RAILWAY COMPANY
(All figures in millions)

Balance Sheet Comparisons

	1948	1949	1950	1951	1952
Assets:					
Investment:					
Road.	$375.3	$377.2	$386.5	$387.3	$391.8
Equipment.	191.4	213.5	210.4	234.9	226.5
Other Investments (net).	16.7	19.5	23.2	23.4	47.4
Current Assets:					
Cash items	63.6	47.2	53.3	55.9	79.6
Other	35.5	29.4	40.0	43.8	41.8
Deferred Assets	1.3	2.1	3.0	1.8	1.7
Unadjusted debits.	3.9	3.7	3.8	2.6	3.0
Total.	687.7	692.6	720.2	749.7	791.8
Liabilities and Net Worth:					
Preferred Stock, 5% ($50 par) . . .	60.0	60.0	60.0	60.0	60.0
Common Stock (no par)	129.8	129.8	129.8	129.8	129.8
Funded Debt	194.7	194.3	192.6	188.4	188.2
Equipment Obligations	47.4	58.2	48.9	68.0	86.4
Due affiliated companies.	0.6	0.6	0.6	0.6	---
Current liabilities	57.9	51.4	73.4	75.3	80.3
Deferred liabilities.	3.6	3.6	3.5	3.3	4.5
Unadjusted credits	13.1	12.9	14.4	17.6	16.0
Surplus	180.7	181.8	197.1	206.8	226.6
Total.	687.7	692.6	720.2	749.7	791.8

Income Account Comparisons

	1948	1949	1950	1951	1952
Operating Revenues:					
Freight.	$207.3	$178.6	$201.9	$221.1	$230.7
Other	37.7	34.2	38.0	41.2	40.9
Railway operating revenues	245.0	212.8	239.9	262.3	271.6
Operating Expenses:					
Maintenance of way & structure. .	33.1	30.6	30.5	36.6	34.5
Maintenance of equipment.	43.2	40.8	42.2	49.4	48.6
Traffic.	4.2	4.2	4.2	4.8	5.2
Transportation.	94.7	81.6	82.4	90.7	88.7
Misc. & general	9.5	9.2	9.3	10.4	2.6
Railway operating expenses	184.6	166.4	168.6	192.0	188.1
Net railway operating revenue. . . .	60.4	46.3	71.3	70.3	83.5
Federal income taxes	12.8	8.1	20.2	20.6	26.8
Other taxes.	14.9	14.0	14.9	15.3	16.5
Railway operating income	32.7	24.2	36.2	34.5	40.2
Net equipment & joint facility					
rentals (dr.).	3.5	2.3	4.3	6.5	3.8
Net railway operating income	29.1	21.9	31.9	27.9	36.4
Other income.	3.1	3.3	3.5	3.9	4.7
Gross income	32.3	25.2	35.5	31.9	41.1
Miscellaneous deductions	0.3	0.3	0.3	0.4	0.3
Available for fixed charges	32.0	24.9	35.2	31.5	40.8
Rents of leased roads	2.3	2.2	2.0	2.0	2.0
Interest on funded debt	10.4	10.7	10.7	10.6	11.0
Other fixed charges	---	0.1	0.1	---	---
Net income.	19.2	11.9	22.4	18.9	27.8
Preferred dividends	3.0	3.0	3.0	3.0	3.0
Common dividends	5.2	1.0	1.3	1.3	5.5
Balance to surplus	11.1	7.9	18.1	14.6	19.0
Maintenance:					
Way & structure.	30.6	28.1	27.9	34.0	31.8
Equipment	37.2	33.2	34.3	41.3	39.5
Total	67.8	61.3	62.2	75.3	71.3
Depreciation:					
Way & structure.	2.5	2.5	2.6	2.6	2.7
Equipment	6.0	7.6	8.0	8.2	9.1
Total	8.5	10.1	10.6	10.8	11.8

<u>Operating Statistics Comparisons</u>

	1948	1949	1950	1951	1952
Miles operated.	6,466	6,324	6,346	6,332	6,305
Average haul.	209	215	215	215	210
Revenue freight density (thous.) . .	2,132	1,800	2,053	2,203	2,144
Avg. Rev. Frt. Train Loan (tons) . .	705	780	894	969	1,041
Train mile earnings	$ 8.12	$ 8.57	$ 9.83	$10.72	$12.02
Avg. revenue per ton-mile (cents) .	1.50	1.59	1.55	1.59	1.71
Gross ton-miles per train-mile . .	1,739	1,965	2,124	2,227	2,376
Net ton-miles per train-mile . .	788	848	957	1,028	1,092
Gross ton-miles per train-hour . .	29.6M	34.1M	35.8M	37.3M	40.5M
Operating ratio	75.35%	78.22%	70.26%	73.19%	69.25%
Operating ratio, freight	67.3	68.2	61.9	64.6	60.3
Operating ratio, passenger	125.6	137.6	120.4	126.6	126.6
Wages (millions).	$120.6	$110.1	$113.2	$127.6	$126.6
Freight revenues: (percent of total)					
Agriculture	11.3%	12.9%	11.6%	11.4%	11.1%
Animals	1.9	2.2	1.7	1.5	1.5
Mines	20.5	18.7	21.1	20.9	20.6
Forests	8.5	8.0	8.7	8.7	8.0
Manufactures & miscellaneous . .	44.7	47.0	47.5	49.1	50.5
L. C. L.	13.1	11.2	9.4	8.4	8.3

78. A Commentary on Municipal Bond Analysis

This problem takes up the analysis of municipal credit in the light of changing conditions that may make ineffective the standard, established types of analysis.

The Guaranty Trust Co. of New York, in its monthly "Survey" for January 1949, takes up the problem of methods of appraisal and selection in municipal securities.[1] Quite different methods are held necessary because of broad changes that have occurred to the pre-war composition of municipal revenues.

In the first place, the ratio of current tax collections to the total real estate tax levy, a long-established yardstick for credit appraisal

---

[1] *Journal of Commerce*, Dec. 30, 1948.

of a municipality, may not be reliable as a criterion of the over-all financial operations of the unit. Property tax revenues now produce, on the whole, considerably less than half of the total income needed to balance budgets, against over 80 per cent of municipal revenues two decades ago.

Revenue accounts, therefore, must now be scrutinized more critically than heretofore with a view to ascertaining the degree of dependence on various tax sources that are liable to be affected quickly by adverse economic trends. This dependence is difficult to measure precisely but may be roughly gauged by the ratio of property taxation to total revenue.

Second, the changed composition of municipal revenues has made it necessary also to revise established ideas as to what constitutes a supportable ratio between funded debt and assessed valuations. Because this ratio formerly stated the debt burden in terms of available income with reasonable accuracy, it was of considerable importance. Now it is less reliable, since it gives no consideration to the large amounts of new revenue that often supplements the property tax levy. A more accurate gauge under present conditions would be "the ratio of interest and amortization requirements to the total revenues available to meet them."

Municipalities have been forced to turn to new sources of revenue because of the prolonged period of inflation in wages and materials costs and in striving for these new revenues they have had to cope with the general apathy of the average municipal citizen toward its affairs. To overcome this hurdle the cities have begun public education programs in co-operation with influential groups. But the record indicates that until a new tax has survived the initial period of strong opposition it usually meets, such new taxes may be in some peril. This is particularly true of municipal sales tax levies that are intended to secure a major portion of revenues.

The amount of debt per capita is a third credit indicator that needs re-examination. Under present conditions total municipal revenue per capita, "considered in connection with the amount of debt per capita, provides a more significant measure of the debt burden than the per capita debt figure alone."

1. Where would you be able to secure data on the personal income of a municipality with which to measure ability to pay? Would this be a good measure in all cases?
2. Are the points discussed above of importance in the analysis of general obligations or revenue bonds? Why must a distinction be made?

79. Analysis of Municipal Securities

*This introductory problem to a most sophisticated area of invest-
ment is intended to point out some of the facets that must be in-
vestigated rather than give a detailed methodology.*

"There is no easy, infallible method of evaluating the credit
rating of individuals, corporations, or municipalities," states one
of the best introductory studies in municipal securities.[1] A municipality's ability to pay depends on a combination of economic, geo-
graphic, financial, legal, and moral factors. Yet a debtor usually
pays if it is able to do so.

Since there are two principal types of municipal security, there
must be two types of analysis, one for general obligations, one for
revenue bonds. The third type of municipal, guaranteed revenue
bond, requires the use of both types of analysis.

Over half of all State and municipal bonds are general obligations
of the issuer backed by the full faith and credit of the borrower.
The borrowing community pledges its tax and all other revenues
to the payment of principal and interest. Doubts about the borrower's ability to meet its obligation generally result in higher yields
to investors, rather than any real loss. Few municipalities have
ever defaulted on their debts, although some have been forced to
secure debt readjustments with bondholders. This has generally
occurred in one-industry towns, or communities dependent on
resorts or an extractive industry. In all cases, the constitutional
limits set by the state or municipality on the amount of debt which
may be incurred or the taxes which may be levied is a controlling
factor. Any extraordinary outlays might hazard the borrower's
ability to pay.

Commentary might be made on the usual measures of analysis.
One-industry towns are not necessarily bad, particularly if the industry is large, financially sound, and performing an essential service. It is important to know who pays the taxes, and their financial
status, rather than who does not pay taxes. Municipal debt ratios

---

[1] John Nuveen & Co., ". . . Of the People, By the People, for the People,"
Chicago, 1949, p. 86.

and per capita debt ratios are important when viewed in the light of trends. In particular, population trends are important, since census data are available only at ten year intervals.

The usual measures of ability to pay have been summarized in a recent text: ratio of net debt to assessed value, net debt per capita, debt service requirements, trend of debt and debt retirement policy, limitations of debt and tax rate, the actual tax rate, the tax collection record, general economic factors, and the character of public administration.[2] A longer list is available in *Fundamentals of Investment Banking*.[3]

Turning to revenue bonds, a recent article in the *Journal of Commerce* fairly summarizes the importance, types, and methods of analysis of municipal revenue bonds.[4]

One of the most spectacular developments in the municipal bond field in the last decade or two is the way in which revenue bond financing by State and local governments, and especially by public authorities, has increased. In 1940, only about 12.5 per cent of all new municipal bonds were dependent for their security on the revenues of the properties against which they were issued, but by 1946, 17 per cent of all municipal offerings were revenue bonds, and by 1951, the proportion increased to 22 per cent, while the volume was more than treble that of 1946.

In 1952, the upward swing became very pronounced, and volume was about double that of 1951, with $1,463,350,500, or 33.2 per cent of all new municipal bonds offered during the year, being secured by revenues from turnpikes, utility systems, and other revenue-producing properties. During 1953, offerings during the first eight months were below those for the corresponding period of 1952, being $786,979,570 as compared to $1,015,872,500. However, by late September, the volume had climbed to $809,730,000, $165,760,000 more were on the calendar for the months ahead, and another $708,228,000 of prospective issues had been authorized and could possibly come out before the end of the year, thus making a potential year's total of over $1,683,718,000, more than were offered during 1952, and once again about a third of the year's total of municipal offerings.

Plainly, here, as with municipal bonds generally, we are in the presence of something like a historic trend—a trend within a trend, as it were, for not only do we have the basic trend of more Government services, but an

---

[2] David F. Jordan and Herbert E. Dougall, *Investments* (6th ed.), Prentice-Hall, 1952, pp. 354-8.

[3] Investment Bankers of America, *Fundamentals of Investment Banking*, Prentice-Hall, 1949, pp. 374–88.

[4] Dirck Keyser in *Journal of Commerce,* Oct. 9, 1953, pp. 4, 8.

increasingly large proportion of these are provided for a fee and financed by bonds secured by these fees.

In other words, in some cases State and local governments and their creature authorities are going into the business of selling services to the public: providing the use of an especially fine highway or of a bridge, selling electric current or water, and many other things. The Port of New York Authority sells the use of airports, tunnels, bridges, piers, warehouses, and terminals. Pennsylvania School District authorities actually build schools, which are then rented to the school district.

In general, revenue bonds, or "revs," as they are familiarly termed, are issued against three primary types of revenues—revenues from publicly owned and operated utility systems, those from transportation facilities such as toll roads and port facilities, and rentals. Most revenue bonds are of the utility or transportation type. The rare bonds backed by rentals are a special case and will be treated separately.

The most common type is the utility revenue issue. Many communities own and operate their own water, electric, gas, and transit systems. In fact, there are probably more municipal water systems owned and operated by municipal water departments than there are privately owned and operated. The public ownership of electric and gas systems is much rarer.

There was a distinct tendency in recent years for cities to take over their ailing private transit systems, but town fathers found them to be white elephants, and now there is a tendancy on the part of the city governments to try to keep such companies on their feet. Nonetheless, nearly three-fifths of the nation's transit investment is publicly managed, and about 15 per cent of the national transit industry is financed by the issuance of transit revenue bonds. The best known of these are the bonds of the Chicago Transit Authority. The nation's biggest transit system, the New York City Transit Authority, cannot issue bonds in its own name, however.

From the point of view of the investor, the utility revenue bonds issued against publicly owned utility revenues are exactly like those issued by privately owned utilities, with the sole difference that the interest is exempt from Federal taxation and usually from taxation by the State in which the bonds were issued. In other words, the same rules as to the soundness of the financial condition of the utility in question must be considered by the potential investor. With this in mind, many investment houses point out that a sound municipal water, electric, or gas department is often as good an investment as the municipality itself. In some cases, a town's water revenue bonds have been rated Aa or A by Moody's Investors Service, while its general obligation bonds have been rated A or Baa.

The point is, a man will often pay a water bill that comes to a few dollars a quarter when he is unable to pay his taxes, which may come to several hundred dollars a year. In many cases failure to pay a water bill will result in discontinuation of service, while failure to pay taxes may not necessarily entail any action on the part of the community for anywhere up to a year.

As for transit bonds, suffice it to say that the revenues of the nation's transit business are declining generally and that, while the private companies have made an attempt, perhaps successful, to reverse this trend, the public agencies are losing more each year. Moody's rating of the bonds of the Chicago Transit Authority, which has been doing better than the publicly owned transits in general and has been making profits, is Ba, which Moody's defines as applying to bonds "judged to have speculative elements; their future cannot be considered as well assured."

Revenue bonds issued against income from transportation facilities include those issued for highways, including toll roads, bridges, tunnels, ferries and parking bonds, and those issued for port facilities, including docks, airports, warehouses, terminals of various sorts, and other purposes.

Although most revenue issues are for utilities, in recent years highway issues have dwarfed all others, and there are probably more toll road and bridge bonds on the market today than any other kind. Most of the coming volume in revenue bonds which may make 1953 a record year for this type of financing will be in turnpike and toll bridge bonds. While the average utility issue may run up to $10 or $20 million on the outside, the average toll road issue will begin at that size, and the largest revenue issue to date has been the $326 million Ohio Turnpike issue sold in June, 1952. Toll roads are a rather special field. No other type of bond, either in the municipal field or out of it, is similar. While toll roads were originally built by private companies, and were still in existence under private management in Pennsylvania as late as the 1920's, they are a relatively new development under public management.

In general, the security behind a toll revenue bond depends on the amount of traffic the road is carrying. Toll revenues should generally be in a two-to-one ratio to the annual amount of principal and interest due on the bonds, in order to provide a good margin of protection. A particularly sound type of toll road has a high proportion of commercial traffic. In time of war, gasoline rationing may seriously reduce the amount of passenger vehicle traffic, which in general will run around 60 per cent of the total volume. Passenger traffic is also vulnerable to depression, since much of it is pleasure riding. If the proportion of passenger traffic is too high, the revenues will be particularly vulnerable.

A particularly strong position exists where the State concerned is a corridor State, as in the case of New Jersey or Connecticut, with much of the traffic being out-of-State through traffic. Such vehicles, especially trucks, can usually effect a substantial saving by using the toll road, and will do so. The Pennsylvania and New Jersey turnpikes have been particularly successful in this respect. Toll bridges and tunnels in metropolitan areas, which carry much commuter traffic, are rather vulnerable. In World War II the Triborough Bridge suffered a great loss in traffic to the subways, and the authority had temporarily to suspend payments on its bonds.

Port and terminal facilities are relatively scarce, but the original port authority, that of the Port of New York, is the prototype for all public authorities which issue bonds. Founded in the early Twenties, the Port of New York Authority has become a colossus which operates the world's third largest office building, three airports under lease—Newark, La Guardia, and Idlewild—owns docks and bridges—including George Washington Bridge—and does over $50 million worth of business per year. Such multitudinous activities have naturally raised a question about such authorities, which are increasing in number every year, and there is a certain amount of opposition to them at present, although it is not very vocal or effective.

Least important in point of volume are those bonds issued against rental revenues. These are, indeed, rather a fringe case. Yet here are some of the worst abuses of revenue bonds. There are in general three kinds—housing bonds, industrial revenue bonds, and bonds issued for the purpose of building public works which are then rented to State and local governments, and which are known as quasi-revenue bonds.

The housing bonds are generally guaranteed by the Federal Government under the terms of the Housing Act of 1949, and are therefore rather a special case, not being generally considered to be revenue bonds. In Massachusetts and other States, local housing authorities may issue housing bonds which are guaranteed by the State. In all cases, the first source of revenue is from rentals in public housing projects.

Quasi-revenue bonds are issued in Pennsylvania, Georgia, Louisiana, and Kentucky. In the case of Georgia, they are issued because the State Constitution forbids the issuance of general obligation bonds by the State. Various State authorities—the Georgia State Office Building Authority, for instance—build projects which are then rented to the State, financing the projects by the issuance of revenue bonds backed by rentals. In Pennsylvania, school building authorities build schools and rent them to school districts, a device used to bypass the school district's debt limit, and one which has drawn some fire from a number of critics.

Criticism has been directed at the issuance of industrial revenue bonds. In Mississippi, for instance, a municipality may construct a factory, financing the work through the issuance of bonds payable only from revenues received from the rental of the factory to a private concern. The purpose is to attract industry. The effect is, as in the case of utility revenue bonds, to exactly parallel ordinary industrial bonds in security, with the added attraction of tax exemption providing lower interest. The criticism stems from the fact that the municipality is, in effect, selling to the private company its privilege of tax exemption, on the one hand, and, on the other, that the community is presenting other towns with what is regarded by them as unfair competition.

In general, revenue bonds are sold at a lower price than general obligations, and if the proposition is a sound one, the investor may pick up some handsome returns. Turnpike issues, especially, may offer good interest as a result of their monumental size. Underwriters are forced to offer especially attractive rates in order to place such big issues.

1. In appraising general obligation bonds, is it wise to rely solely upon tax payments, or must the proportion of debt service to other costs of municipal services be reckoned with? Is this factor measurable?
2. Why would a one-industry town's general obligation often be better than that of a city dependent on durable goods production? Investigate the cases of Mannheim School District (No. 111), Illinois, of Midland, Michigan, and compare them with New London, Connecticut.
3. Compare the experience of the Triborough Bridge with that of the Golden Gate Bridge during the years 1941–1946.
4. Compare the experience of the Maine Turnpike Authority with that of the Oklahoma Turnpike Authority. Does this evidence show anything about the quality of turnpike bonds in general?
5. Compare the experience of Los Angeles Department of Water and Power with the various Public Utility Districts of the State of Washington. Is the net income of such utility revenue systems the source of bond interest and retirement provisions?
6. Why are the housing revenue bonds generally given a high rating?
7. Why are most general obligation and revenue bonds issued in serial form? Is this of importance to the investor? What must he be aware of with regard to maturities?

80.   Municipal Bond Analysis

This advanced problem requires collection of data, and its interpretation in rating city and county bonds.

Customary measures that are used in municipal bond prospectuses include the following:

(a) Population, 1950 and 1940 comparisons
(b) Assessed valuation of property and full valuation, with the

statutory rate of assessment and per capita valuations

(c) Net debt, total and per capita, and per cent of assessed and full valuations

(d) Net direct and overlapping debt, total, per capita, and per cent of assessed and of full valuations

(e) Tax collections last year

(f) Type of obligation

1. For a selected variety of currently offered issues, or from the following list, collect the proper information on the issue and the issuer. Then appraise the issue in terms of ability to pay. Cincinnati, Ohio; Buffalo, N. Y.; Detroit, Mich.; Houston, Tex., or Springfield, Mass.; Des Moines, Iowa; Tulsa, Okla.; Knoxville, Tenn., or Fairfax County, Va.; Cook County, Ill.; Dade County, Florida or Richland County, S. Carolina.

81. Estimating Earnings of Fire and Casualty Companies

/ Due to the nature of the industry, actual net profit figures for fire and casualty insurance companies are difficult to compute. This advanced problem presents methods of various analysts in their attempts to solve this problem.

Victor F. Morris, in two articles in the *Journal of Commerce*, March 15 and 16, 1950, presented clearly the difficulties involved in computing earnings of fire and casualty insurance companies, and the resultant difficulties of investing in such issues, even by sophisticated security buyers. The two articles follow:

I

Insurance stock specialists, the Securities and Exchange Commission, the National Association of Insurance Commissioners and various statistical organizations in the industry are at odds concerning methods of computing fire and casualty company earnings.

To some extent this has long been the case, but the divergence has recently become so serious that stockholders are now getting as many as six different versions of the operating results of their companies. Regardless of which method is employed, the 1949 profits of most companies were highly satisfactory — in fact they were of record proportions. Yet the lack of uniformity in the figures is disconcerting.

For example, on the statutory basis prescribed by the insurance commissioners, the consolidated net operating earnings of Aetna Insurance Co. and subsidiaries in 1949 were equal to $8.12 per share, compared with $6.14 in 1948, while on the basis employed by A. M. Best Co., a leading statistical organization, Aetna's consolidated earnings are boosted to $10 a share in 1949 and $8.60 in 1948. According to Geyer & Co., a securities firm specializing in bank, insurance and public utility shares, Aetna's earnings should be $9.08 and $7.38, respectively, while if the earnings were to appear in a prospectus approved by the SEC they would either have to agree with the statutory figure, which is the most conservative of all, or they would be adjusted to $9.24 and $7.67, respectively, which differ from any shown above.

There are other variations. The parent company basis is still used by some insurance companies in their reports to stockholders. In fact, the statutory method calls for individual "convention form" statements for the parent company and for each of the subsidiaries, and as no consolidation is shown one might say that the statutory procedure is also on the parent company basis. On this basis, per share earnings of Aetna in 1949 and 1948 were only $6.75 and $3.49, respectively.

Aetna's report to stockholders was on a consolidated basis, but nowhere did it sum up the net operating earnings. It showed underwriting and investment accounts, Federal income taxes and dividends paid, and then showed the change in surplus for the year. The reader is left to derive his own figure by any method he chooses, as in the case of a conventional statement.

There is general agreement that consolidated figures are more meaningful to stockholders than parent company figures. The most serious dispute, however, revolves around the unearned premium reserves. The law requires a fire or casualty company to set up reserves equal to the full amount of all unexpired premiums, so that if a company were obliged to do so it could cancel every policy on its books and return the pro rata portion of the premiums to the policyholders. Such reserves are obviously excessive in terms of normal operations. They assume that losses will equal premium income, yet premiums are ordinarily sufficient to absorb not only losses but expenses as well and still leave a profit. It is generally acknowledged, therefore, that every well-managed company has an equity in its unearned premiums roughly equal to the percentage of the premiums written consumed by the cost of acquiring the business, and that in attempting to arrive at the true underwriting results the increase or decrease of his equity must be taken into account. This is especially true in a period of rising or falling premium volume, when statutory results are most misleading.

Up to this point, virtually all insurance stock analysts, statistical organizations and the SEC are in agreement. The insurance commissioners do not specifically dissent from these views, but they ignore the problem of the fluctuating equity in the unearned premium reserve because they are primarily concerned with the balance sheet position of the policyholder rather than the earnings' picture. The companies themselves generally recognize the premium reserve phenomenon and they mention it in their annual reports to stockholders. But they are reluctant to compute an actual adjustment to the statutory figure.

It is in the actual computation that the difficulty lies. How much of an equity is there in the unearned premium reserves? The companies pay Federal income taxes on the basis of the statutory figures, but if an adjustment is made for an increase in premium reserve equity, why should not an adjustment be made for the taxes that will have to be paid on this equity when it is realized as actual earnings?

A. M. Best Co., the insurance statistical organization, has been carrying footnotes in its earnings reports to the effect that "no adjustment has been made for contingent Federal income tax liability on unrealized equities." The SEC has apparently taken the position that a footnote of this sort is sufficient for ordinary statistical material, but in a prospectus it insists that the contingent tax be deducted if the companies wish to claim an increase in unearned premium reserve equity as an adjustment to underwriting earnings. Thus in a recent prospectus by United States Fidelity & Guaranty Co., the increase in premium reserve equity is taken into account "less allowance for Federal income and excess profits taxes which would have been payable upon realization of such increases."

II

Security dealers are convinced that the confusion resulting from the lack of uniformity in fire and casualty company statistics tends to discourage investment in insurance shares. Unlike the stockholder of an industrial company, who typically sees one undisputed earnings figure representing the operating results for a given period, the holder of insurance stocks is faced with a bewildering array of official and unofficial reports and estimates.

The divergent aims of the insurance regulatory bodies and investors are the underlying cause of the difficulty. The regulatory authorities are primarily concerned with the present strength of the company. Since the impact on the balance sheet is to them the decisive factor, unrealized appreciation or depreciation of securities in the company's portfolio is deemed as important as underwriting earnings or net investment income, if not more so. The fact that one is recurrent and the other non-current is irrelevant. Thus even in reports to stockholders a company will sum up its operating results by reference to changes in surplus rather than net operating earnings.

The investor, on the other hand, is primarily interested in earnings and the dividends which may be declared therefrom. True, all the accounts are shown separately in most reports, and the analyst can derive the net operating figure by any method he thinks best. But the average stockholder is not an analyst. His complaint is not that he gets too little information, but that he gets too much. It is what the French call an *embarras de richesse.*

Practically all analysts make an adjustment to reflect the equity in unearned premiums, but there is disagreement as to the treatment of the contingent tax liability on the unrealized equity and the method of determining the equity.

This year Geyer & Co. statisticians are deducting the contingent tax liability from both the earnings and the liquidating value of insurance companies. Vinton C. Johnson of the First Boston Corp. says he, too, is deducting the tax from earnings, but not from liquidating values. He believes the present method of computing liquidating values is too conservative anyway, as it does not take into account the value of agency organizations and other intangibles which do not appear on the balance sheet. These assets, he says, will more than offset the tax liability on unrealized equities.

George Leming, bank and insurance stock specialist with Merrill Lynch, Pierce, Fenner & Beane, is apparently in agreement with Mr. Johnson on both counts. These analysts feel that failure to deduct the contingent tax from adjusted earnings is especially misleading when one compares a company which has little or no statutory underwriting gain and a large increase in premium reserve equity with a company reporting a large statutory gain and a small increase in premium reserve equity. The adjusted underwriting results are presumably the same, but the latter company is subject to a heavy tax while the former gets off with a relatively light tax, and the comparative net earnings after taxes are left entirely out of line—unless the analyst makes a deduction for the contingent tax liability.

But other analysts take a different position. Robert S. Burns of A. M. Kidder & Co. and Frank Elliot of Paine, Webber, Jackson & Curtis are continuing with the method practiced by A. M. Best Co., the insurance statistical organization, and are not deducting a contingent tax. "There is not enough progress involved to justify a change," Mr. Elliot says, but he concedes that, since the Securities and Exchange Commission wants the tax adjustment to appear on prospectuses, there is a strong argument for using it in all statistical material on insurance companies.

Joseph P. Byrne of A. M. Best Co. explains his firm's reluctance to deduct a hypothetical tax as follows:

1. The tax may not be incurred for several years, and meanwhile the tax rate may be changed.

2. In a period of falling premium volume the companies would have to be given a hypothetical tax credit, if consistency is to be maintained.

This "credit" may never materialize, but would merely offset the hpyothetical contingent tax which was "charged" (by the analyst) in previous periods.

3. The funds represented by the contingent tax liability are earning money as invested assets, and may continue to do so for years. Yet under the proposed change they are written off entirely, and no account is taken of the additional investment income.

This is too confusing to justify the change. Robert S. Burns believes the problem can be met adequately by separating clearly the statutory figures from the estimated premium reserve equity, so that the analyst can make his own appraisal. As a matter of fact, this is done in all of Best's literature.

The other important point of contention is the method of computing premium reserve equity before taxes. A. M. Best Co. and most insurance stock analysts have been using 40 per cent of unearned fire premiums and 35 per cent of unearned casualty premiums, with some variation where it is felt that acquisition costs are unusually high or low.

Geyer & Co., on the other hand, is now basing its figures on what it believes are the definitely ascertainable acquisition costs, namely the agents' commissions, premium taxes and field supervision expenses. Robert Chaut, who heads the firm's statistical department, concedes that there are other acquisition costs that are not accounted for by this method, as considerable home office activity revolves around the processing of new business. But he prefers the more conservative figure, particularly one that can be defended by reference to actual accounts in the convention statements, and not merely by rule-of-thumb estimates.

Strong exception is taken to this in other quarters. Aside from the practical problem of pinning down all acquisition costs, it is argued that the Geyer innovation involves a basic conceptual error. The method assumes that the premium reserve equity is equal to the cost of acquiring the business. But what if these costs were excessive? Would that mean the company earned more?

Vinton C. Johnson of the First Boston Corp. cites the case of a casualty company that nearly went bankrupt a few years ago, partly because it paid excessive commissions for substandard risks. According to the "prepaid expense" approach, the company would have appeared to be realizing large underwriting earnings, although subsequent examination by the insurance commissioners proved otherwise.

The position taken by A. M. Best Co. and virtually all other analysts is that the premium reserve equity exists only because the reserve is set too high in terms of probable future losses. The 40 per cent or 35 per cent figure is an estimate, of course, but it is not entirely arbitrary, as it indicates (roughly) what would be left after reinsurance of the business. The dispute turns on a question which has concerned economic theorists for some time, namely whether the value of an asset is determined by its cost, by what it will command in the market (in this case the reinsurance market) or by some other criterion.

1. Are the analytical decisions in the controversies above the result of the basic approach? For example, A. M. Best Co. may be analyzing for safety of the company for policyholders, while stock analysts are interested in earnings as a factor in the determination of market price fluctuations.

2. Of what importance are underwriting profits of an insurance company to the investor? Is he not interested solely in investment income? Look up the price records of some insurance stocks and their relation to: (a) investment income, (b) net income, and (c) book value.

82. Analysis of Insurance Company Securities

This problem presents data for two comparable companies and offers the basic data often available in investment dealers' literature. The analytical problem is quite simple.

As an investor of some means, Mr. Lyon has been approached by an investment dealer with a proposal to purchase a block of shares in either of two well-known, national insurance companies. Both firms operate in all lines of insurance except life insurance. Both have established brokerage accounts of value in writing insurance, and have capable management. The differences in policy are shown adequately in their financial statements, which were given to Mr. Lyon in summarized form. He presents the data to you and asks for a written report as to whether the insurance company stocks are of long-term growth potential which he desires. He has been impressed by the dealer's exhibits showing that substantial gains have been recorded in the period from 1946 to 1952.

You are asked to submit the required report, telling which, if either, issue you would believe suitable for his purposes, assuming the current price for N is 28, and for S is 36.

TABLE V-9
COMPARATIVE FINANCIAL DATA

Company N:	1952	1951	1950	1949	1946
Total assets (millions).	$125.9	$108.5	$103.3	$ 91.2	$ 56.5
Capital stock ($5 par)	10.0	10.0	10.0	10.0	9.4
Bonds held (amortized value)	26.9	24.3	24.3	22.8	11.5
Stocks held (market value).	75.1	63.4	60.0	51.8	32.0
Net premiums in force.	96.2	85.6	78.7	N.A.	N.A.
Underwriting gain (millions).	d$0.5	d$2.5	d$0.6	$9.3	d$3.6
Unearned premium reserve (debit) .	10.3	8.7	3.5	4.9	13.8
Net income.	4.6	3.3	3.9	8.5	d 0.7
Dividends paid	1.9	1.7	1.5	1.3	1.0
Loss ratio (parent co. only)	54.18%	55.88%	59.42%	44.69%	57.49%
Expense ratio (parent only)	38.58%	40.03%	40.01%	39.33%	40.88%
Per share results					
Underwriting gain (before taxes) . .	d$0.22	d$1.26	d$0.28	$4.63	d$2.29
Investment gain (" ") . .	3.14	2.94	2.75	2.36	1.31
Premium reserve (" ") . .	2.03	1.69	0.71	0.94	2.40
Total . . . . . . (after taxes) . . .	4.34	3.33	2.67	5.18	1.40
Dividends paid	0.85	0.75	0.65	0.55	0.50
Liquidating value per share	45.52	39.49	37.14	33.57	22.41
Price range . . . . . . High	28	22 3/4	23 1/8	20 1/8	17 1/8
Low	22 7/8	19 7/8	18 5/8	15	11 1/8
Company S:					
Total assets (millions).	$129.6	$117.5	$110.5	$100.8	$ 71.2
Capital stock ($6.25 par).	20.0	20.0	10.0	10.0	10.0
Bonds held (amortized value)	62.1	55.8	52.6	49.7	32.5
Stocks held (market value).	47.8	42.5	40.6	63.8	42.0
Net premiums in force.	78.7	73.4	68.1	N.A.	N.A.
Underwriting gain (millions)	$5.0	$3.4	$3.0	$5.4	d$1.0
Unearned premium reserve (debit) .	2.2	2.7	3.5	2.8	4.5
Net income.	6.7	7.0	5.4	6.1	1.6
Dividends paid	2.7	2.5[1]	2.4	2.0	1.6
Loss ratio	50.07%	52.69%	51.79%	48.18%	58.32%
Expense ratio	38.11%	37.86%	37.93%	35.69%	37.65%
Per share results					
Underwriting gain (before taxes) . .	$1.27	$0.15	$5.58	$8.69	d$1.13
Investment gain (" ") . .	1.71	1.56	5.76	5.21	3.58
Premium reserve (" ") . .	0.69	0.85	2.78	2.43	3.76
Total . . . . . . (after taxes) . . .	2.91	2.52	11.78	12.37	6.03
Dividends paid	0.85	1.15[1]	3.00	2.50	2.00
Liquidating value per share	31.95	28.89	106.12	97.85	68.37
Price range . . . . . . High	35	35	116	107	82
Low	30 1/2	28 3/4	97	76 1/2	62 1/2

[1]   Plus 100% stock dividend.
d   Deficit.
N.A.   Not available.

83. Analysis of Investment Company Results

This advanced problem in analysis of investment companies can be quite strenuous for the field is wide and the reasoning rather tricky for the amateur.

Mr. Palmer, an executive with a large industrial corporation, has become interested in buying securities with the $20,000 savings which he currently has in a savings and loan account on which he receives a current return of 3 per cent as well as a 1 per cent bonus in each of the last three years. A local investment dealer has been talking to Mr. Palmer about the merits of investment company securities, both for income and for building up an estate. Mr. Palmer is somewhat puzzled by the differentiation between closed- and open-end companies and wonders which offers the better potentials for (a) income, or (b) growth. But Mr. Palmer also realizes that he could invest directly in issues which are held by the investment companies, yet could not achieve the same diversification. He wants to investigate the cost of this management to him, the price of securing diversification, for he thinks that the 4 to 4½ per cent return from income achieved by investment companies is not sufficiently better than what he now gets from the savings and loan account. On the other hand, he might get an average return of 5 to 5½ per cent from holding stocks himself.

The investment dealer had been talking of the following groups of investment companies:

A. Closed Companies, with leverage:
    1. Carriers and General Corp.
    2. General American Investors
    3. Tri-Continental Corp.
B. Closed Companies, without leverage:
    1. Adams Express Co.
    2. Lehman Corp.
    3. Petroleum Corp. of America
C. Open-end Companies, balanced fund:
    1. Axe-Houghton Fund A, Inc.
    2. Boston Fund, Inc.
    3. Eaton & Howard Balanced Fund
    4. Fidelity Fund

    5. Selected American Shares
    6. Wellington Fund
  D. Open-end Companies, stock fund:
    1. Affiliated Fund
    2. Bullock Fund
    3. Fundamental Investors
    4. Keystone Income Common Stock Fund
    5. Massachusetts Investors Trust
    6. National Investors Corp.

1. Mr. Palmer asks you to help him decide on his investment problem. You have available at the library *Moody's Banks*, Weisenberger's annual *Investment Companies*, and *Standard Corporation Records*. Look up either (a) all of the companies in one of the categories given above, or (b) one from each of the categories. Examine the objectives of the company's investment program, its portfolio, its income record, its price record against book value (for the closed companies), and other pertinent details, covering a period of at least ten years. At present-day prices which of these companies studied offers the best chance for (1) income, or (2) growth?

2. Relate the income received in interest and dividends to the value of the portfolio held for each of the companies studied. Then find the percentage of management and operating expenses to (a) investment income, and (b) value of the portfolio. Do you find any significant relation between cost of management and size of company? between cost of management and return achieved? between cost of management and any other factor of interest to the investor? Write a short commentary on the cost to the investor of management received from an investment company.

84.   Analysis of Bank Stocks

Although bank stocks are generally looked upon as an unsatisfactory investment medium for the individual of limited means, it would appear necessary to look into the reasons for such a conclusion. This problem approaches the question on a critical basis.

Analysis of bank stocks is at best a hazardous undertaking. The paucity of data, compared to even the most parsimonious of industrial firms, gives little to work with. It is no wonder, then, that the investment fraternity look somewhat askance at analysis by other than a few highly-trained specialists in the field.

As one writer has said,[1]

To the analyst bank stocks still present a serious accounting problem. Comparative statistics have a tendency to be misleading—sometimes grossly so. It is only to be hoped that some rationalization of accounting will take place. . . . If the results of its (the Committee on Corporate Information of the National Federation of Security Analysts Societies) work turn out to be a real impetus toward reform, the investment status of bank stocks should improve. Many bankers are cognizant of their failings in regard to accounting, and the slowness of change is often ascribable to traditions of so-called conservatism. It is more than probable that pressure from the outside toward rational uniformity would be welcomed by enough managements to force the hands of reaction. And, in many cases, banks want to give stockholders appropriate information but just do not seem to know what is required of them.

What information is necessary for analysis of bank stocks? The Committee studied annual reports of banks for 1951, and of the 28 major banks of the nation examined found that most of them were lacking in sufficient analytical detail in their reports.[2] Ratings were given as excellent, very good, good, fair, poor, unsatisfactory and "?"! Ratings were made on various bases: net current earnings (one bank received an excellent rating), non-operating income and reconcilement of capital funds and reserves (again only one excellent rating), information on assets and reserves (no excellent ratings), and useful detail (several excellent ratings). On the whole, the banks received fair to unsatisfactory ratings from the professional analysts. For their part the banks believed, quite correctly, that (1) a bank need not give out much of its quasi-confidential information, and (2) that only a few stockholders would want such details in an annual report. It might be argued that the standards of the analysts were set too high and that there is no uniform statement procedure among banks which would lend itself to comparative analysis.

But what can be done with the available information, admitting

---

[1] F. E. Elliott Farr, "The Pros and Cons of Bank Stocks under Present Conditions," *Analysts Journal*, vol. 9 (Feb. 1953), p. 83.

[2] *Journal of Commerce*, July 30, 1952.

that in many cases even the minimum essentials are lacking? The relation of net income to gross revenues is important for measuring earning power of a bank. The character of operating expenses, the sources of income, the tax burden—these cannot be analyzed for the typical bank. Published statements of condition are relatively useless, so only annual reports have any utility. But even these often lack income statement data.

One measure of bank stocks that can be found is the ratio of capital to deposits and of risk assets to deposits. Risk assets may be defined as loans and non-government investments. (Yet even U.S. Government bonds are "something less than a perfect haven.") The trend of these ratios over a period of years can indicate the adequacy of capital funds to meet recession or depression conditions. Many banks show quite unfavorable trends due to the inability to retain earnings after taxes in sufficient amount to keep up with deposit expansion and to the heavy cost of acquiring new capital in the market. The effect of both factors is to reduce dividend payments to meager amounts, thus giving only a very small return to investors.

On the other hand, there are some banks that appear to have overcapitalization and have difficulty earning enough to give a reasonable return to investors. The impact of investment and loan regulation and of taxes must be realized as limiting factors on bank earning power. This is in strict contrast to the conditions applying in the insurance fields.

1. Examine the statistical data available in Moody's or Standard & Poor's or Studley-Shupert for the following banks, presenting the data in comparative form: Chase National Bank, National City Bank, Guaranty Trust Co., Irving Trust Co., all of New York, Continental Illinois, First National, and Northern Trust of Chicago, Bank of America, First Bank Stock Corporation of Minneapolis, and Security First National of Los Angeles.

   (a) Are adequate earnings data presented?
   (b) Are loans, investments, and reserves broken down into categories suitable for analysis?
   (c) Are reconciliations of capital accounts available?
   (d) Are all of these of great importance to the analysts? Why?

2. For a selected pair of banks chosen from the list above, but representing two cities, prepare a comparison of deposits, risk

assets, and capital for the period 1929 to date. Compute the ratios of deposits to capital and risk assets to capital. Do you find significant differences in trends? What effect can you trace through to earnings or to stock price?

3. For the same banks, compare earnings, book values, dividends, and stock prices. What relationships do you find? Are the standard yardsticks of the past of great significance? Would you suggest any additional ones?

85. Comparative Analysis of Bank Stocks

This relatively simple problem will bring out the important facets in the analysis of bank shares, particularly those found in these two large, aggressive institutions.

The analyst for a sizable investment institution was asked in 1953 to give an opinion as to the relative merits of purchase of the stock of two national banks, both of which had shown a good record of progress since 1946. The vice-president of the organization asked for a report which could be forwarded to the investment committee with a definite recommendation of one of these two banks.

Bank C is the older of the two banks. Both are widely known and act as correspondents for smaller banks throughout their respective regions; they are not directly competitive. The management of Bank C declared a 25 per cent stock dividend in 1950 and another 20 per cent stock dividend in 1953. Bank D secured additional capital through periodic sales of stock from 1946 through 1952 at $40 a share; in 1953, there was a 5-for-3 split, followed by rights to buy a new share at $30 for each 7 shares held. Fortunately, both banks issue rather complete financial statements which are summarized in the appended tables. Both are known as aggressive, but conservatively managed; both operate in all phases of banking, but reports do not give a comparable division of deposits.

1. As the analyst in this case, you know the policy of your institution is to buy long-term holdings, with income as a secondary consideration. Assuming that Bank C stock sells at 390, and Bank D shares are 35, prepare the desired report.

TABLE V-10
COMPARATIVE INCOME ACCOUNTS
(in millions of dollars)

	1952	1951	1950	1949	1946
Bank C:					
Operating earnings.	$15.5	$13.8	$12.0	$10.5	$ 9.2
Net operating earnings after taxes .	3.8	3.2	3.1	2.6	3.9
Net earnings	2.9	2.7	2.4	2.1	1.9
Earned per share	$29.28	$26.68	$23.56	$26.15	$23.91
Dividends per share	12.00	12.00	12.00*	12.00	12.00
Price range:					
High	410	315	301	335	399
Low	300	280	262	292	360
Bank D:					
Operating earnings.	$12.9	$10.8	$ 9.3	$ 7.3	$ 5.3
Net operating earnings before taxes.	6.5	3.4	2.7	2.5	2.0
Net earnings	4.3	4.1 ‡	2.6	2.3	2.1
Earned per share	$4.08	$4.57	$3.80	$3.87	$4.24
Dividends per share	2.28	2.28	2.00	2.00	2.00
Price range:					
High	54 1/2	50 1/2	46	45	59
Low	46	43	41	38	50

*Plus 25% stock dividend.
‡0.8 extraordinary profit included.

TABLE V-11
COMPARATIVE BALANCE SHEETS
(in millions of dollars)

	1952	1951	1950	1949	1946
Bank C:					
Cash and in banks.	176.4	207.7	182.6	180.8	123.4
U. S. securities.	182.5	168.6	182.8	203.6	172.7
Other securities	65.2	72.0	74.7	75.6	36.0
Loans and discounts	270.3	246.6	209.8	151.4	160.3
Other assets	7.9	6.3	7.5	5.0	4.2
Total assets	702.3	701.2	657.4	616.4	496.6
Common stock ($100 par)	10.0	10.0	10.0	8.0	8.0
Surplus & undiv. profits	23.6	20.9	19.4	20.2	17.3
Reserves	14.3	13.3	12.5	10.7	10.3
Other liabilities.	1.0	1.4	2.9	0.5	2.3
Deposits	653.3	655.7	612.6	577.1	458.8
Total.	702.3	701.2	657.4	616.4	496.6
Book value per share.	$336.46	$309.18	$294.50	$352.17	$316.58
Bank D:					
Cash and in banks.	184.5	166.7	139.3	114.6	85.9
U. S. securities.	95.4	81.5	56.9	63.4	42.2
Other securities	9.6	7.6	5.9	3.0	3.2
Loans and discounts	241.3	212.8	191.7	184.2	136.8
Other assets	56.9	53.0	53.3	12.9	8.5
Total assets	587.7	521.6	447.1	378.1	276.8
Capital stock ($20 par)	21.0	18.0	13.5	12.0	10.0
Surplus & undiv. profits	26.2	23.1	17.6	15.4	12.2
Reserves	7.8	6.1	5.1	3.4	1.6
Other liabilities.	18.4	15.2	9.7	7.4	5.2
Deposits	514.3	459.2	401.3	339.9	247.9
Total	587.7	521.6	447.1	378.1	276.8
Book value per share.	$44.93	$45.68	$46.03	$45.67	$44.30

Appendix

The stock price indexes are based on the weekly indexes of the Securities and Exchange Commission, converted into monthly averages. The prices of individual security issues were computed from the ranges published in the *Commercial and Financial Chronicle* annually. Financial statements were prepared from statistical materials of Moody's Investors Service, and Standard and Poor's Corporation. All data are shown in thousands of dollars. The student of investment analysis is encouraged to trace back these data in order to become familiar with the difficulties of using such sources.

All responsibility as to classification of accounts and errors in transcription or calculation must be assumed by the author of this volume.

The ten companies chosen for presentation are:

Chemicals: Air Reduction and Union Carbide and Carbon
Steel and Iron: Bethlehem Steel and United States Steel
Automobiles: Chrysler and General Motors
Foods: General Foods and National Biscuit
Textiles: American Woolen and Celanese

S. E. C. STOCK PRICE INDEXES, MONTHLY, 1939-1954

(1939 equals 100)

	Com-posite	Manu-facturing	Durable Goods	Non-durable Goods	Transpor-tation	Util-ities	Trade, Finance, Service	Mining
1939								
Jan.	102.1	103.5	104.5	102.3	103.7	95.8	100.0	106.6
Feb.	102.2	103.1	104.9	101.4	99.5	99.1	102.2	104.3
Mar.	102.7	102.8	104.3	101.2	104.8	101.0	102.5	106.2
Apr.	90.5	89.6	86.9	92.3	86.4	94.8	91.5	96.8
May	94.0	92.6	90.4	94.8	90.8	99.1	97.3	100.4
June	96.1	94.5	92.3	96.7	92.4	100.8	102.4	102.6
July	96.7	95.1	93.6	96.7	92.6	101.3	103.8	101.5
Aug.	96.3	94.7	93.8	95.6	91.5	102.2	102.2	100.0
Sep.	104.6	106.5	107.4	105.7	106.5	99.0	97.4	96.7
Oct.	106.7	108.1	110.0	105.9	115.1	101.5	101.2	96.2
Nov.	106.0	106.7	108.5	105.0	111.7	103.7	102.1	95.8
Dec.	103.7	104.1	105.2	103.1	107.0	103.7	99.5	92.6
1940								
Jan.	103.0	102.9	101.7	104.1	105.0	104.8	100.0	92.8
Feb.	103.2	103.1	101.9	104.3	105.0	105.5	100.4	90.5
Mar.	103.1	102.9	101.2	104.6	105.8	105.4	101.0	86.6
Apr.	104.8	104.7	103.1	106.2	109.4	106.4	101.9	87.4
May	92.2	91.9	88.6	95.2	93.5	97.6	86.6	73.1
June	83.7	82.4	79.3	85.5	86.0	93.2	78.2	62.2
July	85.8	83.8	80.4	87.1	91.2	97.2	82.0	62.1
Aug.	85.0	86.4	84.9	87.9	93.4	97.6	84.4	63.0
Sep.	91.3	90.0	89.4	90.6	99.2	98.3	88.3	69.8
Oct.	92.1	90.9	92.3	89.5	101.6	97.9	88.8	70.9
Nov.	94.1	93.3	96.4	90.3	103.7	98.5	88.8	77.8
Dec.	91.2	90.1	92.6	87.7	98.2	97.7	86.4	74.5
1941								
Jan.	91.9	90.4	91.7	89.1	102.4	98.2	88.0	75.3
Feb.	85.7	83.7	84.0	83.4	96.1	94.4	82.3	70.2
Mar.	85.8	83.9	84.3	83.6	97.0	94.3	81.8	69.8
Apr.	83.6	81.6	79.8	83.4	97.1	91.3	79.5	69.5
May	82.2	80.9	77.7	84.0	95.8	86.8	78.2	70.3
June	85.4	84.4	81.2	87.5	95.6	90.1	81.0	72.4
July	89.0	88.9	84.7	93.1	99.4	90.3	83.9	76.4
Aug.	89.1	88.8	84.4	93.2	100.9	89.1	84.9	75.6
Sep.	89.2	88.9	84.8	93.0	98.6	89.2	87.3	75.2
Oct.	86.3	85.7	80.6	90.8	97.1	87.5	84.6	71.9
Nov.	83.0	82.7	75.9	89.5	93.7	83.7	80.1	66.5
Dec.	77.5	78.5	71.3	85.7	83.9	74.6	72.7	60.5

	Composite	Manufacturing	Durable Goods	Nondurable Goods	Transportation	Utilities	Trade, Finance, Service	Mining
1942								
Jan.	77.5	77.9	74.2	81.6	93.5	73.5	72.7	62.9
Feb.	75.1	75.0	73.2	76.8	93.6	72.6	70.6	62.3
Mar.	70.2	70.4	71.1	69.9	86.0	67.4	65.6	54.5
Apr.	68.2	68.7	68.9	68.4	81.7	64.8	63.3	51.7
May	68.7	69.1	68.3	69.8	82.1	65.5	64.3	54.1
June	71.8	72.5	71.1	73.9	80.9	67.3	69.7	59.3
July	74.1	75.2	73.5	75.3	86.6	66.8	71.8	61.0
Aug.	74.1	74.7	72.7	76.7	90.0	67.5	72.8	60.2
Sep.	74.8	75.3	73.2	77.3	92.3	68.6	73.3	61.0
Oct.	80.2	81.2	79.4	83.1	101.9	72.8	74.7	60.5
Nov.	81.8	82.2	79.5	84.9	101.4	76.0	77.9	64.3
Dec.	82.3	83.3	79.3	87.3	98.2	74.9	79.4	65.4
1943								
Jan.	86.8	88.0	84.1	91.9	104.6	78.4	82.1	71.1
Feb.	92.1	93.5	89.9	97.1	110.2	82.5	87.4	76.2
Mar.	95.1	96.1	93.4	98.8	120.5	84.5	91.4	80.8
Apr.	97.8	98.3	95.2	101.3	128.8	86.5	96.3	85.5
May	102.1	102.2	98.5	105.8	135.1	91.8	101.7	85.6
June	104.6	104.9	101.2	108.6	132.7	93.0	107.3	85.9
July	105.8	105.6	101.1	110.0	136.6	95.4	110.5	86.9
Aug.	101.2	100.4	94.4	106.1	127.8	93.8	106.8	84.4
Sep.	103.7	101.7	97.2	108.3	131.0	95.9	110.9	89.2
Oct.	102.5	101.7	96.3	106.8	130.3	95.4	107.2	87.7
Nov.	98.2	97.2	91.3	103.0	121.0	93.8	103.1	83.1
Dec.	99.7	98.8	93.4	104.1	121.5	94.0	106.3	85.7
1944								
Jan.	102.2	101.3	96.8	105.7	127.8	94.9	108.9	88.8
Feb.	101.6	100.1	96.0	104.1	134.0	95.6	107.3	86.3
Mar.	104.5	103.2	99.7	106.6	137.6	96.7	111.8	88.8
Apr.	103.3	101.9	98.4	105.4	135.3	96.0	109.9	89.4
May	104.5	103.5	99.9	107.0	135.7	96.4	110.7	90.4
June	109.1	108.5	106.0	110.9	139.4	98.7	117.6	95.8
July	112.2	111.5	109.8	113.1	144.5	101.0	120.0	100.7
Aug.	111.2	110.2	108.8	111.5	142.8	101.4	120.5	98.5
Sep.	109.5	108.3	107.8	108.9	138.9	100.6	120.8	94.8
Oct.	112.1	110.9	110.4	111.4	144.7	101.8	124.8	95.0
Nov.	111.4	109.9	108.6	111.2	144.9	101.7	125.0	93.9
Dec.	114.0	112.1	111.3	112.8	158.6	102.3	128.3	96.2

235

S. E. C. STOCK PRICE INDEXES, MONTHLY, 1939-1954
(1939 equals 100)

	Com-posite	Manu-facturing	Durable Goods	Non-durable Goods	Transpor-tation	Util-ities	Trade, Finance, Service	Mining
1945								
Jan.	117.2	115.7	114.3	117.0	165.7	102.9	128.0	103.6
Feb.	120.4	119.4	118.6	120.3	168.1	103.8	131.1	109.3
Mar.	120.5	119.4	118.2	120.5	169.6	102.2	131.7	109.1
Apr.	124.0	122.9	122.1	123.6	177.1	106.0	136.0	109.7
May	128.2	126.9	126.7	127.0	186.4	108.5	141.9	111.2
June	129.7	126.8	127.6	126.3	196.8	112.3	146.4	112.2
July	127.0	123.6	124.0	123.2	191.4	114.7	141.6	109.6
Aug.	127.4	124.7	125.8	123.6	183.4	114.4	144.7	106.6
Sep.	135.9	133.3	136.3	132.4	191.1	117.2	155.9	111.4
Oct.	143.1	141.2	141.0	141.5	205.2	119.8	166.3	120.0
Nov.	146.8	143.6	142.2	145.0	215.4	124.7	176.9	129.9
Dec.	151.0	147.9	147.8	148.0	224.1	124.5	186.0	136.2
1946								
Jan.	153.8	151.0	150.9	151.1	227.9	126.0	199.1	135.8
Feb.	158.0	154.3	157.0	151.5	230.7	127.2	212.5	137.4
Mar.	152.6	148.3	146.3	150.2	219.2	124.6	211.6	131.5
Apr.	161.9	158.3	152.0	164.5	221.8	127.3	234.8	137.4
May	163.2	159.6	150.6	168.4	219.1	128.0	239.9	136.5
June	163.8	161.0	153.0	168.9	225.6	129.6	225.2	137.3
July	158.3	156.1	146.2	165.9	214.6	127.2	209.8	131.7
Aug.	154.8	152.8	141.2	164.2	206.4	124.2	207.4	128.8
Sep.	133.7	130.7	119.9	141.3	172.1	112.7	185.0	108.9
Oct.	129.6	127.5	114.0	140.7	158.8	108.5	178.7	105.2
Nov.	129.0	127.1	114.0	140.1	163.2	107.3	174.0	106.3
Dec.	132.9	131.7	118.6	144.6	167.8	109.2	174.3	109.2
1947								
Jan.	132.6	131.7	119.9	143.4	160.2	112.2	169.7	110.4
Feb.	137.8	137.5	128.6	146.2	168.2	113.3	176.1	115.7
Mar.	131.0	130.9	121.2	140.4	155.3	109.5	164.7	114.4
Apr.	126.1	126.3	115.5	137.0	146.8	106.8	155.6	112.1
May	123.3	123.8	111.8	135.7	138.4	105.2	150.5	111.9
June	128.2	129.7	115.3	143.9	140.9	103.7	161.4	117.0
July	135.8	138.2	123.2	152.1	153.9	105.3	174.6	122.9
Aug.	133.0	135.2	120.6	149.3	149.7	104.3	167.8	120.9
Sep.	129.7	131.8	117.5	145.7	144.1	104.7	158.8	117.9
Oct.	133.3	136.3	123.4	148.8	148.1	104.3	162.3	119.8
Nov.	131.3	135.2	122.3	147.6	141.8	100.2	160.0	119.2
Dec.	129.7	133.9	120.8	146.5	144.0	97.3	154.7	124.3

	Com-posite	Manu-facturing	Durable Goods	Non-durable Goods	Transpor-tation	Util-ities	Trade, Finance, Service	Mining
1948								
Jan.	128.9	132.3	119.9	144.3	150.8	98.6	150.2	129.6
Feb.	121.1	123.4	111.1	135.1	143.0	96.3	141.1	121.9
Mar.	124.3	126.8	114.7	138.4	147.9	97.0	145.3	128.9
Apr.	132.4	135.8	123.4	147.6	159.8	98.9	157.9	139.5
May	139.4	143.2	129.3	156.2	168.7	102.4	168.7	149.8
June	143.8	149.3	135.5	162.2	171.0	103.1	169.3	148.4
July	140.0	145.4	131.6	158.4	168.1	102.0	162.1	142.4
Aug.	135.9	140.8	128.4	152.5	163.2	100.1	157.5	133.5
Sep.	133.8	138.0	127.2	148.1	163.8	100.1	158.2	127.8
Oct.	135.5	140.9	129.8	151.4	163.7	99.7	160.3	132.0
Nov.	127.6	131.4	120.0	142.2	148.5	96.9	154.7	118.2
Dec.	127.8	132.0	119.6	143.6	147.2	96.2	154.8	122.3
1949								
Jan.	128.6	133.0	120.3	145.0	147.0	96.3	155.4	125.6
Feb.	122.8	126.2	114.0	137.7	136.9	96.2	149.7	118.5
Mar.	125.0	128.9	115.4	141.6	136.7	97.0	152.6	124.0
Apr.	124.9	128.4	113.2	142.6	137.2	97.1	155.1	131.9
May	123.6	126.8	110.7	141.7	135.3	95.8	156.8	129.7
June	117.4	119.9	104.1	134.7	125.9	93.8	150.3	122.1
July	122.8	126.3	110.5	141.0	128.8	95.3	159.6	121.9
Aug.	128.3	132.4	115.0	148.7	134.2	98.7	165.5	129.4
Sep.	129.7	134.4	115.2	152.4	133.9	99.7	165.9	133.7
Oct.	132.6	138.4	119.5	156.0	136.8	100.4	168.9	140.1
Nov.	135.5	142.2	123.9	159.3	137.5	102.2	169.9	137.3
Dec.	138.8	145.8	128.2	162.3	141.7	104.1	174.9	135.9
1950								
Jan.	141.1	148.1	132.5	162.6	149.4	105.9	177.2	133.9
Feb.	143.7	151.2	137.7	163.8	151.2	107.7	179.1	133.0
Mar.	145.4	152.5	138.2	165.9	152.0	112.0	179.2	133.0
Apr.	149.9	159.1	142.7	171.7	151.4	112.8	178.4	133.9
May	154.7	165.4	149.4	180.2	152.8	115.0	180.6	142.7
June	158.3	171.1	156.0	185.0	149.5	114.8	182.4	143.0
July	146.7	157.9	142.6	172.2	150.0	105.5	170.3	133.7
Aug.	154.4	167.6	151.8	182.2	164.5	105.9	176.6	146.4
Sep.	159.3	173.3	157.5	187.9	168.2	107.1	187.8	150.3
Oct.	164.9	180.3	166.0	193.7	171.4	107.8	198.3	154.5
Nov.	165.9	181.8	166.0	196.5	171.1	107.4	200.8	157.6
Dec.	165.2	180.4	161.7	197.9	184.4	106.5	195.7	159.7

S. E. C. STOCK PRICE INDEXES, MONTHLY, 1939-1954

(1939 equals 100)

	Com-posite	Manu-facturing	Durable Goods	Non-durable Goods	Transpor-tation	Util-ities	Trade, Finance, Service	Mining
1951								
Jan.	176.8	194.4	174.9	212.4	202.1	110.3	205.1	175.9
Feb.	184.0	203.0	181.6	222.8	213.1	112.1	213.2	184.2
Mar.	179.9	198.4	178.2	217.0	200.0	112.9	209.7	176.7
Apr.	183.1	203.8	181.2	224.8	201.9	111.4	207.8	183.4
May	181.7	202.8	175.6	228.1	196.7	110.5	206.0	187.7
June	178.9	200.0	169.1	228.7	188.3	109.9	200.9	186.0
July	182.0	204.7	170.8	236.3	187.9	111.2	202.2	195.2
Aug.	189.3	214.4	178.3	248.0	195.1	113.9	205.5	217.4
Sep.	194.1	220.2	185.2	252.8	202.3	114.9	213.3	229.4
Oct.	191.7	216.0	185.7	244.3	203.3	114.5	214.2	243.6
Nov.	185.3	207.8	179.0	234.6	194.0	114.0	208.0	238.8
Dec.	190.5	214.8	182.7	244.6	203.6	115.2	209.1	238.1
1952								
Jan.	195.8	222.1	186.1	255.4	210.6	116.6	210.0	245.8
Feb.	193.6	218.7	182.9	251.5	208.6	117.0	206.8	258.0
Mar.	188.9	216.8	182.2	248.8	214.0	116.8	203.7	294.9
Apr.	191.3	214.8	181.7	245.2	217.1	116.1	202.9	298.4
May	190.4	213.7	181.7	243.3	215.9	116.7	201.3	283.2
June	196.0	221.6	187.1	253.4	224.6	116.8	203.8	290.5
July	198.7	225.3	191.7	256.3	226.3	116.9	208.3	288.9
Aug.	198.7	225.2	194.3	253.7	227.9	118.6	209.5	278.2
Sep.	194.1	219.3	190.9	245.6	221.3	118.3	206.3	274.8
Oct.	190.3	214.4	188.1	238.8	218.9	117.4	201.9	265.0
Nov.	195.7	221.3	194.8	245.8	223.9	120.6	204.3	260.4
Dec.	203.5	230.8	204.7	254.9	237.7	123.2	212.2	266.9
1953								
Jan.	204.7	232.4	207.7	255.3	239.2	124.1	211.9	261.2
Feb.	201.9	228.6	203.6	251.7	234.8	124.3	210.4	255.8
Mar.	203.9	232.2	206.8	255.6	238.1	124.3	212.4	262.7
Apr.	193.9	220.2	193.8	244.5	223.2	120.4	207.0	252.0
May	194.1	220.9	195.9	243.8	225.7	120.0	208.8	247.0
June	187.3	212.7	186.8	236.4	219.2	116.6	203.8	237.4
July	190.4	216.7	188.0	242.9	223.2	118.9	205.5	236.8
Aug.	190.2	216.6	185.9	244.7	217.2	120.7	205.8	236.3
Sep.	181.0	205.1	175.2	232.3	198.9	118.8	197.5	219.2
Oct.	187.1	213.5	184.4	240.2	202.4	121.4	200.8	218.8
Nov.	191.2	218.7	190.4	244.8	203.8	123.3	206.5	231.5
Dec.	193.4	221.6	192.1	249.1	200.0	124.5	208.7	229.6

TABLE A-1 (Concluded)
S. E. C. STOCK PRICE INDEXES, MONTHLY, 1939-1954
(1939 equals 100)

	Com-posite	Manu-facturing	Durable Goods	Non-durable Goods	Transpor-tation	Util-ities	Trade, Finance, Service	Mining
1954								
Jan.	198.4	228.4	198.8	255.5	206.2	126.1	212.5	238.6
Feb.	203.1	233.9	204.2	261.2	214.6	128.4	216.0	250.3
Mar.	207.1	239.8	209.6	267.5	212.3	130.4	214.6	259.2
Apr.	215.8	252.9	223.2	280.3	211.6	131.8	219.8	265.9
May	223.3	262.9	232.5	290.8	220.6	134.2	225.6	269.6
June	223.9	263.4	236.6	288.0	225.4	134.3	228.3	266.3
July	233.0	273.3	254.3	294.4	233.5	138.6	236.0	257.2
Aug.	237.1	280.0	257.0	301.0	237.1	140.8	243.1	262.6
Sep.	240.4	285.7	260.2	308.8	236.0	139.8	247.2	267.8
Oct.	243.6	291.2	267.4	312.8	240.4	138.2	248.6	269.4

INDIVIDUAL STOCK PRICES, MONTHLY AVERAGE OF HIGH AND LOW
(All prices shown in eighths)

BETHLEHEM STEEL

Year	Jan.	Feb.	Mar.	Apr.	May	June	July	Aug.	Sep.	Oct.	Nov.	Dec.
1939	70.1	70.3	67.3	57.7	55.7	55.0	58.6	58.1	77.2	90.1	84.0	81.5
1940	76.6	76.2	75.3	80.4	76.5	72.7	77.4	76.5	79.0	83.3	88.6	86.7
1941	85.3	79.0	78.5	73.7	70.5	72.2	75.6	72.0	68.3	63.2	60.0	58.7
1942	64.6	61.5	60.0	57.0	53.0	51.7	58.3	54.0	54.4	56.7	57.0	55.1
1943	58.1	59.7	64.2	65.4	65.5	63.3	62.6	59.2	59.0	59.1	57.2	56.0
1944	58.3	59.0	60.1	58.2	58.6	60.5	63.4	62.1	61.6	63.6	62.6	63.7
1945	69.1	71.0	73.3	76.2	78.5	80.2	80.0	79.7	86.5	93.6	94.6	95.3
1946	101.5	104.4	102.0	105.3	105.7	109.0	109.0	108.1	96.7	95.5	91.4	90.5
1947	93.7	94.7	92.3	86.5	81.6	82.2	88.5	88.2	86.7	94.0	99.2	100.6
1948	*33.6	32.5	32.6	35.0	35.3	36.5	36.0	35.3	36.1	37.4	35.7	33.5
1949	32.5	31.6	31.5	30.5	28.1	24.5	26.2	27.2	27.7	29.1	29.6	31.7
1950	32.2	33.3	34.0	35.5	36.7	36.2	37.7	41.6	41.7	44.7	44.4	46.2
1951	54.3	57.4	53.7	55.4	54.1	49.1	49.5	52.2	55.0	53.5	50.4	51.0
1952	52.4	51.4	50.3	49.4	47.4	49.6	51.5	51.3	50.0	48.0	50.6	53.5
1953	56.0	54.5	54.0	51.4	52.2	50.4	51.7	50.2	46.4	49.0	50.2	50.7

*3-for-1 stock split, or equivalent.

UNITED STATES STEEL

Year	Jan.	Feb.	Mar.	Apr.	May	June	July	Aug.	Sep.	Oct.	Nov.	Dec.
1939	61.5	61.1	57.6	48.7	47.1	47.0	49.6	47.3	63.0	76.1	70.2	67.3
1940	62.1	59.0	56.4	62.2	52.6	49.4	52.4	52.4	56.4	59.2	71.3	69.2
1941	66.5	59.5	57.6	54.1	53.0	55.6	58.0	57.6	56.7	53.2	52.2	50.5
1942	54.0	52.1	50.6	48.0	46.0	46.2	48.3	47.3	46.5	49.0	49.4	47.7
1943	49.6	51.5	54.5	56.3	56.0	55.4	56.4	52.3	53.1	52.6	52.3	50.7
1944	52.4	52.1	53.1	51.2	51.5	55.4	60.5	59.2	56.7	58.4	57.4	59.0
1945	61.4	62.3	63.7	65.1	67.1	69.6	68.4	70.7	72.6	79.2	79.3	82.4
1946	87.4	89.0	82.2	83.5	86.4	88.4	89.3	86.3	74.4	69.5	71.2	71.3
1947	72.7	76.0	78.4	70.1	66.5	66.4	71.5	71.6	69.7	74.6	76.0	76.5
1948	75.3	72.0	71.1	75.6	77.5	80.5	80.1	77.4	80.0	83.2	77.2	71.3
1949	73.6	74.0	72.7	72.1	69.5	*21.2	22.3	22.7	23.1	24.0	24.5	25.4
1950	27.1	30.1	31.3	32.1	31.3	34.0	34.3	37.2	38.5	40.2	40.0	40.1
1951	44.7	45.5	42.7	43.2	42.7	39.7	39.5	42.0	43.4	42.4	40.4	40.1
1952	40.7	40.0	39.3	38.6	38.1	38.7	40.3	40.3	39.1	38.1	38.4	41.4
1953	43.2	41.4	41.1	39.2	39.4	38.2	38.5	37.5	34.7	36.5	37.5	39.5

*3-for-1 stock split, or equivalent.

CHRYSLER

Year	Jan.	Feb.	Mar.	Apr.	May	June	July	Aug.	Sep.	Oct.	Nov.	Dec.
1939	75.1	76.6	76.1	62.2	67.0	69.2	76.1	77.7	82.3	91.2	86.1	86.4
1940	85.4	89.0	85.7	88.0	70.4	60.3	68.4	72.0	77.7	80.6	80.3	75.1
1941	68.2	65.3	65.6	60.6	55.4	57.5	57.0	57.3	58.4	56.4	54.0	47.3
1942	46.6	49.1	53.1	53.5	56.5	60.1	61.2	59.6	60.4	63.7	65.7	67.3
1943	69.2	72.4	73.4	73.3	75.5	81.2	80.3	77.4	81.3	79.3	76.6	78.2
1944	80.2	78.7	83.3	82.5	85.0	92.5	93.3	92.1	90.2	92.0	89.3	92.7
1945	94.0	99.1	99.5	104.7	114.1	112.2	108.7	115.7	124.5	124.7	129.5	134.5
1946	135.5	128.5	124.4	132.1	130.2	128.7	123.1	112.5	93.5	88.0	84.1	86.7
1947	92.4	101.1	98.1	91.5	98.6	103.6	113.4	*58.4	58.3	62.3	62.2	61.7
1948	60.6	55.6	57.0	60.3	61.2	64.0	62.1	60.1	58.2	59.1	55.7	53.0
1949	54.4	54.0	53.3	51.4	50.3	46.0	49.2	52.0	52.0	55.1	58.2	63.7
1950	65.5	64.7	65.4	66.5	69.3	74.3	67.4	68.2	71.4	79.0	72.5	67.7
1951	74.0	77.4	78.3	79.2	75.1	68.5	67.4	69.7	71.6	71.4	68.2	69.7
1952	70.0	70.1	72.4	74.2	74.3	76.6	77.4	81.5	82.4	82.3	85.2	90.7
1953	93.3	90.6	84.6	79.3	77.5	72.5	71.3	69.6	66.0	66.3	64.4	61.3

*2-for-1 stock split, or equivalent.

GENERAL MOTORS

Year	Jan.	Feb.	Mar.	Apr.	May	June	July	Aug.	Sep.	Oct.	Nov.	Dec.
1939	46.6	47.5	46.2	40.3	43.2	43.2	45.4	45.4	48.5	55.1	54.2	53.6
1940	53.2	53.6	53.5	54.6	46.1	41.7	44.1	46.4	47.7	49.3	51.6	49.7
1941	45.6	42.6	43.3	40.3	38.3	38.2	38.4	38.7	40.3	40.0	37.2	33.0
1942	32.1	33.0	33.7	33.7	34.5	37.1	38.2	38.1	38.0	40.2	42.0	42.5
1943	45.4	47.2	48.6	49.2	51.5	54.4	53.1	51.5	52.3	51.6	50.5	51.2
1944	53.1	53.3	57.3	57.1	59.1	62.5	63.3	61.7	61.2	62.5	62.1	63.3
1945	63.5	62.0	61.4	67.0	69.0	68.4	67.0	69.2	71.5	72.7	72.7	74.7
1946	77.2	75.1	72.2	74.1	72.6	72.1	69.0	64.4	55.4	50.7	51.2	51.4
1947	56.0	62.4	60.2	57.1	56.2	57.2	60.0	59.3	58.2	60.0	58.6	57.1
1948	55.6	53.7	52.6	56.5	59.5	63.3	61.5	62.7	61.6	63.1	61.0	57.6
1949	59.2	59.4	58.7	58.4	57.2	54.1	59.1	61.6	62.2	65.1	68.5	69.1
1950	70.7	75.7	76.0	81.1	85.2	92.1	82.5	90.2	94.1	*52.0	49.2	45.3
1951	48.1	50.6	51.3	52.4	51.7	47.6	47.7	48.6	51.1	50.6	50.2	51.1
1952	51.4	51.4	52.6	53.7	54.3	56.4	58.6	60.3	60.1	59.4	62.5	66.7
1953	67.0	67.1	65.4	61.3	62.3	60.0	59.2	58.2	55.0	58.3	59.5	59.4

*2-for-1 stock split, or equivalent.

AIR REDUCTION

Year	Jan.	Feb.	Mar.	Apr.	May	June	July	Aug.	Sep.	Oct.	Nov.	Dec.
1939	60.0	58.4	53.5	48.7	49.7	50.6	53.3	52.7	57.4	62.3	57.4	55.3
1940	54.1	50.3	49.6	50.4	42.3	39.0	40.4	41.1	41.2	41.5	42.0	41.0
1941	41.0	38.7	38.0	37.0	38.7	41.0	42.7	42.0	42.4	39.5	36.5	36.7
1942	36.5	34.3	32.5	31.7	31.0	31.3	32.1	32.6	33.6	36.5	37.1	39.1
1943	40.3	42.2	43.3	43.1	45.6	46.3	45.1	47.4	42.7	42.2	41.1	40.3
1944	40.5	41.2	41.5	39.6	38.7	40.2	41.4	40.5	39.7	39.4	38.7	39.0
1945	40.6	43.3	46.0	46.0	46.3	45.1	43.0	43.2	46.4	50.0	49.0	52.3
1946	55.3	54.0	53.3	56.7	54.7	53.6	52.2	48.6	41.7	36.4	35.2	35.3
1947	36.2	37.0	35.2	32.4	31.3	31.4	32.6	30.4	28.4	29.4	27.4	26.1
1948	25.7	24.4	24.1	26.2	26.1	25.2	23.3	22.4	22.1	23.1	21.6	19.5
1949	20.4	20.6	20.7	21.1	22.6	22.1	22.4	22.4	22.0	22.1	22.2	22.3
1950	24.0	23.3	22.5	23.0	23.6	22.6	22.4	24.2	24.6	25.6	26.7	27.2
1951	29.1	29.5	28.3	28.7	29.3	27.7	27.5	29.4	29.4	27.4	25.4	26.5
1952	26.7	26.0	26.0	25.2	24.7	25.5	26.0	26.5	26.5	26.1	25.2	27.5
1953	28.5	27.4	28.3	27.2	27.2	25.4	24.4	24.0	23.1	23.2	23.0	24.0

UNION CARBIDE

Year	Jan.	Feb.	Mar.	Apr.	May	June	July	Aug.	Sep.	Oct.	Nov.	Dec.
1939	85.7	83.3	80.4	70.1	74.1	76.5	78.1	78.6	83.7	89.3	86.6	86.4
1940	84.2	81.6	83.5	82.6	71.5	65.4	69.3	70.3	74.3	73.6	73.2	69.6
1941	67.7	62.6	66.0	65.1	67.1	70.7	75.4	78.2	77.6	73.3	70.4	71.4
1942	70.4	65.3	62.3	59.7	61.3	64.7	67.2	68.2	70.2	73.6	74.4	79.0
1943	80.7	81.2	83.1	83.1	84.3	84.2	83.6	82.2	82.1	81.3	79.1	88.5
1944	81.0	79.3	78.7	78.6	79.0	80.7	80.6	79.4	78.0	79.7	79.4	79.2
1945	80.0	84.1	85.7	88.1	91.7	89.3	88.4	91.4	97.3	97.4	98.4	100.3
1946	104.7	104.2	106.7	117.7	116.4	114.7	110.0	106.6	94.6	91.7	91.4	93.0
1947	93.2	96.7	98.0	97.1	97.2	102.4	108.0	106.4	104.3	110.0	109.6	100.6
1948	97.5	96.6	100.1	109.6	118.7	*41.7	41.1	40.4	40.5	41.2	40.2	40.4
1949	40.3	38.3	38.5	37.6	37.5	35.3	37.4	39.2	39.3	40.4	41.3	43.7
1950	43.7	43.4	43.3	45.4	49.0	47.3	43.1	45.5	46.3	47.2	50.3	52.6
1951	55.0	57.6	55.2	56.5	59.0	60.0	62.3	64.4	62.4	59.0	56.1	59.6
1952	62.2	59.0	60.3	60.1	60.0	65.4	66.6	65.5	64.2	63.1	61.2	69.6
1953	71.3	70.3	69.1	66.2	66.6	63.6	64.1	64.5	64.3	67.3	70.2	73.2

*3-for-1 stock split, or equivalent.

INDIVIDUAL STOCK PRICES, MONTHLY AVERAGE
(All prices shown in eighths)

GENERAL FOODS

Year	Jan.	Feb.	Mar.	Apr.	May	June	July	Aug.	Sep.	Oct.	Nov.	Dec.
1939	38.3	39.5	40.6	40.5	43.3	44.0	45.1	45.0	40.5	42.4	45.1	46.5
1940	46.7	47.5	47.6	48.3	42.5	39.4	41.4	40.6	40.5	38.5	36.4	36.1
1941	37.7	35.0	35.4	36.1	36.0	36.2	38.3	39.2	41.2	40.5	39.2	39.3
1942	37.6	33.4	29.5	26.7	27.7	30.5	31.2	32.3	33.0	33.6	33.6	35.2
1943	35.4	37.1	37.6	38.4	38.1	41.5	42.0	40.6	40.6	41.3	40.3	41.5
1944	42.1	42.0	42.1	41.5	41.6	41.5	42.6	42.3	41.7	41.7	41.1	41.1
1945	41.2	41.2	41.4	41.7	44.3	46.3	44.3	44.6	46.5	49.3	52.4	51.0
1946	53.6	52.7	51.6	53.4	53.1	51.0	53.0	52.0	46.3	42.5	44.0	43.3
1947	44.0	42.6	42.1	41.7	40.5	40.1	40.6	39.6	38.6	39.0	37.5	37.6
1948	37.6	36.0	35.6	37.7	39.0	40.0	39.0	39.3	38.0	38.7	39.0	38.7
1949	41.1	40.4	42.3	41.4	42.5	41.7	42.7	44.5	44.3	46.0	46.3	47.6
1950	48.6	49.2	50.0	50.1	50.1	49.7	47.7	46.3	46.1	48.4	47.6	46.5
1951	46.2	45.2	45.3	44.6	44.3	42.4	42.1	43.7	44.0	43.2	41.4	42.6
1952	43.5	43.4	43.2	42.3	43.4	45.1	47.2	48.2	48.5	49.3	51.1	52.7
1953	53.3	53.4	54.1	53.4	54.2	52.4	54.5	55.1	56.0	56.1	59.3	60.3

NATIONAL BISCUIT

Year	Jan.	Feb.	Mar.	Apr.	May	June	July	Aug.	Sep.	Oct.	Nov.	Dec.
1939	24.4	24.7	26.4	24.4	26.2	26.7	27.0	25.6	23.5	23.1	22.7	22.2
1940	23.5	24.1	24.0	23.5	20.3	18.2	19.1	19.1	19.6	18.6	18.2	17.2
1941	17.5	17.1	17.4	16.5	15.6	16.2	17.1	16.7	17.3	17.5	16.4	14.7
1942	15.3	15.5	14.7	13.4	13.6	14.6	14.6	15.0	15.1	15.6	16.1	15.5
1943	16.4	18.2	19.1	19.6	20.6	21.3	22.0	21.2	21.7	21.4	20.3	20.3
1944	21.3	21.3	21.4	21.0	21.0	21.6	22.7	22.7	22.4	23.4	23.7	24.1
1945	24.2	25.0	24.4	24.5	25.5	25.4	25.2	25.3	27.7	32.0	33.0	33.2
1946	32.6	32.4	32.2	34.3	35.7	33.4	33.7	32.2	29.2	27.5	28.0	28.0
1947	28.1	32.6	31.4	29.6	28.4	28.2	30.2	31.2	30.5	31.2	32.2	31.1
1948	29.6	27.4	27.4	28.1	28.4	29.1	29.1	29.3	30.6	31.3	30.5	30.4
1949	31.6	32.0	33.2	33.6	34.2	33.1	33.7	34.5	34.6	35.6	37.1	38.1
1950	38.6	39.0	38.4	36.5	36.3	36.1	33.1	34.7	36.0	36.0	34.3	32.5
1951	34.0	34.3	34.4	34.0	33.0	32.0	32.5	32.6	32.6	32.0	32.0	30.2
1952	31.1	32.0	30.7	30.1	31.0	32.0	33.0	34.0	33.5	32.6	33.4	34.6
1953	35.6	36.4	37.0	36.6	36.5	35.5	35.5	36.0	34.7	34.7	35.2	36.0

TABLE A-2 (Continued)
INDIVIDUAL STOCK PRICES, MONTHLY AVERAGE
(All prices shown in eighths)

AMERICAN WOOLEN COMMON

Year	Jan.	Feb.	Mar.	Apr.	May	June	July	Aug.	Sep.	Oct.	Nov.	Dec.
1939	5.7	5.3	5.0	4.0	4.3	4.3	4.5	4.4	10.0	13.1	10.6	9.2
1940	8.6	8.1	7.6	9.7	8.7	8.1	8.7	8.6	9.1	9.4	9.5	8.5
1941	7.7	7.0	7.2	6.5	5.7	6.4	7.1	7.7	7.5	6.5	5.6	4.5
1942	4.7	5.0	4.8	4.2	4.0	4.0	4.3	4.0	4.1	4.4	4.1	3.7
1943	4.3	5.6	6.5	7.4	7.4	7.5	7.5	6.6	6.5	6.5	6.0	5.6
1944	4.3	4.4	4.6	4.4	4.3	5.0	5.4	5.0	4.5	4.7	4.5	5.3
1945	10.7	11.4	10.3	10.3	11.0	20.3	24.0	20.1	21.6	23.3	26.6	30.2
1946	43.2	45.4	45.4	47.6	59.3	65.6	59.5	58.1	47.1	48.3	49.1	41.7
1947	30.5	42.3	40.0	33.0	31.2	31.2	37.7	44.5	42.4	47.4	45.7	42.5
1948	43.1	41.5	40.4	46.4	52.3	51.6	53.6	53.4	48.3	44.7	39.0	36.5
1949	36.1	36.5	32.4	27.3	26.5	24.2	27.0	25.5	24.6	25.4	24.7	27.0
1950	29.6	27.0	23.2	23.4	24.2	24.7	30.2	33.6	34.1	31.3	31.1	39.0
1951	43.7	44.3	41.3	38.2	38.6	33.3	33.7	38.4	38.2	40.6	39.4	37.4
1952	35.6	33.2	31.5	28.3	28.7	30.1	29.4	28.6	27.6	24.7	24.0	26.3
1953	26.5	24.7	25.2	21.7	21.0	21.3	20.1	17.6	15.5	15.4	15.3	16.2

CELANESE COMMON

Year	Jan.	Feb.	Mar.	Apr.	May	June	July	Aug.	Sep.	Oct.	Nov.	Dec.
1939	21.0	21.7	19.2	15.7	17.4	20.6	24.5	24.5	24.0	26.6	26.2	27.4
1940	28.3	28.5	30.0	33.0	27.6	24.5	28.0	28.4	29.2	28.1	28.2	27.3
1941	26.3	24.0	23.3	21.5	20.3	21.2	26.2	27.2	25.3	23.3	22.0	20.6
1942	20.4	19.1	18.4	16.4	17.2	18.4	18.6	20.1	20.4	27.5	25.3	28.2
1943	28.2	29.3	32.1	35.3	37.3	39.1	38.5	36.3	36.5	35.3	32.3	34.1
1944	38.1	37.5	37.0	34.0	33.4	35.3	36.1	35.0	35.1	34.7	35.2	37.3
1945	38.0	40.5	43.7	48.3	49.4	48.6	46.6	49.6	53.2	52.4	58.2	63.1
1946	63.2	60.5	64.4	72.6	76.4	75.5	67.3	67.3	57.4	*21.4	20.2	20.6
1947	19.5	19.7	19.1	19.1	18.4	20.7	23.6	24.4	25.3	26.4	25.4	26.7
1948	26.3	28.5	24.6	27.4	30.6	36.5	34.1	33.5	34.0	33.4	31.3	31.2
1949	30.1	27.2	26.4	25.5	25.5	25.3	26.7	26.7	28.1	28.5	31.1	33.1
1950	32.6	33.3	31.6	31.6	34.5	35.2	33.4	37.2	38.4	37.7	40.2	44.1
1951	45.7	51.6	50.6	49.4	48.7	51.1	52.1	55.2	54.4	50.1	46.5	50.5
1952	48.7	45.6	43.6	41.7	38.1	40.5	43.3	44.1	41.4	35.1	36.3	37.0
1953	36.2	33.1	31.6	28.1	27.2	25.6	24.0	24.5	22.2	20.6	21.2	19.6

*5-for-2 stock split, or equivalent.

243

TABLE A-3
BETHLEHEM STEEL CORPORATION

Year	Net Sales	Goods Cost	Gross Profit	Sales etc. Exp.	Deprc. Depl.	Oper. Income	Other Inc.	Total Inc.	Fin. Chgs.	Int. Pd.	Net	Fed. Tax	Net Income	Net com. sh.	Div. com. sh.
1929	342.5	N.A.	N.A.	N.A.	14.0	60.2	7.3	67.5		11.0	42.2	nil	42.2	11.01	3.50
1932	98.5	83.0	15.5	7.7	13.1	d 1.2	1.8	0.6		3.1	d19.4	nil	d19.4	d8.11	.50
1935	197.2	153.8	43.4	10.6	14.6	10.2	1.4	11.5		7.1	5.4	1.1	4.3	d0.70	nil
1936	288.1	231.7	56.4	11.5	28.9	22.9	0.9	23.7		6.5	16.9	3.0	13.9	2.09	1.50
1937	418.6	332.6	85.9	14.5	29.7	44.6	0.8	43.4		6.9	38.0	6.2	31.8	7.64	1.00,4.00a
1938	266.0	214.4	51.6	12.3	28.1	12.9	0.7	13.6		7.1	6.2	0.9	5.3	d0.70	nil
1939	414.1	324.1	90.1	14.7	32.6	38.0	0.7	38.7		7.5	30.8	6.2	24.6	5.75	1.50
1940	602.2	453.6	148.6	18.7	34.9	80.1	0.9	81.0		7.6	72.1	23.4	48.7	14.04	5.00
1941	961.2	742.8	218.4	22.6	49.6	129.8	1.0	130.7		6.0	119.8	85.3	34.5	9.35	6.00
1942	1516.7	1221.8	289.9	21.1	43.3	194.7	2.0	196.7		5.6	176.9	151.5	25.4	6.31	6.00
1943	1902.8	1604.4	298.4	22.5	47.2	183.9	3.3	187.2	4.8	5.7	161.7	129.6	32.1	8.58	6.00
1944	1746.7	1474.9	271.8	23.5	45.9	155.2	3.6	158.8	4.8	5.3	148.2	112.0	36.2	9.93	6.00
1945	1326.6	1132.5	194.1	25.3	74.7	58.5	2.9	61.4	10.3	4.0	47.1	12.2	34.9	9.52	6.00
1946	787.7	672.6	115.1	29.5	20.7	55.8	4.0	59.8	0.1	2.5	57.2	15.5	41.7	11.79	6.00
1947	1032.3	864.6	167.7	33.5	23.1	86.4	2.5	88.9	0.4	3.5	85.0	33.9	51.1	4.98	6.00
1948	1312.6	1064.7	247.9	40.2	30.2	155.2	2.6	157.9	1.4	3.5	153.0	62.7	90.3	9.36	2.40
1949	1266.8	982.9	283.9	42.9	33.0	172.5	4.2	176.6	0.5	4.8	171.4	72.1	99.3	9.68	2.40
1950	1439.8	1061.4	378.4	46.4	35.7	253.2	5.6	258.8	0.2	4.9	253.8	130.8	123.0	12.15	4.10
1951	1793.1	1365.4	427.7	49.8	45.9	282.4	6.4	288.8	0.6	5.6'	282.6	176.1	106.5	10.43	4.00
1952	1691.7	1377.2	313.5	51.5	54.5	168.4	9.8	178.3	0.2	7.8	164.4	73.5	90.9	8.80	4.00
1953	2082.0	1583.4	498.6	60.3	73.7	307.4	12.9	320.3	0.2	10.3	309.7	175.8	133.9	13.30	4.00

N.A. - Not available

d - deficit

a - before and after stock split

244

TABLE A-3 (Continued)

Year	Total Assets	Cash Items	Rec. Acct.	Inven- tory	Curr. Assets	Curr. Liab.	Work. Cap.	Invest- ment	Fix. Assets net	Fund Debt	Appro- priated Resve.	Pfd. Stocks	Com.	Sur- plus
1929	801.6	117.5	41.5	69.1	228.2	48.9	179.2	8.9	455.3	184.3	9.4	100.0	315.9	134.6
1932	659.3	47.0	12.6	51.5	111.1	15.2	95.8	9.6	515.3	126.2	9.1	93.4	315.9	89.2
1935	673.1	31.8	19.2	57.7	108.7	26.4	82.4	8.8	491.4	99.7	9.0	93.4	315.3	74.5
1936	676.1	36.8	32.7	75.8	145.6	40.6	105.0	8.1	470.0	141.1	9.6	93.4	303.2	57.6
1937	715.8	49.4	35.4	104.1	189.1	47.2	141.9	7.7	492.1	166.2	8.8	93.4	302.6	67.2
1938	699.5	37.2	34.2	108.9	180.3	37.5	142.8	8.8	484.3	161.4	9.4	93.4	302.5	64.9
1939	732.9	75.6	48.6	116.5	244.2	56.9	187.3	7.5	462.9	181.3	8.6	93.4	283.6	78.2
1940	763.7	84.0	63.5	135.1	287.3	91.6	195.7	6.7	454.3	177.2	9.6	93.4	283.6	96.3
1941	862.6	117.5	111.0	139.4	388.8	176.3	212.5	6.4	456.5	173.2	17.0	93.4	283.6	106.9
1942	1005.6	195.5	137.2	168.1	523.8	321.7	202.2	6.1	442.1	162.2	32.4	93.4	283.6	107.8
1943	1044.9	264.5	146.3	142.4	558.5	338.0	220.5	6.0	431.4	156.5	47.2	93.4	283.6	121.3
1944	1032.7	296.3	158.1	135.2	589.7	298.1	291.6	9.4	383.2	162.7	55.8	93.4	283.6	133.3
1945	880.9	296.6	101.7	155.8	514.2	174.8	339.3	5.8	335.5	120.9	56.6	93.4	283.6	144.8
1946	867.7	259.0	70.9	128.6	458.5	150.4	308.2	6.8	376.2	125.8	45.9	93.4	283.6	162.0
1947	948.8	206.5	105.4	164.2	486.1	196.0	290.1	9.4	441.1	123.8	57.0	93.4	283.6	188.5
1948	1029.0	189.7	116.0	199.9	505.6	225.0	280.6	11.4	495.3	121.8	30.3	93.4	283.6	268.2
1949	1155.5	314.5	93.0	189.2	596.7	214.2	382.4	14.9	524.6	169.6	30.3	93.4	303.5	337.3
1950	1314.3	346.4	139.1	214.5	700.0	298.8	401.1	24.3	572.4	166.1	30.0	93.4	303.5	414.8
1951	1541.7	473.6	141.9	257.6	873.1	408.8	464.4	30.5	616.6	220.3	30.0	93.4	303.5	476.8
1952	1610.1	402.9	167.1	281.7	851.8	352.1	499.7	33.8	701.1	298.3	30.0	93.4	303.5	522.8
1953	1783.0	511.4	173.9	293.6	979.0	577.3	401.7	34.4	746.3	154.9	30.0	93.4	303.5	611.9

TABLE A-4
UNITED STATES STEEL CORPORATION

Year	Net Sales	Goods Cost	Gross Profit	Sales etc. Exp.	Deprc. Depl.	Oper. Income	Other Inc.	Total Inc.	Spec. Chgs.	Int. Pd.	Net	Fed. Tax	Net Income	Net com. sh.	Div. com. sh.
1929	N.A.	N.A.	N.A.	47.2	63.3	N.A.		N.A.		14.9		N.A.	197.6	21.19	8.00
1932	N.A.	N.A.	N.A.	35.0	39.3	N.A.		N.A.		5.3		N.A.	d71.2	d11.08	.50
1935	776.3	645.0	131.3	34.6	47.8	4.3	6.4	10.7	0.4	4.9	5.1	3.9	1.1	d 2.76	nil
1936	1099.9	889.9	210.0	39.4	55.5	63.4	5.2	68.6	0.4	4.9	61.8	11.2	50.6	2.91	nil
1937	1086.8	790.0	296.8	44.7	59.6	124.2	8.1	132.3	0.9	5.1	124.4	29.5	94.9	8.01	1.00
1938	632.5	488.4	144.1	41.0	48.5	d 2.2	5.3	3.1	cr.0.3	7.9	d 4.8	2.9	d 7.7	d 3.78	nil
1939	904.2	667.1	237.1	51.1	60.6	60.0	4.8	64.8		8.9	54.1	13.0	41.1	1.83	nil
1940	1145.6	804.2	341.4	54.5	69.1	139.7	6.6	146.3		7.9	130.4	28.6	102.2	8.84	3.00
1941	1620.5	1112.1	508.4	58.5	93.4	266.8	5.0	271.8	1.9	5.8	238.7	122.5	116.2	10.45	4.00
1942	1863.1	N.A.	N.A.	N.A.	133.7	261.5	4.0	265.5	4.4	5.4	229.9	158.1	71.8	5.35	4.00
1943	1973.2	1512.3	440.9	47.8	128.8	183.6	5.2	188.8	5.2	4.6	153.5	90.1	63.4	4.39	4.00
1944	2082.0	1645.7	436.3	49.4	137.8	153.3	1.3	154.6	1.1	4.1	126.9	66.2	60.8	4.09	4.00
1945	1740.5	1398.0	342.5	53.1	121.4	84.0	7.2	91.3	2.1	3.4	88.3	30.3	58.0	3.77	4.00
1946	1485.7	1207.0	278.7	62.0	68.7	85.6	11.2	96.8		3.1	121.3	32.7	88.6	7.28	4.00
1947	2116.6	1643.8	472.8	70.6	114.0	213.8	7.0	220.8		2.5	220.8	93.7	127.1	11.70	5.00
1948	2473.7	1938.3	535.4	81.3	146.0	231.5	8.4	239.8		2.4	242.3	112.7	129.6	11.99	5.00
1949	2293.3	1721.5	571.8	90.2	119.7	282.6	9.6	292.2		2.3	295.3	129.4	165.9	5.39	3.75,1.00a
1950	2947.4	2073.8	873.6	93.2	143.9	445.1	9.9	455.0		2.2	454.6	239.1	215.5	7.29	3.45
1951	3509.7	2467.2	1042.5	112.7	162.1	577.3	14.4	591.7		2.0	591.5	407.1	184.4	6.10	3.00
1952	3131.7	2404.3	727.4	114.8	176.9	256.8	5.7	262.5		1.9	265.1	121.4	143.7	4.54	3.00
1953	3853.1	2714.6	1138.5	140.7	236.6	548.5	8.0	556.5		2.1	554.4	332.3	222.1	7.54	3.00

d – deficit
cr. – credit
N.A. – Not available
a – before and after stock split.

TABLE A-4 (Continued)

Year	Total Assets	Cash Items	Rec. Acct.	Inven-tory	Curr. Assets	Curr. Liab.	Work. Cap.	Invest-ment	Fix. Assets net	Fund Debt	Appro-priated Resve.	Pfd. Stocks	Com.	Sur-plus
1929	2286.2	195.5	78.2	288.6	562.2	121.4	440.9		1541.5	134.2	103.1	360.3	813.3	745.7
1932	2158.7	112.0	27.2	258.4	397.5	47.0	350.5		1650.8	114.7	84.4	360.3	870.3	680.4
1935	1822.4	141.7	52.7	258.8	453.2	72.3	380.9		1338.5	91.1	74.3	360.3	870.3	331.8
1936	1864.0	124.6	74.5	286.0	485.2	103.6	381.6		1350.0	97.7	78.1	360.3	870.3	333.9
1937	1918.7	86.0	63.3	331.5	480.7	117.3	363.4		1410.4	106.5	83.5	360.3	870.3	361.5
1938	1711.3	138.1	64.7	307.5	510.3	79.3	431.1		1166.5	230.4	84.3	360.3	870.3	285.8
1939	1768.5	185.5	95.8	294.6	575.9	143.9	432.0		1122.2	216.5	84.9	360.3	652.7	301.7
1940	1854.6	215.1	110.6	309.0	634.6	163.3	471.3		1110.2	191.7	87.0	360.3	652.7	343.9
1941	2045.0	351.2	140.6	291.7	783.5	287.7	495.8		1107.1	181.2	120.9	360.3	652.7	400.5
1942	2123.5	429.4	157.8	319.6	906.8	383.5	523.3		1062.6	139.7	154.4	360.3	652.7	412.2
1943	2106.1	375.4	157.4	334.4	867.3	347.9	519.3		1010.9	129.0	182.8	360.3	652.7	415.1
1944	2082.4	421.6	158.2	307.4	887.2	334.9	552.3		913.2	92.9	206.9	360.3	652.7	415.0
1945	1890.8	429.4	117.8	270.6	817.8	217.0	600.8		702.5	78.6	169.1	360.3	652.7	413.0
1946	2003.5	533.4	137.9	283.4	954.6	325.6	629.1		826.9	81.2	142.2	360.3	652.7	441.6
1947	2162.6	527.0	148.8	289.2	964.9	416.3	548.6		940.5	77.2	158.3	360.3	652.7	497.8
1948	2535.0	439.2	196.0	339.2	974.4	504.9	469.5	0.1	1300.8	71.6	125.5	360.3	870.3	602.5
1949	2556.4	400.1	166.6	372.4	939.1	455.3	483.8	0.1	1356.0	65.9	117.5	360.3	870.3	687.0
1950	2829.2	472.9	215.4	391.1	1079.3	637.5	441.8		1386.6	61.8	114.7	360.3	870.3	784.6
1951	3140.7	560.1	252.8	399.8	1212.7	877.8	334.9		1571.3	54.9	112.0	360.3	870.3	865.4
1952	2988.4	322.3	263.7	424.8	1010.7	684.2	326.6		1851.6	61.0	117.2	360.3	870.3	905.5
1953	3247.5	431.9	237.0	505.4	1174.3	828.3	346.0		1970.0	64.5	100.1	360.3	870.3	1024.1

TABLE A-5
CHRYSLER CORPORATION

Year	Net Sales	Goods Cost	Gross Profit	Sales etc. Exp.	Main-tain Exp.	Deprc. Depl.	Oper. Income	Other Inc.	Total Inc.	Int. Pd.	Net	Fed. Tax	Net Income	Net com. sh.	Div. com. sh.
1929	375.0	316.2	58.8	34.6		N.A.	24.2	3.7	27.9	3.5	24.3	2.4	21.9	4.93	3.00
1932	136.5	126.6	9.9	20.1		13.2	d10.1	1.7	d8.5	2.8	d11.3	---	d11.3	d2.58	1.25
1935	516.8	431.0	85.8	40.9		17.0	44.9	1.4	46.3	2.4	43.9	8.9	35.0	8.07	2.00
1936	667.1	546.0	121.1	47.7		14.2	73.4	2.8	76.2	0.1	74.9	12.8	62.1	14.25	12.00
1937	769.8	661.9	108.0	47.9		15.6	60.0	3.0	63.0	---	61.7	11.0	50.7	11.66	10.00
1938	413.3	352.2	61.1	40.4		13.9	20.7	1.8	22.5		22.5	3.7	18.8	4.32	2.00
1939	549.8	459.7	90.1	43.1		18.4	44.5	0.9	45.4		45.4	8.5	36.9	8.47	5.00
1940	744.6	633.6	111.0	49.8		20.6	57.6	3.7	61.3		61.3	23.4	37.8	8.69	5.50
1941	888.4	772.3	116.1	46.2		25.1	68.2	0.6	68.8		68.8	28.7	40.1	9.22	6.00
1942	623.7	553.3	70.4	21.8		12.5	48.9	3.6	52.5		37.5	22.0	15.5	3.57	3.50
1943	886.5	790.4	96.1	25.5		8.7	68.4	6.5	74.9		55.9	32.6	23.3	5.36	3.00
1944	1098.1	980.4	117.7	31.6		10.3	83.4	2.4	85.8		71.0	46.2	24.8	5.70	3.00
1945	994.5	901	93	36.4	34.1	9.5	55.0	0.6	55.5	1.3	57.1	19.6	37.5	8.61	3.00
1946	870	766	104	50.3	26.0	21.0	32.1	0.7	32.8	0.6	33.1	6.2	26.9	6.18	3.00
1947	1363	1165	198	66.2	30.0	13.6	133.9	5.2	119.2	0.7	118.5	51.3	67.2	7.72	4.00
1948	1568	1336	232	75	34.0	15.4	135.6	9.3	144.9	0.3	144.7	55.5	89.2	10.25	4.00
1949	2085	1772	313	87.4	41.7	19.4	197.3	16.0	213.4	0.3	213.2	81.0	132.2	15.19	5.25
1950	2191	1824	367	90.4	40.2	20.0	256.2	16.6	272.8	---	250.9	123.0	127.9	14.17	9.75
1951	2547	2256	291	103.1	53.3	25.9	142.1	8.9	151.0	---	151.0	79.0	72.0	8.27	7.50
1952	2601	2195	406	105.7	61.6	36.6	239.8	7.9	247.7	---	247.7	169.0	78.7	9.04	6.00
1953	3348	2936	412	144.5	72.4	47.0	193.2	6.6	199.8	---	199.8	125.0	74.8	8.59	6.00

d – deficit

248

TABLE A-5 (Continued)

Year	Total Assets	Cash Items	Rec. Acct.	Inven- tory	Curr. Assets	Notes Pay.	Curr. Liab.	Work. Cap.	Invest- ment	Fix. Assets net	In- tang.	Fund Debt	Appro- priated Resve.	Com.	Sur- plus
1929	209.7	38.7	13.5	38.1	90.3		18.9	71.4	1.1	83.6	25.0	49.8	10.5	73.8	56.8
1932	138.4	42.6	4.7	18.4	65.7	–	16.4	49.3	1.2	61.7	– –	42.3	4.5	21.8	53.3
1935	193.5	59.1	20.3	48.8	128.2	5.0	66.9	61.3	2.9	53.6		5.0	9.6	21.7	90.3
1936	210.7	60.9	19.6	60.6	140.1	– –	75.1	65.0	2.8	60.2		– –	12.2	21.8	101.5
1937	188.8	48.3	14.3	50.1	112.7		38.7	74.1	2.9	66.1			19.7	21.8	108.7
1938	212.0	71.0	16.5	46.6	134.2		55.9	78.2	1.6	70.0			15.6	21.8	118.8
1939	222.5	75.1	15.5	54.9	145.5		50.7	94.7	1.4	67.7			16.1	21.8	133.9
1940	267.6	117.1	18.1	59.2	194.4		77.8	115.6	2.7	63.4			25.4	21.8	141.6
1941	255.3	69.8	38.9	78.0	186.7		59.4	127.2	3.8	58.3			18.5	21.8	155.6
1942	323.8	87.5	100.9	71.2	259.6		118.2	141.4	3.6	55.1			26.6	21.8	155.9
1943	418.5	131.8	141.4	84.0	357.2		188.8	168.3	3.4	51.5			40.1	21.8	166.2
1944	509.5	154.3	216.8	77.5	448.6		255.8	192.8	3.4	48.4			51.9	21.8	178.0
1945	414.2	164.8	96.9	72.5	334.2		139.2	195.0	3.4	71.6			24.7	21.8	228.6
1946	390.4	139.5	49.1	106.3	294.9		107.6	187.3	3.9	85.3			– – –	21.8	261.1
1947	487.2	206.2	61.4	111.6	379.2		162.1	217.1	4.1	103.6				21.8	302.2
1948	541.4	201.2	44.9	141.3	387.4		156.7	230.7	3.8	149.7				21.8	362.9
1949	637.3	322.9	43.6	139.4	505.9		166.1	339.8	3.1	127.5				217.6	253.7
1950	743.8	347.1	47.6	168.7	563.4		229.5	333.9	5.8	169.9				217.6	296.7
1951	758.0	195.2	80.4	210.9	486.5		236.9	249.6	15.3	254.9				217.6	303.5
1952	913.9	167.0	203.3	219.9	590.2		366.4	223.8	13.7	309.0				217.6	330.0
1953	897.9	120.5	121.2	278.0	527.3		327.8	199.5	24.3	345.5				217.6	352.6

TABLE A-6
GENERAL MOTORS CORPORATION

Year	Net Sales	Goods Cost	Gross Profit	Sales etc. Exp.	Main-tain Exp.	Deprc. Depl.	Oper. Income	Other Inc.	Total Inc.	Spec. Chgs.	Int. Pd.	Net	Fed. Tax	Net Income	Net com. sh.	Div. com. sh.
1929	1504.4	N.A.	N.A.	N.A.	N.A.	35.2	N.A.	N.A.	301.9			275.4	28.1	247.3	5.44	2.50,3.30a
1932	432	N.A.	N.A.	N.A.		37	N.A.	N.A.	6			0.5	0.3	0.2	d .21	1.25
1935	1156	900	256	82	74	35	207	5	211			197	30	167	3.69	2.25
1936	1439	1093	347	93	80	39	253	48	301			282	44	238	5.35	4.50
1937	1607	1286	321	98	108	44	223	41	264			246	49	196	4.38	3.75
1938	1057	872	195	84	69	47	111	43	154			130	28	102	2.17	1.50
1939	1377	1056	321	99	95	43	222	38	260			228	45	183	4.04	3.50
1940	1795	1388	407	100	128	46	307	43	350			321	125	196	4.32	3.75
1941	2437	1850	587	101	165	53	486	32	528		1	492	290	202	4.44	3.75
1942	2250	1882	369	55	212	59	265	33	297		1	263	99	164	3.55	2.00
1943	3796	3229	567	75	309	60	427	28	455		5	401	251	150	3.23	2.00
1944	4262	3664	599	91	320	64	446	30	476		5	441	270	171	3.68	3.00
1945	3128	2812	316	99	269	68	171	36	207		6	214	26	188	4.07	3.00
1946	1962	1793	169	119	216	45	12	15	28	cr. 30	3	13	cr.44	88	1.76	2.25
1947	3815	3068	747	156	286	84	590	22	612	29	7	554	266	288	6.24	3.00
1948	4702	3564	1138	197	324	99	841	44	885	49	8	802	361	440	9.72	4.50
1949	5701	4199	1502	225	373	110	1166	45	1211	60	9	1125	468	656	14.64	8.00
1950	7531	5315	2216	246	439	122	1847	64	1912	68	9	1812	978	834	9.35	7.00,2.50a
1951	7466	5575	1891	245	482	125	1485	73	1558	53	2	1489	982	506	5.63	4.00
1952	7549	5656	1893	271	498	138	1484	101	1584	59	2	1502	944	559	6.25	4.00
1953	10028	7894	2134	328	850	178	1628	98	1726	63	3	1653	1055	598	6.71	4.00

N.A. - Not available
d - deficit
a - Before and after stock split
cr. - credit

TABLE A-6 (Continued)

Year	Total Assets	Cash Items	Rec. Acct.	Inven-tory	Curr. Assets	Notes Pay.	Curr. Liab.	Work. Cap.	Invest-ment	Fix. Assets net	In-tang.	Fund Debt	Appro-priated Resve.	Pfd. Stocks	Com.	Sur-plus
1929	1325	127	49	188	365		118	248	N.A.	416	51		58	139	435	381
1932	1115	173	32	76	280		58	222	N.A.	328	52		22	188	435	238
1935	1414	199	69	196	465		145	320	303	319	50		40	188	435	332
1936	1518	196	93	226	514		174	340	259	388	50		49	188	435	368
1937	1567	151	63	279	493		146	347	271	408	50		62	188	435	395
1938	1598	243	78	200	520		133	387	260	396	50		55	188	435	423
1939	1523	290	84	234	618		183	434	241	386	50		37	188	435	446
1940	1536	433	126	265	824		346	478	239	403	50		61	188	435	471
1941	1747	481	176	340	998		498	500	266	410	50		81	188	435	505
1942	1980	345	503	466	1314	100	662	652	203	372	50		70	184	435	573
1943	2265	554	525	564	1644	---	815	829	185	327	64		110	184	441	650
1944	2183	596	511	499	1606		703	903	186	298	63		102	184	441	680
1945	1814	378	437	348	1163		388	775	180	350	63		30	184	441	726
1946	1983	335	212	549	1096		328	769	167	608	63	125	38	284	441	703
1947	2473	520	278	693	1490		625	865	169	723	63	125	53	284	441	846
1948	2958	880	223	787	1889		802	1087	163	775	63	125	86	284	441	1076
1949	2824	779	251	722	1752		486	1266	170	778	63	---	90	284	441	1368
1950	3444	961	430	889	2280		773	1506	211	802	63		118	284	441	1663
1951	3672	550	559	1141	2250		793	1457	212	942	63		168	284	441	1806
1952	4001	312	534	1297	2142		951	1191	233	1263	63		145	284	441	2002
1953	4405	367	543	1447	2357		1121	1236	243	1536	63		125	284	443	2256

N.A. - Not available.

TABLE A-7
AIR REDUCTION COMPANY

Year	Net Sales a	Goods Cost	Gross Profit	Sales etc. Exp. c	Deprc. Depl. b	Oper. Income	Other Inc.	Total Inc.	Int. Pd.	Net	Fed. Tax	Net Income	Net com. sh.	Div. com. sh.
1929	21.8			15.3	2.2	6.5	--	6.5		6.6	0.6	6.0	7.75	4.00
1932	11.7			9.9	1.6	1.8	0.7	2.5		2.5	0.2	2.3	2.72	3.00
1935	20.9	7.4	13.5	7.6	1.1	5.8	0.4	6.2	0.1	6.2	0.9	5.3	6.29	5.50
1936	27.8	9.7	18.1	10.2	1.4	7.9	0.4	8.3	0.1	8.3	1.2	7.1	2.79	2.00,1.50e
1937	31.0	15.2	15.8	7.1	1.3	8.5	0.2	8.7	0.1	8.6	1.3	7.3	2.85	3.00
1938	23.7	13.0	10.7	6.3	1.2	4.4	0.1	4.5		4.5	0.7	3.8	1.47	1.50
1939	27.6	14.9	12.7	6.7	1.3	6.0	0.2	6.2		6.1	1.0	5.1	1.98	1.50
1940	36.4	19.4	17.0	7.9	1.4	9.1	0.2	9.3		9.2	2.8	6.4	2.38	1.75
1941	53.6	29.9	23.7	9.0	1.6	14.6	0.4	15.0		14.9	7.8	7.1	2.68	2.00
1942	75.0	46.0	29.0	9.9	2.9	19.1	0.5	19.6	0.2	19.3	12.5	6.8	2.50	2.00
1943	94.1	63.8	30.3	10.6	3.5	19.6	0.5	20.1	0.2	19.4	12.9	6.5	2.41	2.00
1944	97.9	68.6	29.3	12.4	3.9	17.0	0.5	17.5	0.3	17.0	11.1	5.9	2.15	2.00
1945	80.7	56.6	24.1	13.6	3.7	10.5	0.7	11.2	0.7	10.3	7.0	3.3	3.04	2.00
1946	71.2	49.1	22.1	15.2	2.8	6.5	1.1	7.6	0.7	6.8	2.3	4.5	1.66	1.75
1947	85.5	59.6	25.9	16.6	3.4	9.2	0.8	10.0	0.7	9.2	3.5	5.7	2.08	1.00
1948	94.9	66.4	27.5	17.1	4.0	11.3	0.8	12.1	0.8	11.2	4.7	6.5	2.36	1.00
1949	89.5	61.7	27.8	16.6	4.2	11.2	0.6	11.8	0.8	10.8	4.6	6.2	2.26	1.00
1950	98.1	65.9	32.2	16.1	4.4	16.1	1.4	17.5	0.8	16.6	8.0	8.6	3.15	1.00
1951	118.1	79.5	38.6	18.4	3.9	20.2	1.2	21.4	0.8	20.3	12.8	7.5	2.69	1.40
1952	124.6	88.1	36.5	20.0	5.0	16.4	1.3	17.7	0.8	16.8	9.5	7.3	2.25	1.40
1953	131.4	96.3	35.1	21.3	6.8	13.8	0.8	14.6	0.7	13.8	7.0	6.8	2.06	1.40

a – Includes other income, 1929-33
b – Included in Goods Cost
c – All costs, 1929-33

d – deficit
e – after stock dividend

TABLE A-7 (Continued)

Year	Total Assets	Cash Items	Rec. Acct.	Inven-tory	Curr. Assets	Notes Pay.	Curr. Liab.	Work. Cap.	Invest-ment	Fix. Assets (net)	Fund Debt	Appro-priated Resve.	Pfd. Stocks	Com.	Sur-plus
1929	31.5	10.1	3.1	1.6	14.8		1.7	13.1	4.1	12.4		1.9		19.1	8.8
1932	35.0	5.4	1.9	1.6	11.0		1.3	9.8	12.4	10.8		4.6		22.2	6.9
1935	39.4	15.7	2.9	2.1	20.7		2.7	18.0	4.9	12.7		1.9		24.0	10.9
1936	41.3	16.1	3.3	2.4	21.7		4.2	17.5	4.7	13.7		1.9		24.2	11.0
1937	42.7	13.5	2.9	3.0	19.5		4.3	15.3	5.0	16.4		3.5		25.0	10.0
1938	41.9	12.0	2.9	2.7	17.6		2.5	15.1	5.4	16.9		3.5		25.0	10.9
1939	44.2	13.8	3.5	2.7	20.0		3.4	16.6	5.5	16.6		3.6		25.0	11.3
1940	50.2	14.1	4.4	3.9	22.5		6.3	16.2	5.5	20.8		3.9		28.0	12.0
1941	54.5	10.6	7.1	5.8	23.5		12.0	11.4	4.2	26.1		1.1		28.0	13.4
1942	67.0	12.7	11.5	7.7	31.9	0.6	14.1	17.8	5.2	29.3	9.4	1.0		28.0	14.6
1943	69.6	11.3	13.3	9.9	34.5	0.6	16.5	18.0	5.8	28.3	8.8	1.0		28.0	15.3
1944	90.3	33.1	10.1	9.9	53.1		18.9	34.2	7.8	28.0	24.5	2.3		28.0	16.7
1945	83.1	27.8	9.5	9.8	47.1		10.4	36.8	5.6	28.2	24.0	2.2		28.0	18.5
1946	81.4	18.9	9.1	11.3	39.2		8.6	30.7	6.0	33.9	23.0	2.3		28.0	19.5
1947	91.4	17.6	9.8	12.4	40.4		9.7	30.7	7.7	42.1	30.0	2.3		28.0	21.4
1948	94.5	18.2	10.7	13.1	42.6		11.9	30.7	5.2	45.6	30.0	2.3		28.0	22.9
1949	96.2	21.6	9.5	12.7	44.2		11.1	33.1	5.6	45.4	28.5	2.2		28.0	26.4
1950	107.8	25.3	13.5	13.0	52.5		15.2	37.2	7.9	46.5	27.5	0.6		28.0	36.5
1951	141.1	45.0	16.1	18.8	80.5		23.0	57.5	1.1	58.5	26.5	0.7	24.9	28.0	38.1
1952	135.7	25.9	16.1	21.0	63.8		15.8	48.1	1.3	69.7	25.1	0.6	24.9	28.0	41.4
1933	135.1	16.3	16.0	21.2	54.5		14.8	39.6	1.0	79.0	23.7	0.5	24.9	28.0	43.2

TABLE A-8

UNION CARBIDE AND CARBON CORPORATION

Year	Net Sales	Goods Cost	Gross Profit	Sales etc. Exp.*	Main-tain Exp.*	Deprc. Depl.*	Oper. Income	Other Inc.	Total Inc.	Spec. Chgs.	Int. Pd.	Net	Fed. Tax	Net Income	Net com. sh.	Div. com. sh.
1929	N.A.					7.1	N.A.				0.7	N.A.		35.4	3.94	3.00,1.30a
1932	N.A.					6.2	N.A.				0.7	N.A.		8.8	0.98	1.75
1935	120.0	72.5	47.5	16.5	3.7	7.5	30.7	1.8	32.5		0.8	31.2	4.0	27.3	3.03	1.55
1936	152.1	88.9	63.2	19.4	4.6	8.2	43.4	2.4	45.8		0.8	44.9	8.0	36.9	4.09	2.30
1937	169.1	97.3	71.8	21.9	5.9	9.4	49.8	2.7	52.5		0.8	51.7	8.9	42.8	4.75	3.20
1938	130.5	80.5	50.0	19.8	4.7	10.4	30.0	1.8	31.8		1.0	30.7	5.5	25.2	2.77	2.40
1939	170.3	105.8	64.5	21.5	5.4	11.7	42.9	1.4	44.3		1.2	42.5	6.7	35.8	3.86	1.90
1940	231.4	138.7	92.7	24.9	6.3	15.9	67.7	2.5	70.2	fgn.pr. 2.5	1.2	65.9	23.7	42.2	4.57	2.30
1941	317.8	198.8	119.0	28.6	8.5	20.3	90.3	2.6	92.9		0.8	85.7	43.6	42.0	4.53	3.00
1942	405.0	270.3	134.7	31.6	12.5	32.9	103.1	2.4	105.5		0.9	104.5	66.4	38.1	4.10	3.00
1943	488.4	333.4	155.0	34.6	15.3	37.4	120.4	2.5	122.9		0.8	118.2	79.9	38.3	4.13	3.00
1944	507.9	343.1	164.8	40.0	16.4	33.0	124.8	d0.3	128.1		0.7	117.8	83.3	34.5	4.06	3.00
1945	481.5	345.7	135.8	42.9	17.5	37.7	92.9	4.4	97.3		0.6	96.2	58.2	37.9	4.08	3.00
1946	415.0	279.4	135.6	46.7	16.1	14.8	88.9	4.2	93.1		---	92.9	25.7	57.2	6.10	3.00
1947	521.8	350.7	171.1	54.8	20.9	16.6	115.8	7.1	122.9		0.4	122.2	46.6	75.7	7.98	3.75
1948	631.6	417.2	213.4	58.6	25.6	21.7	155.2	8.8	164.0		4.1	159.5	57.2	102.3	3.55	2.00,1.00a
1949	585.8	384.4	201.4	60.3	23.2	27.5	140.3	9.8	150.1		4.2	145.9	53.7	92.2	3.20	2.00
1950	758.3	464.8	293.5	63.9	27.8	32.7	229.5	14.1	243.6		4.1	237.8	113.7	124.1	4.30	2.50
1951	927.5	589.5	338.0	80.6	39.9	42.9	257.3	16.1	273.4		4.1	268.4	164.5	103.9	3.60	2.50
1952	956.9	652.1	304.8	92.4	46.8	54.3	212.3	21.8	234.1		6.6	227.3	129.0	98.3	3.61	2.50
1953	1025.8	716.5	309.3	91.9	49.5	75.4	207.0	22.8	239.8		11.5	227.8	125.0	102.8	3.55	2.50

N.A. - Not available   d - deficit   a - after stock dividend

* - After 1933, included in Goods Cost and other expenses.

fgn. pr. - write-off of foreign properties

TABLE A-8 (Continued)

Year Dec.31	Total Assets	Cash Items	Rec. Acct.	Inven-tory	Curr. Assets	Notes Pay.	Curr. Liab.	Work. Cap.	Invest-ment	Fix. Assets (net)	Fund Debt	Appro-priated Resve.	Com.	Sur-plus
1929	306.6	68.3	21.8	38.5	128.6	0.1	15.5	113.0	12.5	163.6	12.8		174.2	96.8
1932	234.4	11.3	9.4	41.1	61.8	---	6.6	55.2	12.4	156.5	9.3		172.8	36.4
1935	271.1	30.0	16.3	41.2	87.4	---	16.0	71.5	12.4	167.4	21.2		173.3	58.7
1936	292.6	35.3	20.8	41.0	97.0	---	24.4	72.6	12.8	178.8	21.1		173.3	71.9
1937	292.6	20.1	17.2	52.1	89.4	---	25.7	63.7	8.1	191.3	19.1		173.3	72.6
1938	309.2	33.6	15.7	58.3	107.5	---	17.6	89.9	18.5	181.5	40.0		181.6	70.0
1939	336.8	52.1	25.8	55.5	133.4	---	22.6	110.8	20.0	181.5	40.0		192.9	81.4
1940	364.7	81.3	26.7	50.2	158.2	---	47.0	111.2	17.4	186.8	29.1		192.9	95.6
1941	397.8	68.1	36.1	61.5	165.7	---	76.8	88.8	26.2	203.1	26.4		192.9	100.5
1942	426.6	69.0	52.9	70.0	191.8	---	95.9	95.9	25.7	202.1	24.6	10.0	192.9	101.5
1943	459.5	118.8	55.0	74.4	248.1	---	115.5	132.6	25.4	175.1	22.8	22.5	192.9	104.2
1944	481.2	164.9	54.2	71.4	290.4	---	128.4	162.0	25.4	151.5	21.0	29.0	192.9	108.3
1945	428.1	139.9	42.2	80.1	281.6	---	92.7	188.9	25.6	117.1	---	---	192.9	116.0
1946	439.0	113.5	51.6	91.7	256.9	---	80.3	176.6	26.8	151.1	---	---	192.9	142.2
1947	649.1	201.0	65.4	112.0	378.4	---	102.7	275.8	27.5	238.1	150.0	6.5	193.1	195.2
1948	722.7	158.4	71.5	126.1	356.0	---	124.9	231.0	30.3	330.3	150.0	6.5	194.7	246.5
1949	744.3	142.8	65.8	127.0	335.6	---	111.6	224.0	30.3	373.7	150.0	6.5	197.0	279.2
1950	869.2	214.6	91.9	123.0	429.5	---	177.9	251.5	25.1	409.1	150.0	6.4	201.5	333.3
1951	978.1	197.1	97.0	175.9	470.0	---	237.4	232.6	24.9	478.1	150.0	6.4	204.6	379.8
1952	1072.2	128.1	119.6	225.0	472.8	---	211.0	261.8	19.7	574.5	240.0	6.4	208.8	406.1
1953	1190.6	140.3	107.4	262.7	510.4	---	207.1	303.3	15.7	658.4	330.0	6.4	210.5	436.6

TABLE A-9

GENERAL FOODS CORPORATION

Year	Net Sales	Goods Cost	Gross Profit	Sales etc. Exp.	Main-tain Exp.*	Deprc. Depl.	Oper. Income	Other Inc.	Total Inc.	Spec. Chgs.	Int. Pd.	Net	Fed. Tax	Net Income	Net com. sh.	Div. com. sh.
1929	128.0	71.7	56.3	36.3		N.A.	20.1	1.6	21.7			21.7	2.3	19.4	3.63	3.00
1932	N.A.	N.A.	N.A.	32.4		2.0	11.0	0.9	11.9			11.9	1.6	10.3	1.93	2.50
1935	107.4	66.8	40.7	26.9	1.2	1.7	13.7	0.8	14.5		0.0	14.4	2.7	11.7	2.23	1.80
1936	122.5	77.6	44.9	28.6	1.5	1.7	16.2	1.1	17.3		0.0	17.3	3.0	14.4	2.73	2.25
1937	133.1	93.3	39.8	29.6	1.6	1.8	10.2	0.9	11.1		0.0	11.0	2.0	9.1	1.73	2.00
1938	135.2	88.3	46.9	28.3	1.7	2.4	15.6	0.9	16.5		0.0	16.4	2.8	13.6	2.49	2.25
1939	145.6	94.1	51.6	30.1	2.1	2.9	18.1	0.8	18.9		0.0	18.6	3.4	15.1	2.75	2.25
1940	152.9	99.8	53.1	29.4	2.0	2.7	19.8	0.8	20.6	0.3	0.0	20.5	5.3	15.2	2.77	2.00
1941	180.4	117.1	63.3	32.3	2.2	2.7	27.3	0.9	28.2		0.0	26.7	12.6	14.2	2.57	2.00
1942	231.5	163.3	68.2	31.0	2.3	2.6	33.2	0.9	34.1		0.1	32.5	18.7	13.8	2.50	1.70
1943	259.9	185.9	74.0	33.3	2.9	3.1	36.3	0.7	37.0		0.0	35.5	21.3	14.1	2.42	1.60
1944	296.5	222.2	74.3	38.4	4.1	3.5	30.9	0.7	31.6		0.0	30.1	17.5	12.6	2.14	1.60
1945	307.1	236.9	70.2	37.3	4.4	3.5	28.1	1.0	29.1		0.6	28.4	15.3	13.1	2.36	1.60
1946	330.9	252.9	78.0	43.0	5.8	3.3	33.4	2.3	35.7		0.7	34.8	13.7	21.1	3.79	2.00
1947	407.3	324.8	82.5	51.9	7.4	4.0	28.8	2.1	30.9		0.8	29.8	11.5	18.3	3.19	2.00
1948	463.3	362.8	100.5	59.7	7.8	4.6	38.7	2.1	40.8		0.7	40.0	15.4	24.6	4.25	2.00
1949	474.6	362.6	112.0	66.0	7.4	4.9	43.6	2.5	46.1		1.2	44.9	17.5	27.4	4.77	2.25
1950b	124.1	91.6	32.5	19.5	1.8	1.3	12.4	0.6	13.0		0.2	12.8	4.5	8.3	1.45	0.75
1951	589.2	455.0	124.2	83.7	8.5	5.7	50.5	3.3	53.8		0.8	52.9	26.5	26.4	4.58	2.30
1952	632.5	491.3	141.2	87.7	8.9	6.4	50.8	2.4	53.2	0.4	1.7	51.2	30.8	20.4	3.52	2.30
1953	701.1	536.8	164.3	N.A.	9.1	6.4	59.4	2.1	61.5	4.9	1.9	54.7	29.9	24.8	4.31	2.40
1954	783.0	598.3	184.7	N.A.	N.A.	N.A.	64.7	2.1	66.8	2.2	1.8	62.8	35.0	27.9	4.66	2.65

* - Maintenance and Depreciation are included in Cost of Goods Sold

b - Three months to March 31, 1950; fiscal years thereafter.

N.A. - Not available

256

TABLE A-9 (Continued)

Year	Total Assets	Cash Items	Rec. Acct.	Inven-tory	Curr. Assets	Notes Pay.	Curr. Liab.	Work. Cap.	Invest-ment	Fix. Assets Net	In-tang.	Fund Debt	Appro-priated Resve.	Pfd. Stocks	Com.	Sur-plus
1929	70.5	9.2	6.1	20.2	35.4		10.3	25.1	2.0	23.8	25.3		0.4		47.7	11.8
1932	64.1	10.7	6.1	15.5	32.3		5.2	27.1	3.2	17.4	25.3		0.7		73.7	9.8
1935	67.9	15.4	6.0	20.8	42.2		6.8	35.4	3.1	15.6	25.3		0.7		73.7	17.1
1936	74.2	8.1	7.1	32.0	47.2		10.4	36.7	3.1	16.5	---		0.7		73.7	19.8
1937	76.1	5.6	9.5	30.1	45.3		15.1	30.2	3.1	20.4			0.9		48.4	16.8
1938	89.0	13.9	9.4	29.9	53.2		10.9	42.3	3.1	24.8			0.8	15.0	48.4	19.1
1939	90.9	7.9	9.9	35.9	53.7		10.4	43.4	4.7	30.6			0.5	15.0	48.4	21.5
1940	97.3	14.4	12.4	33.0	59.8		13.0	46.8	5.4	30.7			2.0	15.0	48.4	25.6
1941	118.8	7.5	14.0	57.2	78.7	4.5	30.0	48.8	5.9	32.7			3.5	15.0	48.4	28.5
1942	123.0	28.8	13.4	43.4	85.6		23.8	61.8	2.8	29.6		10.0	4.9	15.0	48.4	35.1
1943	142.6	19.3	18.2	63.8	101.2		30.2	71.0	3.1	32.3		10.0	6.4	15.0	55.4	37.1
1944	155.5	19.7	23.2	73.6	116.5		40.0	76.5	2.4	31.9		10.0	6.4	15.0	55.4	39.5
1945	162.8	38.7	20.6	65.5	124.9		33.4	91.5	2.1	33.6		25.0	6.4	---	55.4	43.4
1946	171.8	21.2	24.3	80.0	125.6		32.4	93.2	2.1	41.9		25.0	9.4	---	55.4	50.4
1947	207.1	20.0	26.6	100.4	148.9	0.2	37.8	111.0	3.4	54.5		27.6	10.1	25.0	55.4	51.9
1948	222.4	24.1	23.9	108.8	160.3	0.1	41.3	119.0	3.7	58.2		27.4	11.6	24.8	55.4	62.9
1949	238.0	31.3	19.8	115.7	170.0	0.6	44.3	125.7	3.1	64.8		26.0	11.7	24.5	55.4	77.0
1950b	246.3	25.6	31.1	116.8	177.5	1.2	52.2	125.3	3.2	65.6		25.3	11.7	24.5	55.4	78.1
1951	292.0	20.1	42.4	147.4	215.9	15.2	83.6	132.3	3.1	73.0		24.0	---	24.3	105.4	55.5
1952	321.2	51.5	41.0	142.1	240.1	1.3	73.2	167.0	3.3	77.4		57.7	0.4	24.0	105.4	61.7
1953	330.7	60.8	45.8	142.3	253.2	1.4	74.3	178.9	3.3	73.7		56.4	---	23.8	105.4	72.4
1954	353.2	26.3	53.2	177.2	261.1		79.2	182.0	3.9	87.8		55.0	---	23.5	119.3	78.2

b – Dec. 31 through 1949, March 31, 1950 and thereafter.

257

TABLE A-10
NATIONAL BISCUIT COMPANY

Year	Net Sales	Goods Cost	Gross Profit	Sales etc. Exp. a	Maintain Exp. a	Deprc. Depl.	Oper. Income	Other Inc.	Total Inc.	Spec. Chgs.	Int. Pd.	Net	Fed. Tax	Net Income	Net com. sh.	Div. com. sh.
1929	N.A.	N.A.	N.A.	N.A.	N.A.	2.6	N.A.	N.A.	24.1			24.1	2.7	21.4	8.20	7.50
1932	N.A.	N.A.	N.A.	N.A.	N.A.	3.2	N.A.	N.A.	23.1			19.9	2.8	17.1	2.44	2.80
1935	81.3	39.8	41.5	30.3	2.0	2.7	11.3	0.4	11.7			11.7	1.7	10.0	1.31	1.70
1936	89.4	44.5	44.9	29.7	1.7	2.7	15.2	0.2	15.6			15.6	2.9	12.6	1.73	1.60
1937	93.7	50.5	43.3	29.2	2.0	2.9	14.0	0.1	14.4			14.3	2.4	11.9	1.62	1.60
1938	90.2	45.0	45.2	29.8	2.0	2.9	15.4	0.2	15.8			15.8	3.0	12.8	1.76	1.60
1939	91.0	44.2	46.8	31.3	2.0	3.1	15.5	0.2	15.9			15.4	3.4	11.9	1.62	1.60
1940	96.1	48.7	47.4	31.3	2.2	3.2	16.2	0.1	16.5	0.5		15.7	5.0	10.7	1.43	1.20
1941	110.8	64.4	46.4	37.2	2.6	3.3	19.1	0.2	19.4	0.7		19.2	8.5	10.7	1.43	1.60
1942	154.8	97.9	56.9	32.5	3.5	3.3	24.3	0.2	24.6	0.2		24.5	15.2	9.2	1.19	1.40
1943	183.0	122.9	60.1	35.2	3.9	3.3	24.8	0.3	25.2	0.2		24.0	15.3	8.7	1.10	1.20
1944	205.3	138.3	67.0	37.4	4.3	3.3	29.4	0.4	29.8	0.2		29.6	20.6	9.0	1.16	1.20
1945	205.0	137.9	67.1	38.1	4.6	3.5	29.0	0.4	29.4	2.2		27.3	16.8	10.5	1.39	1.20
1946	220.2	150.2	70.0	41.2	5.0	3.6	28.8	0.3	29.1	0.0		29.1	11.9	17.2	2.21	1.20
1947	263.9	177.6	86.3	48.2	6.9	3.8	38.2	0.3	38.5	0.0		38.5	15.6	22.9	2.41	1.50
1948	296.2	206.7	89.5	54.2	9.2	4.2	35.4	0.4	35.8	0.2		35.7	14.4	21.3	2.38	2.00
1949	294.4	198.8	95.6	59.0	10.4	5.5	36.7	0.4	37.1	0.2		37.0	15.3	21.7	3.17	2.00
1950	296.4	196.2	100.2	60.5	9.7	6.4	39.7	0.4	40.1	0.0		40.0	18.9	21.1	3.08	2.30
1951	329.9	225.0	104.9	71.6	12.1	6.8	33.3	0.5	33.8	--		33.8	17.6	16.2	2.30	2.00
1952	346.5	229.2	117.3	77.3	12.9	7.2	40.0	0.4	40.4	0.2		40.2	22.4	17.8	2.56	2.00
1953	357.0	235.0	122.0	84.3	13.5	7.5	39.7	1.8	41.5	--	0.2	41.3	23.1	18.1	2.61	2.00

a - Included in Cost of Goods Sold

TABLE A-10 (Continued)

Year	Total Assets	Cash Items	Rec. Acct.	Inven-tory	Curr. Assets	Notes Pay.	Curr. Liab.	Work. Cap.	Invest-ment	Fix. Assets Net	Fund Debt	Appro-priated Resve.	Pfd. Stocks	Com.	Sur-plus
1929	133.2	29.7	4.9	8.9	43.6		7.4	36.2		89.6		8.2	24.8	60.0	34.2
1932	137.1	32.2	3.2	8.5	43.9		8.1	35.8		93.2	0.1	8.2	24.8	62.9	33.1
1935	124.5	24.1	2.4	9.4	35.9		7.3	28.6		87.0		7.7	24.8	62.9	21.8
1936	124.0	26.9	2.4	8.9	38.2		5.9	32.3		84.2		7.7	24.8	62.9	22.7
1937	124.0	27.2	2.5	10.2	39.9		5.8	34.1		82.8		7.7	24.8	62.9	22.8
1938	125.0	30.9	2.6	7.8	41.2		6.5	34.7		82.3		7.7	24.8	62.9	23.1
1939	125.5	30.7	2.5	9.5	42.7		6.9	35.8		81.3		7.7	24.8	62.9	23.2
1940	128.7	33.6	2.9	9.2	45.8		11.1	34.6		81.9		7.7	24.8	62.9	22.2
1941	131.0	31.0	3.5	14.3	48.8		14.7	34.1		81.1		7.8	24.8	62.9	20.7
1942	138.1	30.3	7.4	19.6	57.2		21.6	35.7		79.0		8.8	24.8	62.9	20.1
1943	140.4	31.2	6.5	25.6	63.3		23.4	39.9		74.5		9.9	24.8	62.9	19.4
1944	134.2	41.1	6.1	24.9	72.1		30.2	41.9		57.9		6.6	24.8	62.9	9.7
1945	132.5	47.4	4.7	26.0	78.1		27.2	50.9		52.6		3.4	24.8	62.9	14.2
1946	138.6	43.0	6.7	34.5	84.3		21.7	62.6		52.2		8.7	24.8	62.9	20.6
1947	154.3	46.9	6.8	43.1	96.8		28.8	68.0		54.9		14.7	24.8	62.9	23.2
1948	161.8	44.5	7.2	39.7	91.4		27.9	63.6		67.4		20.7	24.8	62.9	25.5
1949	173.3	34.1	6.4	36.5	89.1	1.6	32.0	57.1		81.8		20.7	24.8	62.9	32.9
1950	183.4	34.1	8.2	40.1	94.6	1.4	35.3	59.3		86.4		20.7	24.8	62.9	39.7
1951	188.0	19.1	8.0	44.3	89.0	0.7	38.0	51.0		96.4		20.7	24.8	62.9	41.6
1952	201.8	40.5	9.2	44.8	94.5	0.9	44.3	50.2		104.4	4.0	20.7	24.8	62.9	45.1
1953	205.2	43.7	9.1	43.4	95.2	---	43.8	51.4	1.1	105.7	4.0	20.7	24.8	62.9	48.9

TABLE A-11
AMERICAN WOOLEN COMPANY

Year	Net Sales	Goods Cost	Gross Profit	Sales etc. Exp.	Deprc. Depl.	Oper. Income	Other Inc.	Total Inc.	Spec. Chgs.	Int. Pd.	Net	Fed. Tax	Net Income	Net com. sh.	Div. com. sh.
1929	N.A.	N.A.	N.A.	N.A.	1.9	d 0.4	1.3	0.9	3.1		N.A.		d 4.2	d19.32	nil
1932	N.A.	N.A.	N.A.	N.A.	1.1	d 4.1	0.9	d 3.2	3.7		d 7.2		d 7.2	d25.40	nil
1935	70.3	62.8	7.5	2.8	1.9	4.7	0.7	5.4		0.1	3.2	0.5	2.7	0.15	nil
1936	71.0	63.4	7.6	3.1	2.0	4.4	0.7	5.1		0.1	2.2	0.3	1.9	d 1.88	nil
1937	75.1	72.0	3.1	2.9	2.1	0.2	0.5	0.7		0.2	d 1.9	0.0	d 1.9	d11.16	nil
1938	42.0	42.6	d 0.6	2.5	2.2	d 5.2	0.5	d 4.7		0.1	d 4.9	0.0	d 4.9	d18.50	nil
1939	64.9	57.6	7.3	2.8	2.1	2.3	0.6	2.9		0.0	2.7	0.4	2.3	d 0.35	nil
1940	76.6	68.8	7.8	2.8	1.2	3.6	0.6	4.2		0.1	4.0	0.8	3.2	1.76	nil
1941	145.7	119.6	26.1	3.7	1.2	20.8	0.8	21.6	2.0	0.2	19.1	12.2	6.9	11.23	nil
1942	196.0	164.2	31.8	3.4	1.3	26.6	1.3	27.9	2.0	0.3	25.1	20.3	4.8	5.93	nil
1943	197.5	156.1	41.4	3.6	1.3	36.3	0.9	37.2	4.0	0.4	32.5	27.0	5.5	7.56	nil
1944	183.0	143.9	39.1	3.9	1.4	33.9	0.9	34.8	4.3	0.1	30.4	25.1	5.3	7.11	nil
1945	162.7	133.2	29.5	4.6	1.4	23.5	0.7	24.2		0.0	24.0	15.7	8.3	14.63	nil
1946	170.8	129.6	41.3	4.7	1.5	35.0	1.9	37.0		0.2	36.4	16.3	20.1	21.86	12.00
1947	176.0	143.6	32.4	5.0	1.6	25.8	0.8	26.6		0.0	26.5	11.2	15.3	15.29	10.00
1948	197.8	163.9	33.9	5.6	1.8	26.6	0.6	27.2		0.1	26.5	10.0	16.5	15.88	8.00
1949	132.1	122.2	9.9	4.5	1.9	3.6	0.4	3.9	2.1	0.6	1.4	cr.0.8	2.2	1.18	3.50
1950	150.1	134.5	15.6	4.7	2.0	8.9	0.4	9.3		0.2	8.7	3.4	5.3	4.39	1.00
1951	253.3	223.6	29.7	5.8	2.0	21.9	0.5	22.4		0.5	19.8	9.7	10.1	9.21	6.00
1952	111.9	118.2	d 6.3	4.6	2.1	d12.9	0.5	d12.5		2.5	d12.9	cr.6.7	d 6.2	d 7.39	nil
1953	73.5	77.7	d 4.2	4.1	1.8	d10.1	0.8	d 9.3		0.2	d 9.8	cr.0.3	d 9.5	d10.74	nil

d – deficit   cr. – credit

TABLE A-11 (Continued)

Year	Total Assets	Cash Items	Rec. Acct.	Inven-tory	Curr. Assets	Notes Pay.	Curr. Liab.	Work. Cap.	Invest-ment	Fix. Assets Net	Fund Debt	Appro-priated Resve.	Pfd. Stocks	Com.	Sur-plus
1929	114.0	11.9	19.2	28.7	59.7		1.3	58.5	3.6	50.3	13.0	1.1	50.0	40.0	9.7
1932	63.9	11.6	3.9	16.9	32.4		0.2	32.2	0.3	31.1	1.2	1.1	41.3	2.0	18.2
1935	71.0	2.0	9.6	30.5	42.2	1.9	4.3	37.9	0.2	28.3	1.1	0.9	38.3	2.0	24.5
1936	78.6	3.0	12.0	33.6	48.6	9.1	11.4	37.2	0.1	29.4	1.1	0.8	38.3	2.0	25.1
1937	65.2	2.2	10.6	22.1	34.9	---	1.1	33.8	0.0	29.8	1.1	0.7	37.3	2.0	23.0
1938	62.5	3.0	8.8	22.3	34.1	2.0	3.9	30.2	0.0	28.0	1.1	0.7	35.6	2.0	19.3
1939	71.0	4.0	13.5	29.8	47.3	11.1	13.5	33.8	---	23.1	1.1	1.7	35.0	2.0	17.8
1940	79.4	4.2	14.7	36.5	55.7	17.4	21.0	34.6		23.1	1.1	---	35.0	2.0	20.3
1941	107.5	8.3	20.3	54.4	83.6	27.6	44.3	39.3		23.0	1.1	2.0	35.0	2.0	23.1
1942	107.2	7.9	19.2	55.1	83.3	5.0	39.8	43.5		23.0	1.1	4.0	35.0	2.0	25.4
1943	109.1	22.4	15.9	45.9	84.6	---	36.3	48.2		22.7	1.0	6.0	35.0	2.0	28.7
1944	119.1	31.5	15.8	44.7	92.6		43.3	49.4	0.0	22.7	1.0	8.0	35.0	2.0	29.8
1945	104.3	29.0	11.6	37.7	80.0		24.9	55.1		22.9	0.9	9.0	35.0	2.0	32.5
1946	104.4	12.5	17.8	48.1	78.6		21.9	56.7		24.4	0.9	3.0	18.9	25.1	28.6
1947	117.6	11.3	18.1	58.5	88.5	10.0	29.0	59.5		27.6	0.9	4.0	17.1	27.9	29.1
1948	122.4	7.3	23.7	59.1	90.4	11.0	30.5	59.9		30.2	0.8	8.0	18.6	30.4	33.0
1949	105.8	7.7	22.3	43.3	73.7	5.8	16.2	57.5		30.5	0.8	5.9	19.6	30.5	32.9
1950	142.5	10.0	29.3	70.9	111.0	37.8	49.7	61.3		30.4	0.7	5.9	19.6	30.5	36.2
1951	142.6	10.2	27.6	73.6	111.9	28.5	46.6	65.3		29.2	0.7	5.9	19.1	30.9	39.4
1952	93.0	7.1	16.4	33.0	56.7	---	4.3	52.4		27.9	0.7	5.9	19.1	30.9	32.1
1953	80.7	11.8	11.7	22.0	45.7	---	2.5	43.1		25.7	0.6	---	19.1	30.9	27.5

d – deficit

261

TABLE A-12
CELANESE CORPORATION

Year	Net Sales	Goods Cost	Gross Profit	Sales etc. Exp.	Deprc. Depl.	Oper. Income	Other Inc.	Total Inc.	Fin. Chgs.	Spec. Chgs.	Int. Pd.	Net	Fed. Tax	Net Income	Net com. sh.	Div. com. sh.
1929	N.A.	N.A.	N.A.	N.A.	0.5	N.A.	0.4	3.5		0.2		3.3	0.4	3.0	1.00	nil
1932	N.A.	N.A.	N.A.	N.A.	0.7	0.9	0.1	1.1		0.1		1.0	0.1	0.9	d0.95	nil
1935	25.0	16.7	8.3	2.2	1.1	4.8	0.0	4.8			0.1	4.7	0.6	4.1	1.99	nil
1936	30.9	21.4	9.5	2.6	1.2	5.2	0.3	5.5			0.2	5.3	0.8	4.4	2.25	1.50
1937	34.0	24.3	9.6	2.7	1.3	5.3	0.0	5.3			0.2	5.1	0.7	4.5	2.04	2.25
1938	28.7	21.2	7.4	2.5	1.4	3.2	0.0	3.2			0.4	2.8	0.4	2.5	0.26	nil
1939	35.5	22.2	13.3	3.2	1.9	8.0	0.7	8.7			0.6	8.0	1.7	6.4	3.67	0.50s
1940	44.5	27.3	17.2	3.6	2.3	11.2	0.1	11.3			0.7	10.5	4.1	6.4	3.38	1.25t
1941	62.3	39.9	22.4	4.6	2.8	15.1	0.0	15.1			0.8	14.1	7.0	7.1	3.43	2.00
1942	86.1	54.0	32.1	7.3	3.8	21.0	0.1	21.1		1.0	1.0	18.8	11.7	7.1	3.42	2.00
1943	94.6	64.9	29.7	7.6	4.2	17.9	0.2	18.1			1.2	16.6	10.4	6.3	2.83	2.00
1944	101.7	68.4	33.3	8.9	4.3	20.1	0.3	20.4			1.2	18.9	11.6	7.2	2.86	0.50u
1945	104.2	68.9	35.3	9.7	4.6	21.0	0.4	21.4	0.8	4.6	1.2	14.7	7.1	7.6	2.82	2.00
1946	135.2	88.9	46.3	11.9	5.9	28.5	0.7	29.2	0.2		1.2	27.8	11.7	16.1	2.36	1.62½, 0.25a
1947	181.1	119.3	61.8	13.3	7.0	41.5	1.0	42.5	0.2		1.9	40.3	16.2	24.2	3.83	1.30
1948	230.4	139.3	91.0	15.0	8.5	67.4	1.0	68.4	0.2		2.1	66.1	26.7	39.5	6.61	2.20
1949	171.3	109.8	61.5	14.6	10.8	35.9	0.9	36.8	0.2		2.4	34.3	13.7	20.6	3.19	2.40
1950	232.5	124.0	108.5	12.8	11.7	84.1	1.1	85.2	0.3		2.2	82.7	42.3	40.4	6.38	2.55
1951	202.7	122.7	80.0	13.3	12.2	54.5	1.1	55.6	0.1		2.3	53.1	28.3	24.8	3.56	3.00
1952	166.7	121.4	45.3	13.1	12.3	19.9	1.3	21.2			3.3	17.8	8.6	9.2	0.77	2.25
1953	166.0	118.1	47.9	13.3	13.4	20.1	1.7	21.8			3.3	18.4	7.7	10.7	1.01	1.25

N.A. - not available
d - deficit
s - plus 2 1/2% stock dividend

a - Before and after stock split
t - plus 2 1/2% and 3 1/2% stock dividend
u - plus 3 for 70 stock dividend

TABLE A-12 (Continued)

Year	Total Assets	Cash Items	Rec. Acct.	Inven-tory	Curr. Assets	Notes Pay.	Curr. Liab.	Work. Cap.	Invest-ment	Flx. Assets Net	In-tang.	Fund Debt	Appro-priated Resve.	Pfd. Stocks	Com.	Sur-plus
1929	37.3	9.1	2.2	6.5	17.8		1.9	15.9	2.1	15.8	0.9		0.2	26.3	5.8	3.1
1932	31.5	4.3	1.7	4.0	10.1		1.4	8.6	1.4	19.7			0.1	26.3	1.0	2.6
1935	44.6	5.7	2.7	6.6	15.0	1.3	2.3	12.6	1.4	27.3		5.6	0.5	26.3	1.0	8.8
1936	51.1	9.4	4.1	6.7	20.2	1.0	3.4	26.8	1.4	28.3		4.9	0.5	31.3	1.0	10.0
1937	50.6	3.9	3.6	7.9	15.4	---	2.2	23.3	1.4	32.3		5.8	0.5	31.3	1.0	9.7
1938	61.0	15.8	3.0	6.5	25.3		2.4	23.0	1.1	32.8		16.2	0.1	31.3	1.0	9.8
1939	66.3	17.6	3.5	5.5	26.7		5.7	21.0	1.7	36.5		14.8	0.0	31.3	1.0	13.3
1940	86.2	29.7	4.1	6.1	40.0		8.9	31.1	1.5	41.5		28.9	0.0	31.3	1.1	15.6
1941	101.0	27.1	6.9	8.4	42.5		12.6	30.0	0.9	54.3		27.7	1.5	35.1	1.4	22.2
1942	103.4	19.5	8.8	10.2	38.6		5.3	33.3	1.2	58.7		34.3	2.5	35.1	1.4	24.2
1943	107.0	25.7	8.4	9.7	43.8		5.2	38.5	1.4	56.1		34.3	2.5	35.1	1.4	25.1
1944	126.7	41.0	8.5	8.5	58.0		6.4	51.6	2.6	58.8		34.3	2.5	48.2	1.6	29.3
1945	137.3	48.0	8.3	9.0	65.4		5.6	59.7	2.7	62.4		40.0	2.5	48.2	1.7	38.4
1946	191.9	68.5	10.8	13.7	93.1		8.3	84.8	4.5	85.7		65.0	3.5	55.2	2.2	56.8
1947	212.0	44.4	15.0	20.7	80.0		18.4	61.6	7.3	118.0		63.5	3.5	55.2	2.2	68.1
1948	256.7	43.8	18.6	24.5	90.1		16.4	73.7	12.3	153.0		86.1	3.5	55.2	2.2	92.4
1949	254.9	45.3	16.8	20.5	85.9		16.6	69.3	14.7	153.2		80.1	3.5	55.2	2.2	96.8
1950	274.4	61.7	22.6	18.8	106.2		25.6	80.7	17.9	149.4		69.2	3.6	55.2	2.3	118.4
1951	335.2	58.7	12.4	45.3	120.0		17.2	102.8	42.0	171.8		98.8	3.6	103.4	2.3	109.9
1952	326.9	29.7	17.5	37.5	88.0		17.7	70.3	48.6	188.6		98.8	3.6	103.3	2.3	101.2
1953	321.8	27.6	12.9	41.1	85.0		14.0	71.0	50.8	184.4		98.8	3.6	103.3	2.3	99.8

SUGGESTED USE WITH CURRENT TEXTBOOKS

The following chart, listing possible suggestions for use of cases and problems in this volume, is offered for convenience of users. Although specific aspects considered by cases and problems may not be covered explicitly in the chapters as listed, I believe that the topic can best be taken up as an extension or amplification of the treatment given by the author of the textbook.

Key to Chart

BG — Badger and Guthmann, *Investment Principles and Practices*, fourth edition. Prentice-Hall, 1951.

B — Bellemore, *Investments: Principles, Practices and Analysis.* Forbes, 1953.

C — Clendenin, *Investments.* McGraw-Hill, 1951.

DF — Dowrie and Fuller, *Investments*, second edition. Wiley, 1950.

GD — Graham and Dodd, *Security Analysis*, third edition. McGraw-Hill, 1951.

G — Grodinsky, *Investments.* Ronald, 1953.

JD — Jordan and Dougall, *Investments*, sixth edition. Prentice-Hall, 1952.

PH — Plum and Humphrey, *Investment Analysis and Management.* Irwin, 1951.

PK — Prickett and Ketchum, *Investment Principles and Policy.* Harpers, 1954.

P — Prime, *Investment Analysis*, revised edition. Prentice-Hall, 1952.

R — Robbins, *Managing Securities.* Houghton Mifflin, 1954.

S — Sauvain, *Investment Management.* Prentice-Hall, 1953.

CHART OF CHAPTERS IN TEXTBOOKS

Prob-lem	BG	B	C	DF	GD	G	JD	PH	PK	P	R	S
1	1	1	1	1	4	1	1, 2	1	1	1	1, 7	1
2	3	1	1	1	4, 8	1	1	1	1	1	—	1
3	3	6	6	3	8	7	5	3	6	2	12	2
4	3	6	6	3	8	7	5	3	6	2	12	2
5	3	5	4, 5	3	8	7	6	4	5	3	20, 21	2
6	5	6	6	3	3	7	4, 5	3	6	2	15	2
7	5	6	6	3	3	7, 20	5	3	6	8	12	8
8	5, 25	4	5	3	3, 8	8, 20	1	2	2	8	11	8
9	5	6	6	3	3	7, 20	5	3	6	8	12	8
10	6, 25	5	4	3	3, 8	—	6	17	5	8	21	8
11	22	7	2	10	—	20	17	AII	7	3, 6	6	—
12	22	7	2	2	—	20	17	3, AII	7	6	6	2
13	22	7	2	30	—	8	17	4, AII	—	2, 6	35	—
14	22	7	2	30	—	—	17	4, AII	—	3, 6	35	—
15	23	10	9	4	—	—	15	7	9, 27	5	2	4
16	23	10	9	4	—	—	16	7	27	6	4	4
17	23	10	9	4	—	—	16	7	27	5	4	4
18	23	10	9	4	—	—	16	7	27	5	5	4
19	23	10	8	4	—	—	15	7	27	5	2	4
20	—	10	9	—	—	—	16	7	—	5	5	—
21	2	3	2	2	1	2	1	1	2	1	8	1
22	2	2	2	2	1	2	1	1	2	1	8, 9	1
23	2	2	2	2	1	2	1	1	2	1	8, 9	1
24	4, 25	4	1	7	1	2	—	2, 16	1	—	9, 15	—
25	4	17	1	8	1	26	7	2, 16	18, 31	—	11	5
26	4	17	1	9	1	26	7	2, 16	18, 31	—	11	7
27	4	17	1	10	1	20	7	2, 16	18, 31	—	11	6
28	4	17	_1	7	1	26	7	2	18, 31	—	11	—
29	4	17	2, 4	29	8	—	23	4	18	—	11	—
30	6	17	2, 10	8	—	3	7	18	5, 31	8	11	13

CHART OF CHAPTERS IN TEXTBOOKS (*Continued*)

Prob-lem	BG	B	C	DF	GD	G	JD	PH	PK	P	R	S
31	6	17	1	6	4	1	8	2	7, 32	8	—	12
32	26	19	18, 24	14	5	27	9	—	25	8, 21	9	16
33	26	20	23, 24	15	5	27	10	—	10	—	9	17
34	26	20	20	15	5	28	—	—	25	8, 22	9	17
35	27	20	24	13	5	28	10	—	—	—	9	19
36	27	20	24	13	5	28	10	—	—	—	9	19
37	27	20	24	13	5	28	10	—	—	—	9	19
38	16	30	19	16	5	28	10, 29	19	26	9	33	18
39	16	30	19	16	5	28	10, 29	19	26	9	33	18
40	28	17	28	12	5	26	10	17	—	8	8	14
41	28	18	23	—	—	—	4	AI	11	—	8	10
42	—	18	25	27	—	—	30	—	17	—	—	10
43	28	18	28	12	5	1	11	—	18	8	8	11
44	28	18	28	12	5	1	11	16	18	8	8	11
45	28	18	28	12	5	—	11	16	18	8	8	11
46	28	18	28	12	5	—	11	—	32	8	8	12
47	28	18	28	12	5	—	11	—	32	8	8	12
48	28	18	28	12	5	—	11	—	32	8	8	12
49	28	18	28	12	5	—	11	—	32	8	8	12
50	28	18	28	12	5	—	11	—	32	8	8	12
51	28	16	10	8	5	26	8	18	32	8	38	15
52	28	16	10	8	5	26	8	18	32	8	38	15
53	28	16	10	8	5	26	8	18	32	8	38	15
54	7	—	13	17	7	4	23	9	4, 8	—	25	9
55	25	15	10, 13	17	53	23	—	17	8	8	1, 37	14
56	7	—	13	17	7	3	23	9	3, 8	—	25, 26	9
57	7	—	13	17	7	3	26	9	3	—	25	9
58	7, 23	13	11	—	6	24	12	8	9	A	10	—
59	7	—	14	18	—	9, 11	26	10	4	13	22, 24	—
60	7	—	14	19, 20	II	9	—	10	4	13	23	—

Prob-lem	BG	B	C	DF	GD	G	JD	PH	PK	P	R	S
61	7	17	14	20	II	9	23	12	4	14	13, 20	—
62	7, 10	17	16	30	II	9	25	—	3	—	25	14
63	9	17	14	29	II	16	23	10	5, 18	—	25	13
64	—	—	14	—	—	9	23	10	4	17	21	—
65	7, 10, 13	17	6	21	III	—	23	12, 13	6, 9	—	12	12
66	—	17	17	29	IV	21	—	18	5, 9, 31	—	25	15
67	7	17	17	29	IV	13	—	18	31-	—	25	15
68	7	17	17	29	IV	22	—	18	5, 31	—	25	15
69	8	28	17	29	II	9	26	9	19	17	26	—
70	8	28	17	29	II	—	26	10	19	20	26	—
71	8	29	17	31	II	10	26	10	20	20	26	—
72	10	25	16	26	III	14	25	13	24	—	27	—
73	10	25	16	26	III	—	25	13	23	20	27	—
74	11	26	16	26	II, III	14	25	14	24	20	28	—
75	13	27	15	25	II	10	24	11	8	—	29	—
76	13	27	15	25	III	14	24	12	22	20	30	—
77	14	27	15	25	III	14	24	12	22	20	30	—
78	20	23	22	23	III	18	21	15	14	12	18	3
79	20	23	22	23	III	18	21	15	14	12	18	3
80	20	23	22	23	III	18	21	15	14	12	18	—
81	15	33	20	—	—	28	28	15	25	22	32	—
82	15	33	20	31	—	—	28	15	25	22	32	—
83	16	31	19	16	—	28	29	19	26	9	34	18
84	15	32	18	31	—	—	27	15	25	21	31	—
85	15	32	18	31	—	—	27	15	25	21	31	—